American Indians and U.S. Politics

A Companion Reader

EDITED BY
JOHN M. MEYER

FOREWORD BY
DAVID E. WILKINS

PRAEGER

Westport, Connecticut
London

Library of Congress Cataloging-in-Publication Data

American Indians and U.S. politics : a companion reader / edited by John M. Meyer ;
foreword by David E. Wilkins.
    p. cm.
  Includes bibliographical references and index.
  ISBN 0–275–97264–X (alk. paper) — ISBN 0–275–97278–X (pbk. : alk. paper)
    1. Indians of North America—Government relations. 2. Indians of North America—
Politics and government. I. Meyer, John M.
  E93.A44 2002
  323.1′197073—dc21   2001054590

British Library Cataloguing in Publication Data is available.

Library of Congress Catalog Card Number: 2001054590
ISBN: 0–275–97264–X
     0–275–97278–X (pbk.)

First published in 2002

Praeger Publishers, 88 Post Road West, Westport, CT 06881
An imprint of Greenwood Publishing Group, Inc.
www.praeger.com

Printed in the United States of America

The paper used in this book complies with the
Permanent Paper Standard issued by the National
Information Standards Organization (Z39.48–1984).

10 9 8 7 6 5 4 3 2 1

Contents

Foreword

Indigenous peoples constitute an integral and distinctive component of North America's diverse human mosaic. Although there are more than 560 recognized native polities, the total cumulative population of Native America is still less than one percent of the total U.S. population. With the exception of those non-Indians who live on or near reservations or other Indian trust lands, or those who plunge into the tempting financial dreams offered by Indian gaming operations, many Americans still know very little about native peoples, their histories, or their cultures.

More distressing still, most Americans, including those in the Academy, know virtually nothing about the sovereign governmental status of indigenous polities as the original national powers with whom various European states, and later the United States, engaged in not only intense and deadly wars but also in diplomatic and commercial relations via ratified treaties, multinational accords, controlled trade and interaction, and other consensual ventures that confirmed the tribes' governmental and landowner status.

The enduring naivete and lack of scholarly acknowledgment or treatment of tribes as sovereign partners with the federal government, and their increasing intergovernmental relations with states, counties, and municipalities, has contributed in no small part to the destabilized and ambiguous nature of tribal political status and to nearly perpetual tension in indigenous-nonindigenous political, legal, cultural, and economic relations.

This compilation of articles, covering a range of topics that will fit easily as a supplemental text for introductory courses in American politics, Native American Studies, and other courses as well, has been expertly organized and introduced by John Meyer. It is an important and timely contribution to the literature and will provide the committed instructor and the interested student with solid knowledge about the dynamic political relationship between First Nations and the U.S. government.

The selections identify and add clarity to the complexity of indigenous nations in their federal and intergovernmental relations in the areas of constitutional history, indigenous political theory, citizenship, civil liberties, interest groups, congressional politics, elections and campaigns, the presidency, the judiciary, bureaucracy, and policy issues. The essays, individually and collectively, serve as a stark reminder that the historical and contemporary experiences of native peoples, both internally and intergovernmentally, cannot and must not be conflated with those of other racial and ethnic minority groups.

First Nations wield increasingly sophisticated governmental systems that exercise a measure of jurisdictional authority over their citizens and noncitizens alike, a characteristic that is unique to Indian tribes and not shared by any other ethnic or racial category. The fact that indigenous citizens also happen to be American citizens is yet another important reason to learn more about tribal nations. Finally, I believe that this compilation, if it is taken seriously and given wide readership, will bring real enlightenment to its readers, because it fundamentally recognizes American Indian governments—and their internal and external political affairs with the other sovereigns that have settled on their ancestral lands—as legitimate and worthy of critical examination and study.

David E. Wilkins
Associate Professor of American Indian Studies,
Political Science, and Law
University of Minnesota

Introduction

The ambitions for this book are simultaneously enormous and modest.

Let's consider the enormous ambition first. This volume reflects an attempt to modify the coverage of the largest, most familiar, and often the most predictably structured course in the curriculum of most U.S. political science departments—the introductory course in U.S. government and politics—by examining the political relationship between American Indians and the U.S. political system. American Indians—as individuals and as tribal nations—receive scant attention in most introductory textbooks,[1] and, frankly, there are far too few political scientists who are confident they have sufficient knowledge or resources to supplement this coverage in their courses. The design of this volume begins with a recognition of these realities. It promotes an ambitious goal by providing material in a format that can be readily incorporated into the syllabus of the introductory course. The readings are keyed to the topics most commonly found on these syllabi, enabling the instructor to include them in conjunction with other assigned readings on these topics (the Constitution, the Courts, the Executive Branch, Federalism, etc.), rather than carving out a separate segment of the syllabus for consideration of American Indian "issues"—or more commonly, giving them no coverage at all.

That this volume's aim is modest is reflected in its slim size. The goal is not to review the rich yet painful experience of American Indian history, nor to explain in detail the character of American Indian beliefs. The chapters are also not presented as an examination of the structure or practices of tribal governments themselves. While careful consideration of all these matters would be necessary for a full appreciation of the contemporary situation of American Indians, it is beyond the scope of this volume. The limited goal here is to enable the student to develop an appreciation for the distinctive relationship between American Indian governments and the U.S. political system. That such a relationship even exists is rarely understood by students of the latter. To the extent that American Indians are considered in the curriculum, it is most frequently in one of two ways. The first is in their role as individuals; noting, for example, Northern Cheyenne tribal member Ben Nighthorse Campbell's election to the U.S. Senate from Colorado. The second is as members of a minority group within the polity, whose interests are presumed largely to parallel those of African Americans and other racial or ethnic minority groups. Yet it is the government-to-government relationship that will be of greatest interest to us here; a relationship that highlights the subject of tribal sovereignty, the doctrine of federalism, and the often unfamiliar questions that these raise about the structure and character of the U.S. political system.

Attention to the relationship between Indian peoples and the U.S. government is, on the face of it, valuable for the understanding it can offer of the unique standing of these tribes and their members. It enables a clearer understanding of contemporary controversies surrounding issues such as Indian fishing rights or gaming casinos. In the context of an introductory course on the U.S. political system, moreover, it allows us to see topics already discussed, such as the U.S. Constitution, the structure of federalism, citizenship, and civil liberties from a fresh and distinctive perspective: that of groups that often sought—and were often promised—a protected place *outside* the U.S. polity rather than inclusion within it.

There are many supplementary readers currently available for a U.S. politics course and their editors have adopted a variety of formats. Some aim to be comprehensive or exhaustive in their coverage (though even here, there is rarely attention to American Indians); others seek to provoke debate through a "point-counterpoint" format. I have done neither here. This volume offers one or sometimes two essays that reflect something distinctive about the American Indian political experience as it relates to the course topic being covered. I hope this will provoke critical analysis of the topic, but the contrast is not structured into this volume, it will be reflected in the disparity between the concerns covered here and their absence in most other readings on American government and politics. Similarly, while I hope that students will be encouraged to read more about the subjects touched upon here, I have not sought to be encyclopedic in my coverage, for the reasons suggested above.

This reader is an outgrowth of my involvement in the American Indian Civics Project at Humboldt State University in Arcata, California. Supported by a generous, multiyear grant from the W. K. Kellogg Foundation and co-ordinated by the university's Center for Indian Community Development, Humboldt faculty from several departments have sought to learn about American Indians, tribal governance and sovereignty, treaty rights, and U.S. policy making toward Indian nations and to integrate an understanding of these into our teaching of introductory courses in U.S. government and history, among others.

I joined this project in its second year, when I began as a new faculty member at Humboldt. Like most others in political science, I had no for-mal training in this area and I found myself scrambling to deepen my learn-ing about these subjects in order to teach them. The more I bolstered my own knowledge, the more certain I became that this subject was valuable not only for American Indian students or for those specifically seeking to learn about American Indian politics, but for all students seeking a clear un-derstanding of the U.S. political system. Yet, although hearing scholarly pre-sentations and reading books and journal articles lessened the superficiality of my own knowledge, it still left me with one central question: What ma-terials can I use to integrate the teaching of this to my beginning U.S. poli-tics students? In a syllabus so full that I already struggled to keep up with the pace, I found it difficult to figure out how to integrate this complex and multifaceted subject matter into the curriculum. The view that "if today is Monday, we must be studying Congress" does not reflect ideal pedagogy, but it is one that I have shared with many other instructors (and probably many students) in this course. Also, although the materials I read were of-ten stimulating, many were inappropriate, in terms of accessibility or length, for beginning students in a course where First Nations simply could not be the primary subject of attention. So, the question became, how can we in-tegrate a substantial consideration of American Indians into the course in a meaningful yet viable manner?

This volume is one attempt to answer that question. Readings have been selected that address their subject matter in a clear and accessible manner and have been organized to mirror the familiar format of the introductory U.S. politics course. I sought to develop this volume only when I discov-ered that nothing like it already existed. It is an attempt by one who is an eager student of American Indian politics and history but by no means an expert on the subject. Likewise, I am an engaged student of the U.S. political system, yet most of my own academic research lies in the fields of political theory and environmental politics. I "confess" to this lack of expertise not as an apology, but because I believe it mirrors that of many instructors who might consider adopting this volume for their course. The book has been developed and organized with the needs of these instructors and their students in mind.

This volume would never have come to fruition without the hard work and support of a number of people. Foremost among these is my graduate research assistant, Rebecca Robertson, who searched for, pored through, and annotated countless articles in an effort to identify appropriate contributions for this book. Lois Risling and Dee McBroome transformed my complaint that "there simply isn't a neatly packaged source of readings available" into a project to create one. Lois, along with Nancy Hill and the rest of her team at the Center for Indian Community Development, ensured that we had the necessary funds to accomplish this. Sterling Evans and (early on) Steve Prince were valuable collaborators whose plans for similar volumes in their own disciplines of history and economics, respectively, contributed greatly to this one. Ster also found us all a publisher. Sam Sonntag tried out a number of these articles in her American Government class and allowed us to survey students' responses to them. Jae Emenhiser, Melanie Williams, and other HSU faculty affiliated with the American Indian Civics Project provided valuable suggestions and assistance. Sheri Evans did a meticulous job preparing the manuscript. Finally, both David Wilkins and Christopher Miller offered early encouragement for this project and reassurance that there was a place for a volume such as this one. I sincerely wish to thank all of these individuals.

In the interest of brevity and accessibility, I have removed appendices, footnotes and other citations from the essays reprinted here. Students interested in further exploring the source material are encouraged to read the articles in their original form. Finally, I must observe the obvious: this book will be a success only if it is used in classrooms and read and absorbed by students. If instructors or readers have suggestions that might make the volume more effective in this regard, please do not hesitate to forward them to me.

NOTE

1. See Jeffrey S. Ashley and Karen Jarrat-Ziemski, "Superficiality and Bias: The (Mis)Treatment of Native Americans in U.S. Government Textbooks," *American Indian Quarterly*, vol. 23, nos. 3 and 4 (Summer and Fall 1999): 49–62; Franke Wilmer et al., "Including Native American Perspectives in the Political Science Curriculum," *PS: Political Science and Politics*, vol. 27, no. 2 (July 1994): 269–276; Anne Merline McCullough, "Perspective on Native Americans in Political Science," *Teaching Political Science: Politics in Perspective*, vol. 16, no. 3 (1989): 93–98.

I

CONSTITUTION

The U.S. Constitution is the foundational document for understanding the structure of U.S. government as well as the relationship among the various parts of this government and between the states and the federal government. As JeDon Emenhiser makes clear, although the Constitution contains only three references to Indians (and only one remains operative), this document—and its interpretation by the courts—is nevertheless fundamental to an understanding of the relationship between the U.S. government and Indian peoples. This relationship is truly a unique one. In part because of this uniqueness—"peculiarity," as Emenhiser uses the word—it has been understood very differently by different actors and observers over the course of U.S. political history. Given the central role of the Constitution, moreover, it should not be surprising that Emenhiser's essay introduces us to a number of concepts and themes—including tribal sovereignty, trust relationship, state-Indian federalism, and congressional plenary power—that are central throughout this volume.

A Peculiar Covenant: American Indian Peoples and the U.S. Constitution

JeDON A. EMENHISER

Not only is the relationship between American Indian peoples and the United States Constitution often complex, frequently confusing, and rarely unemotional, it is also a *peculiar* one, peculiar in a covenant sense. Like the Torah, which speaks of Israel as God's chosen people, and the New Testament, which extends a covenant to followers of Jesus, the U.S. Constitution provides a peculiar status for American Indian peoples. Today some folks, such as Mormons, use the adjective "peculiar" with pride, as a badge of honor. In this connotation, I believe, Indian peoples, also proud of their differences from other Americans, enjoy their peculiar, covenant relationship with the U.S. Constitution and continue to endure persecution for their beliefs and values. They often take pride in retaining what is precious to them, striving to defend their rights and ways of life.

Using the term *peculiar* rather than, say, *different*, *special*, or *unique*, conveys a significant meaning for us to explore. After briefly questioning the term "Indian people," we shall pursue the U.S. Constitution in search of this peculiar relationship.

Many of the ideas in this chapter were contained in the author's address at a conference sponsored by the W. K. Kellogg Foundation's American Indian Civics Project at Humboldt State University, Arcata, California, in 1999, where Dr. Emenhiser is Professor of Government and Politics.

AMERICAN INDIAN PEOPLES

First of all, it is almost impossible to generalize about Indian people, which is true, of course, not only legally and politically but historically and culturally as well. This should not surprise us, however, if we remember that the very concept of a single Indian people rather than separate nations, separate language groups and living styles, is after all an imposition of European explorers. Thus, one of our problems in trying to understand Indian civics is largely our own making. We often search for generalizations that do not exist. We may be better off learning small, concrete cases rather than trying to paint a big abstract canvas that distorts more than it explains. Most important, we should use the plural term, Indian peoples, to remind us not only of the richness of cultures but the diversity of the constitutional relationships. Let us turn now to the text of the Constitution, then, and examine the doctrines of trust responsibility, tribal sovereignty, plenary power, and state-Indian federalism.

THE U.S. CONSTITUTION

The word "Indian" appears in the U.S. Constitution three times, twice in Article I, dealing with enumeration and commerce, and once in the 14th Amendment, modifying the Enumeration Clause. But only one of these provisions, the Indian Commerce Clause, is still operative, and it has evolved extensively in practice. In addition to these specific references to Indian tribes, the definition of citizenship and the powers to make treaties as well as, some might add, to declare war are also relevant provisions to help us understand the civic relationships with Indian peoples.

The Enumeration Clause

The 14th Amendment, section 2, abolished the so-called Three-fifths Clause of Article I, section 2, clause 3, which dealt with the apportionment of representatives to slave states. It now reads:

> Representatives shall be apportioned among the several states according to their respective numbers, counting the whole number of persons in each state, excluding Indians not taxed.

But, an opinion of the U.S. Attorney General in 1940 stating "that all Indians are subject to taxation" apparently makes this provision obsolete.

Citizenship

The 14th Amendment also generated some confusion regarding the citizenship of Indian peoples. Ratified in 1868, Section 1 reads in part:

All persons born or naturalized in the United States, and subject to the juris-diction thereof, are citizens of the United States and the State wherein they reside.

The Supreme Court ruled that this provision did not give Indian peoples citizenship, since they were not generally considered to be under the juris-diction of the United States.

The alien and dependent condition of the members of the Indian tribes could not be put off at their own will without the action or assent of the United States. They were never deemed citizens of the United States, except under explicit provisions of treaty or statute to that effect, either declaring a certain tribe, or such members of it as chose to remain behind on the removal of the tribe west-ward, to be citizens, or authorizing individuals of particular tribes to become citizens on application to a court of the United States for naturalization and satisfactory proof of fitness for civilized life. (*Elk v. Wilkins,* 112 U.S. 94, 101 [1884])

Citizenship was gradually extended to Indian peoples through treaties and statutes, especially the General Allotment Act of 1887, and ultimately in 1924, revised by subsequent Immigration and Nationality legislation.

The Commerce Clause

In listing one of the most important powers delegated to Congress, Article I, section 8, clause 3, says:

The Congress shall have power . . . to regulate commerce with foreign nations, and among the several states, and with the Indian tribes.

While controversies arise over the meaning of the words "regulate" and "commerce," the Court has said generally that regulation means the power to prohibit or encourage, as well as govern the way in which commerce is conducted. Commerce includes not only the buying and selling of goods and services but also the extraction of raw materials and the processing of prod-ucts prior to distribution and sale. Killian, a senior specialist at the Library of Congress, claims that this clause, "once almost rendered superfluous by Court decision, has now been resurrected and made largely the basis for informing judicial judgment with respect to controversies concerning the rights and obligations of . . . [Indian peoples]."

At first it was used as the authority for the Intercourse Acts of the late 18th and early 19th centuries, which among other things overrode the power of states and banned the sale of alcohol to Indian peoples from 1802 until 1903. It began to evolve in 1885 after the U.S. Supreme Court ruled in *Ex parte Crow Dog,* 109 U.S. 556 (1883), that a U.S. District Court in South

Dakota did not have criminal jurisdiction in the alleged murder of Chief Spotted Tail by another Sioux leader. Congress reacted by explicitly making it a federal crime to commit murder and six other serious offenses by any Indian person, even on Indian land.

Where did Congress get the authority to pass this Major Crimes Act? After all, the nation as opposed to the states is a government of delegated power; it may exercise only those powers granted to it by the people in the U.S. Constitution. Mainly, in domestic affairs, these are the powers to tax and spend and regulate commerce. Unlike the states, the national government does not possess a broad police power to regulate the health, safety, morals, and welfare of its people. Under the Constitution, which went into effect in 1789, and then explicitly stated in the 10th Amendment, ratified in 1791, states retain those "powers not delegated to the national government . . . nor prohibited to . . . [them]." How does the murder of one Indian person by another on a reservation come under federal regulation? Does it affect commerce?

Not exactly, according to the Supreme Court. In *U.S. v. Kagama*, 118 U.S. 375 (1896), a case from the Hoopa Reservation, the Court sustained Congress's power, not on the authority of the Commerce Clause as the government argued, but "on the ground that the Federal Government had the obligation and thus the power to protect a weak and dependent people." This notion of a special trust relationship was first pronounced in 1831, as we shall see below.

Treaties

Europeans made numerous treaties with Indian nations prior to American independence. Then, after 1776, the United States made 26 treaties with tribes under the Articles of Confederation (1781–1788) and continued to make treaties under the Constitution, pursuant to Article II, section 2, clause 1:

> The President shall have power, with the advice and consent of the Senate, provided two-thirds of the Senators present concur, to make treaties.

Further, Article III, section 2, clause 1, stipulates that

> The judicial power shall extend to all cases arising under the Constitution, laws, and treaties.

Moreover, the Supremacy Clause, Article VI, clause 2, declares:

> This Constitution, and the laws of the United States which shall be made in pursuance thereof; and all treaties made, or which shall be made, under authority

of the United States, shall be the supreme law of the land; and the judges in every state shall be bound thereby, anything in the constitution or laws of any state to the contrary notwithstanding.

And finally, as far as treaties are concerned, Article I, section 10, clause 1, firmly proclaims:

No state shall enter into any treaty, alliance, or confederation.

While numerous treaties were negotiated and most of them ratified, Congress called a halt to treaty-making with Indian tribes in 1871. This did not abrogate those treaties in effect. It just meant that future relationships between tribes and the U.S. government would be based on other sources, such as statutes passed by Congress and approved by the President or executive orders under authority granted to the President.

Moreover, it is important to realize that treaties and statutes are coequal under the Constitution. Therefore, just as a statute passed this year may amend or abolish one passed last year, a more recent statute may modify or even replace an older treaty. In 1903 the Court explicitly proclaimed that a statute may abrogate a treaty with an Indian tribe, *Lone Wolf v. Hitchcock*, 187 U.S. 553.

Further, some persons argue that the practice of making treaties with Indian nations gives tribes equal status to states in a 10th-Amendment sense. They say that tribes possessed absolute sovereignty until parts of that sovereignty were removed by treaties. Then, like states under the 10th Amendment, which retain all powers not delegated to the national government nor prohibited to the states, tribes retain all those powers that are not denied to them by treaties. Others point out that treaty-making is not the same as constitution-making. The U.S. Constitution reserves powers to the states, but treaties and statutes may take powers away from tribes. Today, treaties still in effect may account for such practices as allowing special hunting and fishing privileges for members of some tribes, even off reservations, a distinct element of the peculiar covenant.

TRUST RELATIONSHIP

John Marshall, Chief Justice of the U.S. Supreme Court from 1801 until 1834, articulated the twin doctrines of trust relationship and tribal sovereignty. On the one hand, the trust relationship means the U.S. government has an obligation to serve as a trustee to protect a beneficiary, the Indian peoples. On the other hand, tribal sovereignty guarantees that Indian tribes are domestic nations with a substantial degree of independence. To some this sounds like having one's cake and eating it, too, a significant part of the peculiar relationship.

The idea that the national government has a duty to protect Indian people may become paternalistic and degenerate into a ward-guardian relationship, as Marshall's 1831 opinion ominously stated:

> They [i.e., Indian Tribes] occupy a territory to which we assert a title independent of their will, which must take effect in point of possession when their right of possession ceases. Meanwhile they are in a state of pupilage, *Cherokee Nation v. Georgia*, 30 U.S. 1, 17.

The next year Marshall reiterated that tribes are "under the protection of the United States," *Worcester v. Georgia*, 31 U.S. 515, 537.

The Court explained some of the reasons for the trust relationship in 1943 when it pronounced that

> In the exercise of the war and treaty powers, the United States overcame the Indians and took possession of their lands, sometimes by force, leaving them an uneducated, helpless and dependent people, needing protection against the selfishness of others and their own improvidence. Of necessity, the United States assumed the duty of furnishing that protection, and with it the authority to do all that was required to perform that obligation and to prepare the Indians to take their place as independent, qualified members of the modern body politic. . . . *Board of County Comm'rs v. Seber*, 318 U.S. 705, 715 (1943).

In 1974 the Court supported its decision upholding a law giving Indian peoples preference over others in working for the Bureau of Indian Affairs by saying,

> As long as the special treatment can be tied rationally to the fulfillment of Congress' unique obligation toward the Indians, such legislative judgments will not be disturbed, *Morton v. Mancari*, 417 U.S. 535, 556.

Today, questions arise about whether the trust relationship extends to all Indians or only members of a tribe, whether a group meets the legal definition of a tribe, whether an individual is a tribal member, and whether the trust is a permanent relationship or one that may expire when Indian peoples are assimilated.

The Code of Federal Regulations addresses two of the questions. It defines a tribe as

> any Indian or Alaska Native tribe, band, pueblo, village, or community within the continental United States that the Secretary of the Interior presently acknowledges to exist as an Indian tribe.

And it defines a tribal member as

an individual who meets the membership requirements of the tribe as set forth in its governing document or, absent such a document, has been recognized as a member collectively by those persons comprising [*sic*] the tribal governing body, and has consistently maintained tribal relations with the tribe or is listed on the tribal rolls of that tribe as a member, if such rolls are kept.

We have to wait for answers to other questions.

TRIBAL SOVEREIGNTY

John Marshall spoke for the Court in 1832 when he delivered the classic pronouncement on Indian tribal sovereignty:

> From the commencement of our government, Congress has passed acts to regulate trade and intercourse with the Indians; which treat them as nations, respect their rights, and a firm purpose to afford that protection which treaties stipulate. All these acts . . . consider the several Indian nations as distinct political communities, having territorial boundaries, within which their authority is exclusive, and having a right to all the lands within those boundaries, which is not only acknowledged, but guaranteed by the United States, *Worcester v. Georgia*, 31 U.S. 515, 557–558 (1832).

Although there is a strong emotional attachment to the term *Indian sovereignty* and there is a growing political movement to assert it, tribal authority and independence of Indian peoples are, in fact, at the mercy of Congress.

Speaking for a unanimous Court in 1978, Associate Justice Potter Stewart summarized Indian sovereignty when he said:

> The sovereignty that the Indian tribes retain is of a unique and limited character. It exists only at the sufferance of Congress and is subject to complete defeasance. But until Congress acts, the tribes retain their existing sovereign powers. In sum, Indian tribes still possess those aspects of sovereignty not withdrawn by treaty or statute, or by implication as a necessary result of their dependent status, *U.S. v. Wheeler*, 435 U.S. 313, 324.

PLENARY POWER

Since much of Congress's power over Indian affairs comes from the Commerce Clause, the first instance of the Court's interpretation of that provision is instructive. In his opinion Chief Justice Marshall ruled that Congress's power over commerce among the states was "supreme, unlimited, and plenary" (*Gibbons v. Ogden*, 22 U.S. 1, 1824), meaning it was full and complete. In other words, Congress can do whatever it wants to regulate interstate, foreign, and Indian commerce, as long as it does not violate any prohibitions against government action in the U.S. Constitution.

In 1972 the Court ruled that Congress even has the unilateral power to sever the trust relationship if it desires (*Affiliated Ute Citizens v. U.S.*, 406 U.S. 128).

STATE-INDIAN FEDERALISM

Although the Constitution did not create the states, since they were already in existence, it did diminish their power from a supreme position under the Articles of Confederation and increased the strength of the national government, reducing state influence over Indian tribes and peoples.

As we saw earlier in discussing treaties, the Supremacy Clause in Article VI provides a hierarchy of law with the Constitution at the top, national laws and treaties next, then state constitutions and state statutes below. So, the national government, acting within its legitimate sphere, may preempt state law dealing with Indian matters.

Chief Justice Marshall recognized the separation of Indian nations from the states in 1832, when he wrote the following:

> The Cherokee nation, then, is a distinct community occupying its own terri-
> tory, with boundaries accurately described, in which the laws of Georgia can
> have no force, and which the citizens of Georgia have no right to enter, but
> with the assent of the Cherokees themselves, or in conformity with treaties, and
> with the acts of Congress. The whole intercourse between the United States
> and this [Cherokee] nation, is, by our Constitution and laws, vested in the
> government of the United States, *Worcester v. Georgia*, 31 U.S. 515, 562.

Today, this means, for example, that unless Congress gives its permission states may not tax reservation lands or income generated by Indian peoples on a reservation, *McLanahan v. Arizona Tax Comm.*, 411 U.S. 164 (1973). Congress may, if it chooses, prohibit states from taxing anyone doing business with Indian peoples on a reservation, *White Mountain Apache Tribe v. Bracker*, 448 U.S. 136 (1980). But states may tax Indian-owned businesses off a reservation unless Congress acts to prevent it, *Mescalero Apache Tribe v. Jones*, 411 U.S. 145 (1973); and tribes may not try non-Indians for criminal offenses, *Oliphant v. Suquamish Indian Tribe*, 435 U.S. 191 (1978).

The Court has ruled that despite some confusion about the source of national power over Indian matters, "it is now generally recognized . . . that it derives from federal responsibility for regulating commerce with Indian tribes and for treaty making," *McLanahan v. Arizona Tax Comm.*, 411 U.S. 164, 172 n. 7 (1973).

CONCLUSION

The U.S. Supreme Court's interpretation of the fundamental, constitutional relationship between American Indian peoples and their governments has not followed the vacillating pattern of statutory and regulatory relations emanating from legislative and executive actions. Not that the Court has been any more consistent than the political branches of the government, it has just had its own fits and starts largely independent from Congress and the executive branch. While Congressional and executive actions are often categorized in chronological periods designated by the terms Removal (1789–1871), Allotment and Assimilation (1871–1928), Reorganization (1928–1945), Termination (1945–1961), and Self-Determination (1961–present), Supreme Court rulings appear to have their own logic. This logic—derived from the constitutional delegation of powers to make treaties and regulate commerce among the Indian tribes, the concept of a trust relationship, Congress's plenary power, and the doctrine of tribal sovereignty—may be understood in the light of a peculiar covenant.

II

POLITICAL IDEALS, TRADITIONS, CULTURE

"Are you a Canadian?" author Taiaiake Alfred asks a Native American woman living in British Columbia. "No," she answers without hesitation. Her answer reflects a sense that her own political identity is quite distinct from that of the nation-state of Canada. If the question was "Are you an American?" the same answer might be given by a Navajo living in New Mexico or a Yurok in northern California.

In the United States, many have become accustomed to speaking of this as a multicultural society. Even this recognition that history and experience have led to cultural differences among racial and ethnic groups, however, generally assumes that these differences exist within a common political system. Yet Taiaiake Alfred offers a powerful argument that this sort of multiculturalism simply isn't enough where indigenous peoples are concerned. Alfred argues that the *political* traditions of Native peoples are at least as distinctive as their *cultural* traditions. Fully aware that there are differences among tribes, Alfred nonetheless sketches some important political values that set most or all of these tribes apart from the European political traditions that have structured the political systems of Western nations, including Canada and the United States.

Native American Political Traditions

TAIAIAKE ALFRED

Native American community life today is framed by two value systems that are fundamentally opposed. One, still rooted in traditional teachings, structures social and cultural relations; the other, imposed by the colonial state, structures politics. This disunity is the fundamental cause of factionalism in Native communities, and it contributes significantly to the alienation that plagues them. What those who seek to understand and remedy the problems that flow from it often don't realize is that this separation was deliberate. Without a good understanding of history, it is difficult to grasp how intense the European effort to destroy indigenous nations has been, how strongly Native people have resisted, and how much we have recently recovered. Not to recognize that the ongoing crisis of our communities is fueled by continuing efforts to prevent us from using the power of our traditional teachings is to be blind to the state's persistent intent to maintain the colonial oppression of the first nations of this land.

Indigenous people have made significant strides toward reconstructing their identities as autonomous individual, collective, and social beings. Although much remains to be done, the threat of cultural assimilation to the North American mainstream is no longer overwhelming, because substantial pride has been restored in the idea of being Native. The positive effects of this restoration in terms of mental, physical, and emotional health cannot be overstated. But it is not enough. The social ills that persist are proof that cultural revitalization is not complete; nor is it in itself a solution. Politics matters: the imposition of Western governance structures and the denial of indigenous ones continue to have profoundly harmful effects on indigenous people. Land, culture, and government are inseparable in traditional philosophies; each depends on the others, and this means that denial of one aspect precludes recovery for the whole. Without a value system that takes traditional teachings as the basis for government and politics, the recovery will never be complete.

Indigenous people have successfully engaged Western society in the first stages of a movement to restore their autonomous power and cultural integrity in the area of governance. This movement—which goes by various names, including "Aboriginal self-government," "indigenous self-determination," and "Native sovereignty"—is founded on an ideology of Native nationalism and a rejection of models of government rooted in European cultural values. It is an uneven process of re-establishing systems that promote the goals and reinforce the values of indigenous cultures against ongoing efforts by the Canadian and United States governments to maintain the systems of dominance imposed on Native communities in the last century.

Recent years have seen considerable progress toward ending the colonial relationship and realizing the ideals of indigenous political thought: respect, harmony, autonomy, and peaceful coexistence. Many communities have almost disentangled themselves from paternalistic state control in the administration of institutions within jurisdictions that are important to them. Many more are currently engaged in substantial negotiations over land and governance, which they believe will give them significantly greater control over their own lives. Perhaps because of this progress, people in the communities are beginning to look beyond the present to envision a post-colonial future. However, that future raises serious questions in the minds of those people who remain committed to systems of government that complement and sustain indigenous cultures.

To many of these traditionalists it seems that, so far, all of the attention and energy has been directed at the process of decolonization—the mechanics of removing ourselves from direct state control and the legal and political struggle to gain recognition of an indigenous governing authority. Almost no attention has been paid to the end goals of the struggle. What will Native governance systems be like after self-government is achieved? Few people imagine that they will be exact replicas of the systems that governed Native communities in the pre-colonial past. Most acknowledge that all Native structures will have to incorporate modern administrative techniques and technologies. But the core values on which the new government systems will be based remain a mystery.

The great hope is that those systems will embody the underlying cultural values of the communities. The great fear is that they will simply replicate non-indigenous systems—intensifying the oppression (because it is self-inflicted and localized) and perpetuating the value dichotomy at the root of our problems.

What follows will be considered a bold assertion in government and academic circles, though its truth is widely recognized in Native communities. The fact is that neither the state-sponsored modifications to the colonial-municipal model (imposed in Canada through the Indian Act and in the United States through the Indian Reorganization Act) nor the corporate or public-government systems recently negotiated in the North constitute indigenous governments at all. Potentially representing the final solution to the white society's Indian Problem, they use the cooperation of Native leaders in the design and implementation of such systems to legitimize the state's long-standing assimilationist goals for indigenous nations and lands.

Non-indigenous people have always seen indigenous people in problematic terms: as obstacles to the progress of civilization, wards of the Crown, relics of savagery and dregs of modern society, criminals and terrorists. Over the centuries, indigenous people themselves have consistently defended their nationhood as best they could; and they have sheltered and nurtured their cultures, keeping the core alive despite all manner of hostility and degradation. It would be a tragedy if generations of Native people should have suffered and sacrificed to preserve what is most essential to their nations' survival, only to see it given away in exchange for the status of a third-order government within a European-American economic and political system.

Has anything changed in the way white society looks at Native people? It is still the objective of the Canadian and U.S. governments to remove Indians or, failing that, to prevent them from benefiting from their ancestral territories. And by insisting on their ownership of traditional territories, cultural autonomy, and self-determination, the original people of this land remain a problem for the state. Particularly in Canada, where the legal title to large portions of the land is uncertain, the policy goal is to extinguish Aboriginal title and facilitate the exploitation of the natural resources on or under those lands. In the area of culture, folklore and the arts are promoted while traditional political values are denied validity in the process of negotiating new relationships, and the state defends its "right" to create Native communities and determine their membership. In politics, indigenous nations continue to face denial of their international rights to autonomy, imposed wardship status, and intensive efforts to co-opt community leaders. In fact, nothing has changed. Why, then, are we now so accepting of what Canada and the United States have to offer?

Throughout the process of supposed decolonization, many Native politicians have steadily moved away from the principles embedded in traditional cultures toward accommodation of Western cultural values and acceptance of integration into the larger political and economic system. It is as if they had stopped believing that their indigenousness is a holistic state of being. Rather, contemporary Native politicians seem to assume that indigenousness can be abstracted and realized in convenient (and profitable) ways, that being indigenous does not have an inherent political dimension, and is simply a matter of looking the part—possessing tribal blood, singing traditional songs, or displaying tribally correct behavior. They ignore the basic traditional teaching that just as we must respect and honor our songs, ceremonies, and dances, so too we must honor the institutions that in the past governed social and political relations among our people, because they are equally part of the sacred core of our nations. As long as this is the case, the underlying value dichotomy will remain.

An indigenous existence cannot be realized without respecting all facets of tradition: culture, spirituality, and government. Those mystics who ignore politics and live their Indian identity only through ritual and the arts are just as lost as the often vilified yuppie Indians who don't go to traditional ceremonies. This is not to say that people have to immerse themselves in all aspects of tradition in order to be indigenous—simply that the basic values and principles of traditional political philosophy must be respected to the same degree as cultural and spiritual traditions.

Should we as indigenous people consider ourselves as individuals, or as representatives of our cultures and members of our nations representing distinct and identifiable values and worldviews? Many people recognize the obvious injustices and misuses of power, and the absence of traditional values, in the new structures, but they can only point to the problems. The lack of any coherent strategy to solve them suggests that Native people need to go beyond the divisive electoral politics and Western-style institutions recommended by most scholars and develop solutions for themselves from within their own cultural frameworks, reuniting themselves as individuals with their collectivity. Human beings do not exist in isolation—the influence of cultural groups and structures is constant and profound. By ignoring traditional teachings, Native people risk losing what they most need to survive as indigenous people, and move closer still to the cultural vortex of the other, foreign, collectivity.

The alternative to cultural annihilation begins with acknowledging the erosion of pre-contact indigenous cultures and becoming fully aware not only of post-contact history but also of the shifting, evolving nature of culture itself. Knowing the history of European colonialism in North America demands recognition of the damage that has been done to the vitality of our traditional cultures. But we must also honor the fact that indigenous peoples have survived: the frameworks of their value systems remain intact and vital.

Indigenous governance systems embody distinctive political values, radically different from those of the mainstream. Western notions of dominion (human and natural) are noticeably absent; in their place we find harmony, autonomy, and respect. We have a responsibility to recover, understand, and preserve these values, not only because they represent a unique contribution to the history of ideas, but because renewal of respect for traditional values is the only lasting solution to the political, economic, and social problems that beset our people. To bring those roots to new fruition, we must reinvigorate the principles embedded in the ancient teachings and use them to address our contemporary problems.

Within a few generations Turtle Island has been devastated and degraded. The land has been shamefully exploited, indigenous people have borne every form of oppression, and Native American ideas have been denigrated. Recently, however, Native people have come to realize that the main obstacle to recovery from this near total destruction—to the restoration of peace and harmony in our communities and the creation of just relationships between our peoples and the earth—is the dominance of European-derived ideas. The past two or three generations have seen efforts to rebuild social cohesion, gain economic self-sufficiency, and develop structures for self-government within Native communities. They have also seen renewed interest in the wisdom of the traditional teachings that sustained the great cultural achievement of respectful coexistence. Indigenous people have begun to appreciate that wisdom, and much of the discussion about justice within Native communities today revolves around the struggle to recover those values. Yet among non-indigenous people there has been little movement toward understanding or even recognizing the indigenous tradition.

In fact, it is one of the strongest themes within Native American cultures that the modern colonial state could not only build a framework for coexistence but also cure many of its own ills by understanding and respecting traditional Native teachings. The wisdom encoded in the indigenous cultures can provide answers to many questions; many seemingly intractable problems could be resolved by bringing traditional ideas and values back to life. Pre-contact indigenous societies developed regimes of conscience and justice that promoted the harmonious coexistence of humans and nature for hundreds of generations. As we move into a post-imperial age, the values central to those traditional cultures are the indigenous contribution to the reconstruction of a just and harmonious world.

Indigenous people have many different perspectives on what constitutes tradition and what is good and bad about traditional ways. My own views have been shaped by life in Kahnawake, a Kanien'kehaka (Mohawk) community of over 8,000 people located on the south shore of the St. Lawrence River outside Montreal. Our people have come a long way toward recovering their identity and power in recent years, but during my childhood, in the 1960s and early 1970s, we were fractured, dysfunctional, and violently self-destructive, colonized and controlled to a large degree by white men. Yet that period was also a revolutionary time. As my generation awakened politically in the late 1970s, we refused to participate in our own colonization and embarked on the path of tradition, rejecting the identities and power relations that characterized us as a dominated people. It has been an enormous, costly, and sometimes violent struggle, but today the Kahnawakero:non are part of a re-emergent nation, self-confident, cohesive, and assertive in the promotion of their goals. We are not yet free, but we do not hesitate to contest our colonization. In one generation we have accomplished the rebirth of tradition in Kahnawake. The transformation of the community in terms of personal, familial, and collective peace, empowerment, and happiness has been truly amazing.

Yet the return to traditional values and identities is not uniform among Native peoples, either in its pace or in its intensity; it is not even universally accepted as an objective. To gain a better understanding of how different nations are dealing with the internal and external conflicts that are inherent in the process of decolonization, in the summer of 1997 I spoke with a 33-year-old Kwa'kwala'wakw woman living in Victoria, British Columbia, who has worked extensively in various Native political organizations and is active in the revival of traditional culture among her people. We talked about the effects of colonization and shared thoughts on the most serious problems undermining the health and security of indigenous people today. We also considered the lessons and strategies represented in this book, and explored the relevance of a message drawn from the Rotinohshonni tradition to the situations of other indigenous peoples. Our conversation pointed to the particularity of each community's struggle, but also to the underlying similarities that make it possible to speak of a Native American perspective rooted in traditional values. The words we shared captured some of the complex intensity that seems to motivate all those committed to a traditionalist critique of the prevailing colonial structure and mindset.

Interview

Now that I've explained the traditional Condolence ritual, I'd like to know your thoughts about your own traditions and nation. Remember that in "Adding to the rafters" there is a reminder that the longhouse—as a metaphor for our teachings—sometimes needs additions. As the present generation, that's our responsibility: we have to add sections to the longhouse. That's where we're failing now, in my view, and in the book I will deal with that by projecting this traditional perspective onto some key contemporary issues. We have the rafters—the traditions that our grandmothers and grandfathers, great-grandfathers and great-grandmothers built. But there is an explicit instruction in the teachings that someday we will have to add to those rafters. Now it seems we're so jealous and protective of our traditions that we aren't thinking about that, in my nation anyway. From what I've seen in my travels, it's much the same in other nations. We're afraid to change, to update. As in the ritual, that's where I want to leave off: by concluding that what we really need to do is embark on a creative rethinking of ourselves, rooted in tradition.

What I keep doing is looking at the causes of the losses. You know, when you look back on the smallpox and TB and all the different things that contact with white people brought, I don't think the implications of those things over the generations are anywhere near being understood.

Even amongst our own people?

Amongst our own people, that's true. Think about how contact and everything that came with it affected the transference of knowledge. We don't have the skills that we would have learned if everything had stayed the same. People's experience in residential schools is a good example. On one level the family gets broken up; on the next level the community gets broken up. That's a big factor. But on the individual level it's even worse. If you don't have the benefits of the nurturing and the teachings in the first place, when you come out of the school you still don't know how to learn, let alone how to teach. You end up going back home and it's as if the community had blown up, as if a bomb had been dropped in the middle of the village and we were just salvaging the leftover pieces, just trying to stick them back together. But because nobody has the real internal, individual knowledge, nobody's able to work together. So there are all kinds of fragments floating around. When you talk about what's missing—it's some very basic individual, healthy sense of self.

You notice this in a lot of communities because you do a lot of traveling, right?

Right. I've noticed it more this last time around because we were talking about education and traditions, and I became interested in knowing how different parts of the province, different tribal groups, had handled things. Everyone talked about learning from the elders, but on the other hand they recognized that not all elders are the same—some are respected, but there are others who have fallen victim to the system. These elders have been victims in a really bad way for their whole lives, and ended up sort of "faking it." Now they're trying to appear knowledgeable, to sound knowledgeable, but all you have to do is put a couple of their statements together and you realize that they don't know what they're talking about, because it doesn't make sense. The way people were talking about all the things we've been trying to do—economic development, community development, self-government, the whole treaty process . . . I don't think it's going to work because people, at an individual level, don't understand where they're supposed to be going anyway. On a very personal level, people don't know what you mean when you talk about "jurisdiction," they don't know what you're talking about when you say "control"—other than the negative idea of control that they have from their own direct experience of government in the communities. People don't know what it means to really have self-respect. I've talked to lots of women out in the communities who tell me that our young people don't know what it means to make a statement like "I'm going to make a choice about getting involved in drugs or not, and my choice is based solely on the fact that I have enough self-respect that I wouldn't do that to myself." There's always another reason; it's always because "My family says so." It's always very external. The only thing that's holding people together is that, peripherally, they're seeing another way. They see something is there but they don't know what it is, they are just seeing this shadow that kind of follows them around. People keep trying to look at what it is, but they don't have enough . . . I don't know what the words are. . . .

What is it for you, that thing?

I think maybe it's intuition. No. It's not so much intuition itself, as the ability to recognize intuition. And to trust it—to be able to trust yourself and your own choices based on your intuition and your knowledge. It's as if all those little things are sitting there waiting for you, but it's hard getting the connecting factors and finding how they all work together inside. So that's what we're up against.

I'm thinking about our treaty process. I walk in there and I don't know where to begin. You'd have to go through every individual and wipe out all of the superficial ideas that people have about what treaties are going to bring them, and get down to what they believe in, philosophically. When I was up in North Island [Vancouver Island] I asked people, "Philosophically, why are we doing this? Why do you want to negotiate a treaty?" They'd answer, "Because it's the only game in town," and other external reasons, or maybe mention some really cerebral kinds of ideas about what they want to do. You know, it was interesting when you mentioned "seven generations." I asked people at home and in several communities, "What do you really mean by seven generations?" I was sure that that sort of thinking, wherever it comes from, has a full story behind it. But I kept hearing everybody use the words, when it was clear that nobody knew what the hell they were talking about. Yeah, that sounds like a nice buzzword, "seven generations" from now!

Penetrating that superficiality is one of the things I want to do, because what you just described is certainly a problem in our communities as well. Everybody seems to use that expression, because it comes directly from the ceremonies, but we don't really think about it—it just sounds good. The principle of "seven generations" involves children, it involves some foresight, and all of that. But as for living it as a person, either in a treaty or even in your own life—I get the sense that not a lot of people have thought about how it applies, what it actually means. That's one of the things that I want to get at.

In the past, everyone knew who he or she was in relation to one another. I look at the medicine wheel and its message about the different races, and I think that somewhere our teachings probably talk about who we are as the red people in the medicine wheel, that there is a spiritual link. When you look at our ceremonies in the big house, the cedar bark, and things like the spiritual creature that comes from the north end of the world—all those things contain messages that we haven't figured out how to interpret today; but I think it's all there in our songs. The answer to who we are in relation to everybody else is sitting there, and has been sitting there for many generations now, but nobody has quite deciphered what it means because no one has thought to put a little energy into it. And that's because people think, "We're in the 1990s and we've got our potlatches, at least we still have our language, our culture." They think they can just take in whatever else is going on around them and stay true to their traditions too. But if we don't get a sense of who we really are from the old teachings, then all this tradition stuff is just going to become watered down in a couple of generations.

So you think that this might be the gap in the traditional movement—that people are singing the songs without looking at what they really mean?

Yep. For a while it was just surface, then we got a little bit beneath the surface, but nobody's gone any deeper than that. So the traditional movement has the appearance of something that's going to carry on, that's going to last. But the traditional culture is only going to last, I think, as if it were in a glass box. It's all recording, videos—now we even have CD-ROM and Internet connections. All of that doesn't mean anything. The culture is going to sit in a glass box that we'll all go to the museum and see one day, just the way we look at all our other stuff right now.

Well, that's what I call folklore. It's all just folklore unless you act on it. In fact, that's a criticism that's been directed at some "traditionalists." They act as if they're traditional and they sort of parrot what they're supposed to be doing, but then they go and live their lives totally differently and ignore the inconvenient messages— the ones that don't conform to their own choices in life. They ignore the important teachings that they don't like, and then they try to give the impression that those sections are obsolete. I would argue that they aren't obsolete at all. All the basic teachings are part of a unified whole that's crucial to understanding the tradition and the wisdom; we have to understand the way they all interrelate. You can't just ignore sections of it. If you haven't ever got to the real meaning, then I agree with you—in two or three generations it'll just be folklore.

Nobody understands the bottom-line, basic principles that form the framework for everything. All the other stuff—the fact that we use button blankets, the fact that we're videotaping and audiotaping songs—those are just little tools that we've adapted along the way. "The basic principles"—people keep saying those words but nobody's living them. They're not saying that the bottom line is doing what I do in my life with respect and humility and understanding and honor. If I'm doing these things in a serious way, then anything that blossoms out of it is going to be right. Everyone figures, you know, that if we go to enough ceremonies, and get seen enough and have a presence and visibility and appear to be involved in all this culture stuff, then we're truly balancing both worlds. But you don't have to balance both worlds. What you have to do is know your basic principles in the first place, and then blend the contemporary and traditional together—but you have to have the principles right. I grew up watching some people at ceremonies thinking they had all the knowledge, and then when I got into my mid-twenties I went back to ask them what it means. I said, "I watched you do that when I was a kid, I saw you do that in a potlatch." But they didn't even know why! Now I'm finding out in the last five or six years that all along they were just following what they were told, or mimicking what they had seen themselves. They don't know why they're doing anything.

Do you fault them for that?

No.

Or do you see it as an evolutionary thing?

Yeah, I think that there were a lot of factors in the 1950s and '60s that affected that generation. Everyone in that era had a whole bunch of other things to deal with that we're not dealing with now: the right to vote, all the civil rights stuff happening south of the border, the American Indian Movement, and then the Indian Act here. In the late 1960s and early '70s, actually getting band offices and our own councils in the first place, and having our own Native people sitting in Department of Indian Affairs offices serving as Indian Agents. And they believed at that time that we were going to become white. So if there was a potlatch and they were told by their elders, "Here's how you do the dance, just go do it," they did what they were told because they had had enough of the old teachings to know that they had to. But they still weren't getting the consistent, everyday exposure that they would've had in the past. When it came around to potlatch time they would get into it and go through the motions. But every other day of the rest of their lives, it was just—you know—go out, get a job, participate in the economy, make some money, and have a big house.

Some of which might be contrary to the values and the objectives of the potlatch in the first place.

I think it brought about an interesting way of thinking—and I ended up being on the receiving end of it. In the potlatch system there are various ranks— in effect you've got noble people and commoners, and the whole range in between—but everybody has a role, and everybody is acknowledged in that role and you don't actually look down on people, and you don't treat them poorly. In the mentality of the 1960s and '70s, if you potlatched in a really big way, you had the right to call anyone down because you were so great. You were so humble that you would never do it, you had too much respect to do it—but you knew that you could. Another reason I think it happened was that people were getting mixed messages about whether they were Indian or white. They would equate participation in the potlatch with material wealth, as being one and the same. And that meant that if you didn't have a big house, plus a fishing boat, plus $100,000 per year coming in from your job, then you were poor. You were poor materially, and poor in the potlatch system.

I think that's one of the differences between our cultures, even today. Yours is much more hierarchical and divided among families. I believe ours is much more egalitarian. When I was growing up, our identity was always "Mohawk," and not really defined by clan or family. Whenever any of us did something good, people would say, "Way to go, Mohawk!" You know, it was "for the nation." When someone did something good, I would always identify with it. At home it's still that way. People get upset when someone claims to speak as a Mohawk but isn't really part of the society, because for us, when someone says they're speaking as a Mohawk, we expect the message and the perspective to be consistent with what the community thinks. In my basic identification, I don't say I'm from the "Alfred" family, or from Kahnawake, or this clan or that clan. I say I'm Kanien'kehaka, Mohawk. And that's it, there's only one group. Whereas out here, on the West Coast, it seems to me that identity is family- or clan-based. It's very different.

Yes it is. And residential schools are a big part of life out here, too. It's not a just generational thing either; it's not just the individuals who actually went to the schools, it's their entire families. Their parents feel guilty for sending their kids in the first place and finding out it wasn't such a good place after all. So first there are the parents, and then the kids, and then all their children. This "recognizing pain and sorrow" that you talk about, people don't know what to call it, and they don't know what the spin-off effect is when you deprive yourself of the opportunity to grieve. And all the grieving that never happened around the losses from disease. . . . If you don't go through the process of acknowledging what you've lost, you don't have a way to come back and get it . . . get it back again.

Do you feel that some of the efforts that are under way now, with the social-work or social-services approach, are helping?

I think it's all a pile of crap.

Why don't you tell us how you really feel? Try not to hold back, okay? [laughter]. Why is that so? I don't like the dominant social-work approach, either. I think they're using a foreign set of assumptions—goals, even—to address the problem. But why do you think it's crappy? Maybe it comes from experience?

I'll have to smoke on that one. But I'll tell you the image I get in my mind when I think about social work, all the self-help groups, therapy, and all. I think of us trying to make a bike wheel: we've already got the outside rim, we know where the spokes need to go, and all of those spokes are possible, but people have to work together to make them a reality. And everyone has to have an understanding of that, right?

Is that our traditional culture, the wheel that you're talking about?

Everyone describes it in a different way, or visualizes it in a different way. For me it's as if everyone has to understand where the spokes need to go before we can get anywhere, but the information about where the spokes go is scattered right now. So if all the people who understand where just one spoke needs to go came together and put their one spoke on the wheel, we'd have something. But instead, what social work and all these self-help things try to do is create more spokes. And they keep putting them in the wrong place—they're all on one side of the wheel. The social-work approach is taking what's already fragmented and fragmenting it even more. They've got all these spokes on one side of the wheel, and they get frustrated with us because they can't understand why, after they've given us all these spokes, we haven't been able to make the wheel turn. Well, one, it doesn't have any of our spokes, and two, they're all on one side. White people are just starting to discover that yes, we do have a lot of answers, and we did have really elaborate, complex systems that spoke to every aspect of life.

"Excuse the pun," heh?

What pun?

"Spoke" to . . .

At the end of the day, any social workers who've been in our communities for twenty years or more have resigned themselves to the fact that the discipline of social work, or psychology, doesn't have a clue.

I'd like to shift over and talk about the role of women in Native societies, both traditionally and today. In your life right now, you're involved in politics, you're involved with the culture. Is there respect for women?

To be really honest, no. I think that men who are in their forties, fifties, and sixties say the words. But only a rare few really know what it means to show respect and to actually demonstrate it.

How would someone do that? You could give me a positive or a negative example. How would someone disrespect women—if you're comfortable talking about it?

On the positive side, there's one man at home in particular who comes to mind. He was brought up with the old people; he understands the language, understands the culture. His words are so carefully orchestrated, and I don't think that's because he's trying to appear respectful; he is respectful, and it comes out in the way he speaks. Because he has such an understanding of Kwa'kwa'la language, when he translates to English he does it in a very eloquent way. As for guys who aren't respectful, I always hear them talk about "our women," "our women," as if we were possessions still. They keep saying, "We have respect for our women." The biggest insult, to me, is that they go through the motions in the big house, but then when we come out of the big house into our contemporary lives, they don't show any of that respect.

What about the young guys?

I think among the young people that I'm spending the most time with, it's about an 80 percent to 20 percent split. There's 20 percent or so that have had the benefit of the band school, hearing the language in the home, or learning the values and the principles in the home or through the potlatch. So they're okay, they're on the right path, even though they're still being distracted by the contemporary influences. The other 80 percent are doing what the previous generations have done, in that they're using whatever works for them, whatever will serve their personal agenda. A couple of years ago, when a bunch of us women started getting together at night for dance practices and singing practices in the big house, some young guys—16 or 17 years old—were saying things like "First of all, there should be no women sitting up at the log singing"; or "Women shouldn't be learning the songs anyway"; or "When we have our potluck dinners or when we have feasts, we should be served first."

"We" being the men?

They haven't been taught that you will be shown respect when you give respect in the first place. So the women in the community here in Victoria started getting together and thinking about how we could address this. Because we realized that we hadn't succeeded in teaching these boys everything they needed to know. We hadn't carried out our responsibilities either. At first we just thought their families should have done more. Then we started realizing—holy cow, we've got residential schools, and alcoholism, and all kinds of issues around adoption and families getting back together. There were too many things happening at once for any of us to assume that anyone was doing anything outside of our own activities. So we started, just over the last couple of years, rebuilding the whole scheme. We focus first on the young kids, because we can't afford to lose this time with them—they need to learn it the fastest now. A bunch of us are going to focus on that, and some of us are going to take a look at what we are learning in the way of contemporary skills—doing projects, workshops, healing kinds of thing. There's some of us who are proposal writers, ideas people. So we'll sit and think about things. And then over time, whenever we feel like we need to, we'll just get together and brainstorm, piece it together—make it happen.

Who's the leader that you respect most and why? I'm asking you now what you would consider to be a leader. In spite of everything that you've talked about, there are obviously still people, men and women, that you would respect. What is it about them that makes them true leaders? Or maybe I'm making a big assumption. Maybe it's not the case . . .

There are some, but they're very few, and they are all elders. Agnes Cranmer, who just passed away recently, was a hell of a leader because she knew that her upbringing in the potlatch, her understanding of the potlatch, was right. That's all there is to it. She never thought, "Maybe I'm wrong about this." She believed she was right. There was also, in the same time period, a woman we all called Granny. Those two women, along with lots of women in that generation, just believed that it was right to do what they were doing. Regardless of whether there was funding, regardless of whether there was a hall or a place to go and do things, they just kept doing them. They kept teaching their kids, they made sure their kids were brought up in the potlatch way, that they understood what basic principles are, no matter what happened. They lived through the potlatch ban. It was Mrs. Cranmer's husband, Dan Cranmer, who threw the potlatch on Village Island where everybody got arrested and thrown in jail. They lived through all of that, and saw the worst of it, but they kept doing it anyway, because they believed it.

Did she embody all the traditional values . . . ?

She lived them. I think that's what the neat thing was, considering the era she lived in. She made it through the potlatch ban, she lived through the 1960s and '70s and '80s, and throughout all of that she was still carrying on the culture. She opened up her own corner store and pool hall, she ran a business, and at the same time she was working with the community to teach children in the nursery school. She did all these incredible things, and none of them ever interfered with one another; they actually complemented one another. So even though she was very much participating in the local economic activity, she was still one of the foundations of our culture in everything that she did. There was another lady who was I don't know how much older than Agnes. She never involved herself much in contemporary economic stuff, but she supported those who did. She gave them enough common-sense information to go out there and look at business as though it was a traditional activity: "As long as you follow these basic principles you'll be fine." To me, that's all of it right there. I never watched how the old men conducted themselves. To me it was simple—I just had to follow the path that those women led. I'm not going to be able to do what those men do, I'm not a speaker, I'm not a singer, I'm not any of those things, so I didn't pay attention to any of that: just to what those ladies did.

But there are men that you would respect in that category, as well?

The man from home I spoke about earlier. What I think is neat about him is that when he's wrong he comes right out and admits it. He doesn't try to make excuses. He just says, "This is what happened, this is what I understood at the time to be true, this was my action as a result of my thinking. It turned out that it wasn't correct, and now I stand corrected." Then he goes through the traditional way to correct it. I don't know how many male "leaders," or people who are sitting in political positions now, do that. I've seen them do it for the sake of appearing to be humble. And I've seen them do it because if they didn't admit it, the repercussions would be worse, and they stood to lose more in terms of material things. So I've seen them do it. But you know, you can tell when they're just faking.

So how do these internal issues that we've been talking about affect our status relative to other peoples? How have they affected the strength of our nation, vis-à-vis others? Has our "sovereignty" been undermined? Has our nation lost power in a real way because of these problems? Or is it more a matter of other people doing things to us? That's another question I want to address in this book. What is the relationship between our problems and those that have been imposed on us? Maybe we haven't responded well. If so, does that have ongoing implications? Can we rebuild our nations in the midst of these internal issues? Or do we have to resolve those issues first, and then confront the outside?

Well, I think one of the simplest things it comes down to is this: if you don't respect yourself, no one else will. As for rebuilding internally and externally, I think they can be done simultaneously. In fact, they have to be done simultaneously, the healing and the rebuilding. If we stop nation-building now and do nothing but healing, then the whole treaty process—which is going down the tubes anyway—will be down the tubes even faster, because all the resources will get scooped up while we're all busy trying to heal. There is a lot of healing to be done. But the flip side is that there's so much strength; the fact that we're still here is testimony to the fact that we've got some good coping skills. Why don't we pat ourselves on the back for what we've done well? It's amazing that we've managed to survive this far. We should emphasize that instead of always saying, "I'm a victim of residential schools, I'm a victim of alcoholism." You can play that game for a few years, but you're wasting time. In the meantime, you could be learning a little bit about how to run a home-based business and get self-sufficient. If you don't understand what self-sufficiency is in your home, you can't contribute something to the nation. Why would you think you can contribute something to the nation, when you have no concept of it in your own life? That's why I think the rebuilding has to happen simultaneously, inside the community and outside.

In terms of nations, what would be the ideal relationship between your nation and the rest of Canada once things get back on track? If you compare the militancy of Mohawk politics with things here in B.C., where do you stand?

Well, I like to look at all sides of the question. I do think there's a need for us to get militant again, in a big bad way. I think we have to. But at the same time there are people who are nowhere near ready for that. They're scared. And they'll sabotage things for the militants because they're afraid—afraid for a lot of reasons. I'm close to the militant extreme, because I really believe that we have to nail this down—just get on with it. But at the same time I know from the people I've talked to around the province that there are many people who couldn't physically, emotionally, or intellectually bring themselves to that level. They're not prepared to die. Whereas personally, I remember that when Oka flared up, I was thinking, "If this is how it has to be, I'm prepared to die." But lots of people I worked with were saying, "What the hell are the Mohawks doing? They're gonna get us all in shit!"

Are you a Canadian?

No. Actually, I've tried to search for the moment in time when Canada decided legally—at least legally—that we were considered citizens. Which is kind of a joke, because as I've heard someone say, "Legally, yes, we are regarded as citizens. Yet the same legislation—the Indian Act—is always there to remind us that we're not." To me, you can't look at the Indian Act, and look at the precedents in the courts, and then draw the conclusion that we're citizens.

Well, I think legally they gave Indians the vote in the 1960s. Formal citizenship came before that, but not much before. It wasn't asked for: it was given because they realized that in order to tax and do the things they wanted to do for Indians— or to Indians—they needed them to be citizens. They resisted as long as they could, then they made Indians second-class citizens and imposed the Indian Act on them. I'm not a Canadian. I don't believe in that. I think that if you're strong in your nation, then that's what you are. If you have a good relationship with Canada, fine, so much better.

Some of my best friends are Canadians [laughter]. No, I do no regard myself as a Canadian. You see all the things like the Olympics, the Commonwealth Games, all those things that people get excited about it. For what? These people are going to go off to—where is it, Bosnia?—and the government is going to give them $15 million. Somebody just died on one of our reserves this week— someone died on every reserve this week—of malnutrition or infection, because of poor conditions. Oh yeah, we're citizens.

They gave $2 billion to China, to buy nuclear reactors, and they complain about $58 million for a Royal Commission on Aboriginal Peoples.

I was surprised, the commentaries in the papers on the Royal Commission's recommendations were not that bad. They were even a little bit supportive. Got to watch out for that, though. Watch out for—what is it again. . . ?

"Beware the magic."

The magic, and the lurking dangers.

Is there a fundamental or inherent difference between indigenous and white society? This is a relevant question, given the tendency of the dominant Western tradition to draw racial distinctions. Indigenous traditions, by contrast, include all human beings as equal members in the regimes of conscience. Yet some Native people have been influenced by the divisive European approach. Representing this perspective in an academic context, Donald Fixico has claimed that white people can never come to terms with indigenous values because they "come from a different place on earth." He writes:

> Anglo-Americans and Natives are fundamentally different. These differences in
> world-view and in the values that go with them mean that there will always exist
> an Indian view and a White view of the earth.

I believe, on the contrary, that there is a real danger in believing that views
are fixed (and that cultures don't change). Fixico's polarization of Indian and
European values suggests he believes that white people are incapable of at-
taining the level of moral development that indigenous societies promote
among their members with respect to, for example, the land. Not only does
this dichotomization go against the traditional Native belief in a universal
rationality, but it offers a convenient excuse for those who support the state
in its colonization of indigenous nations and exploitation of the earth. If
Fixico is right, they can't help it: their worldview is preordained.

Challenging mainstream society to question its own structure, its acquisi-
tive individualistic value system, and the false premises of colonialism is essential if we are to move beyond the problems plaguing all our societies,
Native and white, and rebuild relations between our peoples. A deep reading of tradition points to a moral universe in which all of humanity is ac-
countable to the same standard. Our goal should be to convince others of
the wisdom of the indigenous perspective. Although it may be emotionally
satisfying for indigenous people to ascribe a greedy, dominating nature to
white people, as an intellectual and political position this is self-defeating.
It is more hopeful to listen to the way traditional teachings speak of the various human families: they consider each one to be gifted and powerful in its
own way, each with something different to contribute to the achievement
of peace and harmony. Far from condemning different cultures, this position challenges each one to discover its gift in itself and realize it fully, to
the benefit of humanity as a whole. It is just as important for Europeans as
it is for Native people to cultivate the values that promote peace and
harmony.

The value of the indigenous critique of the Western worldview lies not in
the creation of false dichotomies but in the insight that the colonial attitudes
and structures imposed on the world by Europeans are not manifestations
of an inherent evil: they are merely reflections of white society's understanding of its own power and relationship with nature. The brutal regime of
European technological advancement, intent on domination, confronted its
opposite in indigenous societies. The resulting near-extinction of indigenous
peoples created a vacuum in which the European regime established its political, economic, and philosophical dominance.

The primitive philosophical premises underpinning that regime were not
advanced or refined in the deployment of microbes and weapons. At their
core, European states and their colonial offspring still embody the same
destructive and disrespectful impulses that they did 500 years ago. For this
reason, questions of justice—social, political, and environmental—are best
considered outside the framework of classical European thought and legal

traditions. The value of breaking away from old patterns of thought and developing innovative responses has been demonstrated with respect to environmental questions. But in fact many of these and other pressing questions have been answered before: indigenous traditions are the repository of vast experience and deep insight on achieving balance and harmony.

At the time of their first contact with Europeans, the vast majority of Native American societies had achieved true civilization: they did not abuse the earth, they promoted communal responsibility, they practiced equality in gender relations, and they respected individual freedom. As the Wendat historian Georges Sioui put it in a lucid summary of the basic values of traditional indigenous political and social thought:

> With their awareness of the sacred relations that they, as humans, must help maintain between all beings, New World men and women dictate a philosophy for themselves in which the existence and survival of other beings, especially animals and plants, must not be endangered. They recognize and observe the laws and do not reduce the freedom of other creatures. In this way they ensure the protection of their most precious possession, their own freedom.

The context of life has changed, and indigenous people today live in a materialistic world of consumerism and corporate globalization—a world diametrically opposed to the social and political culture that sustained our communities in the past. It may be difficult to recognize the viability of a philosophy that originated in an era unaffected by European ideas and attitudes. Nevertheless, revitalizing indigenous forms of government offers a real opportunity to inspire and educate mainstream society, and to create and empower a genuine alternative to the current system.

In my own community of Kahnawake, as part of an effort to determine the cultural appropriateness of various social services in the early 1990s, people were asked to consider a list of statements about traditional values, and to say whether they agreed that those concepts were still important today.

VALUE	% STRONGLY AGREE
Responsibility to all creation	97
Importance of extended family	89
Respect for inner strength or wisdom	88
Importance of educating youth	88
Sacredness and autonomy of children	78
Importance of family unity	78
Wisdom of the past	71
Sharing and cooperation	71

The survey points to the community's recognition of traditional values, despite the imposition of European culture. Indigenous people who seek to

realize the goal of harmonious coexistence within their communities find that
this is impossible within the mainstream political system as it is currently
structured. The Lakota philosopher Luther Standing Bear, writing in 1933,
presaged this frustration with Western values:

> True, the white man brought great change. But the varied fruits of his civiliza-
> tion, though highly colored and inviting, are sickening and deadening. . . . I
> am going to venture that the man who sat on the ground in his teepee medi-
> tating on life and its meaning, accepting the kinship of all creatures, and ac-
> knowledging unity with the universe of things was infusing into his being the
> true essence of civilization. And when native man left off this form of develop-
> ment, his humanization was retarded in growth.

Having had their freedom stolen and their civilizations crushed by colonialism, Native people are well aware of the social and political crisis they
face. But the crucial goal of restoring a general respect for traditional values, and reconnecting our social and political life with traditional teachings,
remains elusive. Standing Bear's thoughts on true civilization are echoed in
conversations all over Indian Country. So why have we not yet rejected the
European ways that hurt us and rejoined the indigenous path to peace,
power, and righteousness?

The answer to this question is the reason why, of all the important issues
we need to address, the most crucial is leadership. Understanding leadership
means understanding indigenous political philosophy: conceptions of power,
and the primary values that create legitimacy and allow governments to function appropriately and effectively. Good indigenous leadership ensures that
government is rooted in tradition, is consistent with the cultural values of
the community. This is a key element in restoring the necessary harmony
between social and political cultures in Native societies. Non-indigenous
political structures, values, and styles of leadership lead to coercive and compromised forms of government that contradict basic indigenous values and
are the main reason our social and political crisis persists.

We have not fully recovered from colonialism because our leadership has
been compromised, and we will remain subject to the intellectual, political,
and economic dominance of Western society until the leaders of our communities realize the power of indigenous philosophies and act to restore respect for traditional wisdom. Leadership is essential if we are to disprove the
rule that societies must hit rock bottom before they begin to realize meaningful change. Is it not possible to reach into the depths of tradition and
begin to build the future now?

Returning to indigenous traditions of leadership will require an intensive
effort to understand indigenous political life within the moral and ethical
framework established by traditional values. Without obscuring the distinc-
tiveness of individual societies, it is possible to see fundamental similarities

in the concept of "Native leadership" among indigenous cultures. Most agree that the institutions operating in Native communities today have little to do with indigenous belief systems, and that striking commonalities exist among the traditional philosophies that set the parameters for governance. The values that underpin these traditional philosophies constitute a core statement of what indigenous governance is as a style, a structure, and a set of norms.

In their most basic values, and even to a certain extent their style, traditional forms of government are not unique: similar characteristics can be found in other systems. The special nature of Native American government consists in the prioritization of those values, the rigorous consistency of its principles with those values, and the patterns and procedures of government, as well as the common set of goals (respect, balance, and harmony) that are recognizable across Native American societies. Adherence to those core values made the achievement of the goals possible; it was because of the symbiotic relationship between the traditional value system and the institutions that evolved within the culture that balance and harmony were its hallmarks. Indigenous governance demands respect for the totality of the belief system. It must be rooted in a traditional value system, operate according to principles derived from that system, and seek to achieve goals that can be justified within that system. This is the founding premise of pre/decolonized Native politics—and we are in danger of losing it permanently if the practices and institutions currently in place become any further entrenched (and hence validated).

On the west coast of Vancouver Island, I spoke with a Nuu-chah-nulth elder who recognized the danger of continuing to think of governance in the terms of the value system and the institutional structures that have been imposed on Native communities by the state. Hereditary chief Moses Smith used to be a band councilor under the Canadian government's Indian Act system, but now he recognizes the harm that system has done to his community. As a leader, he is now committed to teaching his people's traditional philosophy so that an indigenous form of government can be restored. Lamenting the loss both of traditional values and of the structures that promoted good leadership, Moses said that "in the old days leaders were taught and values were ingrained in hereditary chiefs. The fundamental value was respect." In his view, contemporary band councils are not operating according to traditional values, and Native leadership premised on traditional power and knowledge will vanish forever unless "the traditional perspective is taken up by the new generation."

In choosing between revitalizing indigenous forms of government and maintaining the European forms imposed on them, Native communities have a choice between two radically different kinds of social organization: one based on conscience and the authority of the good, the other on coercion and authoritarianism. The Native concept of governance is based on what a great student of indigenous societies, Russell Barsh, has called the "primacy of conscience." There is no central or coercive authority, and decision-making is collective. Leaders rely on their persuasive abilities to achieve a consensus that respects the autonomy of individuals, each of whom is free to dissent from and remain unaffected by the collective decision. The clan or family is the basic unit of social organization, and larger forms of organization, from tribe through nation to confederacy, are all predicated on the political autonomy and economic independence of clan units through family-based control of lands and resources.

A crucial feature of the indigenous concept of governance is its respect for individual autonomy. This respect precludes the notion of "sovereignty"—the idea that there can be a permanent transference of power or authority from the individual to an abstraction of the collective called "government." The indigenous tradition sees government as the collective power of the individual members of the nation; there is no separation between society and state. Leadership is exercised by persuading individuals to pool their self-power in the interest of the collective good. By contrast, in the European tradition power is surrendered to the representatives of the majority, whose decisions on what they think is the collective good are then imposed on all citizens.

In the indigenous tradition, the idea of self-determination truly starts with the self; political identity—with its inherent freedoms, powers, and responsibilities—is not surrendered to any external entity. Individuals alone determine their interests and destinies. There is no coercion, only the compelling force of conscience based on those inherited and collectively refined principles that structure the society. With the collective inheritance of a cohesive spiritual universe and traditional culture, profound dissent is rare and is resolved by exemption of the individual from the implementation and implications of the particular decision. When the difference between individual and collective becomes irreconcilable, the individual leaves the group.

Collective self-determination depends on the conscious coordination of individual powers of self-determination. The governance process consists of the structured interplay of three kinds of power: individual power, persuasive power, and the power of tradition. These power relations are channeled into forms of decision-making and dispute resolution grounded in the recognition that beyond the individual there exists a natural community of interest: the extended family. Thus in almost all indigenous cultures, the foundational order of government is the clan. And almost all indigenous systems are predicated on a collective decision-making process organized around the clan.

It is the erosion of this traditional power relationship and the forced dependence on a central government for provision of sustenance that lie at the root of injustice in the indigenous mind. Barsh recognizes a truth that applies to institutions at both the broad and the local level: "The evil of modern states is their power to decide who eats." Along with armed force, they use dependence—which they have created—to induce people's compliance with the will of an abstract authority structure serving the interests of an economic and political elite. It is an affront to justice that individuals are stripped of their power of self-determination and forced to comply with the decisions of a system based on the consciousness and interests of others.

The principles underlying European-style representative government through coercive force stand in fundamental opposition to the values from which indigenous leadership and power derive. In indigenous cultures the core values of equality and respect are reflected in the practices of consensus decision-making and dispute resolution through balanced consideration of all interests and views. In indigenous societies governance results from the interaction of leadership and the autonomous power of the individuals who make up the society. Governance in an indigenist sense can be practiced only in a decentralized, small-scale environment among people who share a culture. It centers on the achievement of consensus and the creation of collective power bounded by six principles:

- it depends on the active participation of individuals;
- it balances many layers of equal power;
- it is dispersed;
- it is situational;
- it is non-coercive;
- it respects diversity.

Contemporary politics in Native communities is shaped by the interplay of people who, socially and culturally, are still basically oriented toward this understanding of government, with a set of structures and political relationships that reflect a very different, almost oppositional, understanding.

The imposition of colonial political structures is the source of most factionalism within Native communities. Such institutions operate on principles that can never be truly acceptable to people whose orientations and attitudes are derived from a traditional value system. But they are tolerated by cynical community members as a fact of their colonized political lives. As a result, those structures have solidified into major obstacles to the achievement of peace and harmony in Native communities, spawning a nontraditional or anti-traditionalist political subculture among those individuals who draw their status and income from them.

The effort needed to bring contemporary political institutions, and the people who inhabit them, into harmony with traditional values is very different from the superficial and purely symbolic efforts at reform that have taken place in many communities. Symbols are crucially important, but they must not be confused with substance: when terminology, costume, and protocol are all that change, while unjust power relationships and colonized attitudes remain untouched, such "reform" becomes nothing more than a politically correct smokescreen obscuring the fact that no real progress is being made towards realizing traditionalist goals. Cloaking oneself in the mantle of tradition is a shallow façade masking a greed for power and success as defined by mainstream society. Recognizable by its lack of community values, this selfish hunger for power holds many Native leaders in its grip and keeps them from working to overturn the colonial system.

The indigenous tradition is profoundly egalitarian; it does not put any substantial distance between leaders and other people, let alone allow for the exercise of coercive authority. Yet these are fundamental features of the political systems imposed on Native people. The hard truth is that many of those who hold positions of authority in Native communities have come to depend on the colonial framework for their power, employment, and status. How many of them would still hold their positions if the criteria for leadership reflected indigenous values instead of an ability to serve the interests of mainstream society? Very few contemporary Native politicians can honestly claim to possess the qualities and skills needed to lead in a non-coercive, participatory, transparent, consensus-based system. The hunger for power, money, and status prevents many people from seeing what is best for the community in the long run. But even when the people who seek that power do so with the best intentions, for the good of the people, the fact remains that holding non-consensual power over others is contrary to tradition. Whatever the purpose behind the use of arbitrary authority, the power relationship itself is wrong.

Proponents of indigenist government aim to overturn that unjust power relationship along with the government systems that have been imposed on our communities since colonization. Those systems cannot be defended on grounds of history (they are foreign), morality (they are intended to destabilize), or even practice (they do not work). Yet many people who are entrenched politically or bureaucratically within them resist any attempt to recover the traditional basis for governmental organization. Their defense of the status quo reflects a need to preserve the power relationships of contemporary Native politics. This is both a political and philosophical problem, a corruption that must be addressed if the values embedded in the European-American political system are not to form the general criteria for status, prestige, and leadership in our communities.

Efforts to recover the integrity of indigenous societies are not new. The first post-European Native cultural revival, at the start of the nineteenth century, was aimed largely at expunging cultural influences that were seen to be destructive. Various social and religious movements, including the Ghost Dance, Peyoteism, and the Code of Handsome Lake, sought to overcome the loss of spiritual rootedness and refocus attention on Native value systems. Experience since then has shown that cultural revival is not a matter of rejecting all Western influences, but of separating the good from the bad and of fashioning a coherent set of ideas out of the traditional culture to guide whatever forms of political and social development—including the good elements of Western forms—are appropriate to the contemporary reality. It is this rootedness in traditional values that defines an indigenous people; a culture that does not reflect the basic principles of the traditional philosophy of government cannot be considered to be indigenous in any real sense.

In lamenting the loss of a traditional frame of reference, we must be careful not to romanticize the past. Tradition is the spring from which we draw our healing water; but any decision must take into account contemporary economic, social, and political concerns. We seek the answer to one of the basic questions any society must answer: What is the right way to govern? For generations, foreigners have provided the answer to this question. Our deference to other people's solutions has taken a terrible toll on indigenous peoples. A focused re-commitment to traditional teachings is the only way to preserve what remains of indigenous cultures and to recover the strength and integrity of indigenous nations. At this time in history, indigenous people need to acknowledge the losses suffered and confront the seriousness of their plight. There is no time left to wallow in our pain. Instead, we should use it as a measure of how urgent the challenge is. The power of our most important traditional teachings will become evident as they begin to ease our suffering and restore peace.

Reorienting leaders and institutions toward an indigenous framework means confronting tough questions about the present state of affairs. It would be unrealistic to imagine that all Native communities are willing and able to jettison the structures in place today for the romantic hope of a return to a pre-European life. But it would also be too pessimistic to suggest that there is no room at all for traditional values. Mediating between these extremes, one could argue that most communities would simply be better served by governments founded on those principles drawn from their own cultures that are relevant to the contemporary reality. In a practical sense, this is what is meant by a return to traditional government.

The persistence of political apathy, ignorance, and greed does not mean that traditional forms of government are not viable. These problems simply demonstrate that imported forms of government do not work in Native communities. In those places that have embarked on a traditionalist path and still find themselves plagued by these problems, they indicate that there is still too much distance between the idea of traditional government and the reality of the issues that need to be addressed. In both cases, traditional knowledge has to be brought forward and translated into a form that can be seen as a viable alternative to the imposed structures—as the culturally appropriate solution to fundamental political problems.

Some may be tempted to ask why it is so important to return to a traditional perspective. Aren't there other paths to peace, paths that would take us forward rather than back? Some may even see the problems besetting

Native communities as the product not of colonialism but of the people's own failure to adapt to a modern reality shaped by forces that traditional values cannot comprehend, let alone deal with. Tradition, in their view, is a dream no more grounded in reality than clouds that disappear on the first wind—a beautiful dream, unsuited to the harsh realities of the world.

Such people are mistaken. Rediscovering the power of the traditional teachings and applying them to contemporary problems is crucially important to the survival of indigenous people. There is more than one Indian in this world who dreams in the language of his ancestors and wakes mute to them, who dreams of peace and wakes to a deep and heavy anger. If a traditionally grounded nation is a dream, it is one worth pursuing. It has been said before, and it bears repeating: sometimes dreams are wiser than waking.

III

FEDERALISM

Divided sovereignty is the fundamental characteristic of a federal system of government. As virtually every textbook makes clear, it is also a political reality that has been the source of tensions and conflicts central to American political history. Although the balance of power and responsibility between states and national government has clearly changed over time, the federal relationship remains central.

However, our federal system really has more than two types of players in the United States. Tribal governments have also been recognized as a form of sovereign. As Sharon O'Brien's chapter explains, tribal governments play many of the roles for their members that non-Indians expect to be played by either the states or the federal government. Thus, we must recognize a tripartite division of sovereignty in the United States. Just as recognition of state-national federalism doesn't inhibit us from paying attention to the shifting power of these governments but actually encourages us to do so, a recognition of tribal-state-national federalism can allow us to see when tribal sovereignty and governments are acknowledged as having meaningful autonomy and when their sovereign claims are ignored or overshadowed by other governmental players within the federal system.

Tribal Governments

SHARON O'BRIEN

The dispatcher notifies the Reno Sparks, Nevada, tribal police officer of a robbery in progress. The Navajo health care worker drives for an hour over the mesa to make certain an elderly woman is properly taking her prescribed medication. The Quinault tribal biologist attends a national conference to discuss with other experts the latest techniques in salmon hatching. Banging down his beaded gavel, the Sac and Fox judge grants the couple's divorce petition. The Mississippi Choctaw Chief has requested the council to examine the feasibility of constructing a bingo hall on tribal lands. The Yakima delegation is in Washington, D.C., to lobby its congressional representatives for support against the proposed location of a nuclear-waste dump near their reservation in Washington state.

The scenarios sketched above illustrate the numerous roles tribal governments perform daily throughout Indian country. For thousands of years, tribes have served their people, providing for their safety, health, and economic well-being. Their structures, processes, and methods of governing have changed; the responsibilities have not. To best appreciate the current challenges faced by the more than six hundred tribal governments in the continental United States and Alaska, one must first understand the past pressures that tribes have endured.

This chapter is reprinted from *National Forum*, Volume 71, Number 2 (Spring 1991): 18–20, by permission of Sharon O'Brien. Copyright © by Sharon O'Brien.

Historically, tribal governments varied considerably in structure and complexity. The smaller bands of the Basin and California regions approximated truly direct great democracies. The Muscogee Confederacy of the Southeast, on the other hand, possessed an elaborate system of checks and balances guided by a dual clan and town system.

Contact between Indians and non-Indians altered in varying degrees—but without exception—the philosophy, structure, and powers of these traditional governments. The immigrants valued property, material progress, and individualism. Indian nations, with their extensive lands and resources, were both the source of and the obstacle to the attainment of the non-Indians' goals. Tedious negotiations with people who did not view land as a commodity to be sold, who cared little for the individual amassment of wealth, and who practiced consensus decision-making precluded the quick attainment of lands by the non-Indian. The federal government responded to this obstinacy with measures to destroy tribal cultures and sovereignty.

The federal government, like its European predecessors, initially recognized tribes as independent nations, with exclusive sovereignty over their external and internal affairs. England negotiated more than 500 treaties with tribes and the United States more than 370. Recognition for tribal rights declined, however, as the greed for Indian lands intensified and the power balance tipped favorably toward the United States, jeopardizing the tribes' ability to maintain their traditional structures and powers. Tribal governments, such as those of the Choctaw, Cherokee, and other Indian nations of the Southeast, responded to internal tribal demands and changed their governments, modeling them after those of their white neighbors. Other tribes, such as the Lakota (or Sioux), were subjected to continuous federal policies designed to undermine their leaders and governments.

By the late 1800s, the federal government's decision to solve the "Indian problem" by assimilating Indians into the dominant society had emasculated not just the government of the Lakotas, but most other tribal governments. Congress's unilateral decision in 1871 to end treaty making with the Indian nations deprived tribal governments of a voice in their relationship with the federal government. The virtual extinction of the buffalo and other game, a forced reliance on federal rations, and the allotment of reservation lands severely disabled the tribal governments' ability to secure their people's economic well-being. The authority of the Bureau of Indian Affairs agent and the establishment of Indian police forces and courts usurped the tribal government's responsibility to provide for public order and justice. Federal regulations outlawing tribal religious practices, efforts to convert tribes to Christianity, policies to extinguish Indian languages, and the teaching of American values through education obscured the philosophical sources of traditional governments. Federal actions were indeed changing tribes from self-sufficient nations into wards.

By the 1930s, when Congress passed the Indian Reorganization Act, tribal governments had nearly ceased to exist. The Indian Reorganization Act of 1934 offered tribes constitutions drafted by the Bureau of Indian Affairs (BIA) and congressional funds for economic development. Although many experts praised the act for its resuscitation of tribal governments, others criticized it as assimilationist, charging that the government provided tribes with Western-derived political institutions rather than improving traditional systems.

Congressional support of tribal governments, however limited or misdirected, ended in the 1950s and early 1960s with the passage of several termination bills—legislation intended to solve the ever-present Indian problem by abrogating the federal government's relationship with tribes and integrating their lands and peoples into the surrounding states. Pursuant to this objective, Congress terminated its relationship with 109 communities, bands, and tribes before again altering its policies toward tribal governments in the mid-1970s. Congress's current approach toward tribal governments is to acknowledge and promote tribal self-determination. The implementation of this policy has translated into increased funds and training that enable tribal governments to administer programs and services formerly operated by the Bureau of Indian Affairs.

Congress refers to its relationship with tribes as a government-to-government relationship, a term signifying the inherent sovereignty of each party. As sovereigns, tribal governments receive their authority to operate from their own people, not from the United States Constitution as do state governments. (This has led one judge to write that tribal governments, in effect, have a status higher than states.) No longer viewed as wards, tribal governments are recognized by Congress and the states as the official representatives of domestic dependent nations.

As domestic dependent nations, tribes possess the inherent sovereignty to exercise all governmental power unless extinguished by treaty or congressional legislation or unless it is a power that is inconsistent with the tribes' dependent status. In practical terms this means that tribes have retained, with some limitations, the authority to structure their own governments, to administer justice, to regulate domestic relations, to manage and develop their lands and resources, to conduct businesses, and to tax individuals and commercial enterprises.

Differing cultures, histories, resources, and leadership abilities have created a diverse collection of tribal governments, each with its own structure, governing style, objectives, and tribal programs. Approximately half of all tribes operate according to the guidelines of the Indian Reorganization Act. Other tribes, such as the Onondaga and the Seneca of New York, the Yakima of Washington, and several Pueblos, have retained much of their traditional structures.

In general, tribal governments are headed by a council, referred to by some tribes as a legislature, or a business committee. Council members are usually elected, although such tribes as the Warm Springs of Oregon and the Miccosukee of Florida have a combination of elected officials and traditional band or clan chiefs. A community's cultural values may also be apparent in the council's composition, for instance in the ratio of young to old, educated to non-educated, and men to women council members. Governing styles and procedures differ, too. The discussion of an economic-development proposal by one tribal government may continue informally for months until the council has achieved a clear consensus. A neighboring tribe's consideration of a similar proposal may last a shorter time, with discussions occurring according to Robert's Rules of Order, and the final decision determined by majority vote.

Although many are patterned after non-Indian institutions, most tribal governments do not possess clearly separated branches of government. Especially in smaller tribes, the council may be responsible for various, if not all, executive, legislative, and judicial functions. The independence and power of the executive (referred to as a chairperson, chief, governor, or president, depending on the tribe) is determined by a tribe's history, constitution, and mode of election. The relocated Five Civilized Tribes of Oklahoma, who historically have possessed strong executives, elect their principal chiefs by popular vote. The Menominees of Wisconsin have ceded the election of the chairperson to their legislature.

More than 140 tribal governments have established separate judicial systems. These courts vary considerably in complexity, independence, and cultural orientation. Tribal legal systems may include one court or several, such as separate criminal, civil, family, or conservation courts. The Navajo Nation has developed the most elaborate system, consisting of an attorney general's office, a variety of specialized courts, and more than twenty codes, including laws pertaining to commercial enterprises and child welfare. On small reservations the council may serve as the court of first and last resort. Other tribal constitutions vest the council with the right to hear appeals. A few tribes, such as the Lakota, have established a special supreme-court level to decide appeals from any of the several member reservations. Judicial review, a right not given to all tribal courts, and the selection process of judges, elected by the people or appointed by the council, are other factors affecting the independence of tribal judicial systems.

Whatever the particular system, most tribal courts employ and apply a combination of traditional and Anglo-derived procedures and laws. For example, tribal regulations on the Blackfeet reservation require all lawyers and judges to speak the native language and to be members of the tribal bar; other reservations require lawyers and judges to be members of the state bar, while still others provide a more informal conflict-resolution process staffed by respected leaders who may or may not have formal legal training.

Tribal courts no longer exercise complete criminal and civil jurisdiction over all matters and individuals within their territory. Criminal and civil jurisdiction in Indian country is today a patchwork of exclusive and concurrent authority exercised by tribal, federal, and state governments. The federal government has assumed criminal jurisdiction over Indians committing any of fourteen major crimes. In addition, two recent Supreme Court decisions have ruled that the exercise of tribal criminal jurisdiction over anyone but a member is inconsistent with the tribes' status as domestic dependent nations. These court cases and laws, in combination with federal legislation limiting the penalties levied by tribal courts to one year in jail or $5,000 in fines, have severely undermined the ability of tribal governments to protect their people and others living on the reservation. Tribes have retained most civil jurisdiction over Indians and non-Indians within their boundaries. Civil-dispute settlement, marriage, divorce, zoning, and taxation are inherent powers properly exercised by all tribal governments. The Agua Caliente have passed zoning laws for their reservation lands, parts of which are located in Palm Springs, California. The Jicarilla Apache tax energy companies located on their property. Tribal courts, as clarified by the Indian Child Welfare Act of 1978, possess primary jurisdictional rights over state courts in procedures involving the custody and adoption of enrolled Indian children.

Historically, states had no jurisdiction over tribal lands. In the last thirty years, however, the federal government has allowed state governments to exercise increased authority within reservation boundaries. In 1953, Congress granted five (later six) states the authority under Public Law 280 to assume criminal and civil jurisdiction over most reservations within their borders. And as mentioned above, state courts now have the power to try nonmembers for criminal acts committed on the reservation. The states are also permitted to tax and regulate non-Indians hunting and fishing on non-Indian lands within reservation boundaries.

Ironically, as the courts chip away at the edges of tribal autonomy, Indian governments are developing into increasingly experienced and well-trained social-service providers. The Muscogee Creeks of Oklahoma own and operate their own hospital. Head Start, alcoholism, and elderly programs are basic services provided by tribal governments throughout Indian country. Support for cultural activities, the supervision of government housing programs, and job training are among other services administered by tribes.

Given the limited resource base of most reservations, the provision of social services and programs depends heavily upon the availability of federal funding. In communities where unemployment ranges from 20 to 80 percent and half of all jobs are tied to federal programs, budget reductions can have disastrous consequences. Attempting to free themselves from dependence on federal dollars, tribal governments have initiated a variety of entrepreneurial projects. Tribes fortunate enough to have mineral, timber, or fishery resources are investing considerable efforts, both individually and jointly, in their sustained exploitation. The Mescalero Apache, along with forty-three other tribes, compose the membership of Council of Energy Resource Tribes (CERT)—an organization that provides technical assistance to tribes in the development of their oil, gas, and coal reserves. The Pacific Northwest tribes are especially knowledgeable and proficient in all facets of the salmon industry, from hatcheries to processing. Washington tribes now raise more than 30 percent of all salmon produced in the state.

The introduction of gaming operations in Indian country in the last two decades has offered many tribal governments, particularly those poor in land and resources, an opportunity to infuse needed jobs and money into the tribal economy. The tribal council of the Wisconsin Oneidas, to mention one of the more successful examples, has constructed a profitable bingo operation and hotel near Green Bay. With revenue generated from these businesses, the council has supplemented and improved the tribe's educational services, health and elderly care, and economic-development programs.

In addition to their responsibilities to provide social services, ensure public safety, initiate economic development, regulate zoning and taxation, and protect members' rights, tribal governments possess one other extremely important obligation—defense of the tribe's sovereignty and culture. Tribal survival depends on more than improving tribal programs and services. Nor is tribal survival simply an issue of retaining the language, traditions, and crafts. Tribal governments must also adapt and meet outside pressure while maintaining internal cohesion and integrity.

How does a tribal government reinforce its culture's traditional respect for the environment and engender responsibility for collectivity when surrounded by an alien culture that praises domination of the environment, measures progress and self-worth in terms of individual materialism, and emphasizes rights over responsibility?

It is this underlying and constant contradiction that forces tribal governments to analyze every decision for the long-term impact on the tribe's culture and independence, as well as for its pragmatic benefits. Decisions that for state and local governments involve primarily issues of funds and support have greater and more wide-reaching consequences for tribal governments. For example, a tribal council is in the process of establishing a judicial system. Should it resurrect the tribe's traditional mediation model or install an adversarial system? The former is more culturally attuned but may deter investments by outside companies. Should resources be left undeveloped in keeping with traditional teachings, exploited by a tribal business, or leased to individual tribal members? Should a tribal government with limited resources request the county police to provide law and order on the reservation? How does a council balance the need for protection and safety against the potential loss of tribal authority to the state? Should a tribal business strive for maximum efficiency and profits, or sacrifice some degree of both to employ more tribal members?

It is this fundamental tension between two cultures, exacerbated by limited resources, that most challenges tribal governments today. Whether tribes can meet and survive this challenge is perhaps best answered by reference to a letter written by Benjamin Franklin in 1751: "It would be a very strange thing if Six Nations of ignorant savages should be capable of forming a scheme for such a union, and be able to execute it in such a manner as that it has subsisted for ages, and appears indissoluble; and yet that a like union should be impracticable for ten or a dozen English colonies."

Franklin's reference is to the Iroquois Confederacy, a political alliance of the Mohawk, Oneida, Seneca, Cayuga, and Onondaga nations (the Tuscarora joined later), which continues to operate today. Scholars estimate that the Iroquois established their confederacy around 1200 A.D. Whether the Iroquois Confederacy, or the All Indian Pueblo Council, composed today of the nineteen Pueblos of New Mexico, deserves the honor as the oldest continuing political institution in the United States, remains unknown. What these institutions do illustrate is the cultural tenacity, human resourcefulness, and political ability of indigenous governments to survive.

IV

CITIZENSHIP AND POLITICAL PARTICPATION

The story of citizenship and political participation in the United States is commonly told as a progressive one. The franchise (right to vote) was very limited at the time of the founding, this story goes, but it has been expanding ever since. First it was expanded to non-property-owning white males, later to African-American males, then to women, and finally to youth (18- to 21-year-olds). Of course, there are important caveats typically added to this story, most especially the fact that although in principle African-American males were granted the right to vote following the Civil War, it took the civil rights movement of the 1960s to put this into practice for most. Still, the familiar story is one of struggle by a disenfranchised group for meaningful inclusion within the polity and eventually emerging victorious.

Where do American Indians fit into this story? As Jill Martin's chapter makes clear, in many ways they don't. The history of American Indian citizenship upends this familiar progressive story. Citizenship was imposed by the U.S. government on many Indians, not sought after or struggled for by them. Moreover, this status came to be applied to different Indians at different times, reflecting the U.S. government's attempt to eliminate tribal forms of political affiliation. The notion that the right to vote and other manifestations of citizenship might reflect defeat for a group rather than victory is not one that many of us are likely to immediately realize, but it is one that American Indian history forces us all to consider.

"Neither Fish, Flesh, Fowl, nor Good Red Herring": The Citizenship Status of American Indians, 1830–1924

JILL E. MARTIN

INTRODUCTION

Early European discoverers of the North American continent claimed exclusive title to the land upon which they set foot, as the accepted European right of conquest. That Indian tribes and nations had been present at the time of discovery made no difference to this claim of right. The European discoverers admitted and allowed that the Indians had a right to use and to occupancy of the land, but once the European sovereign claimed it, the Indians could not alienate or dispose of the land to anyone else.

The Indians were allowed to use the land and maintain their own governments. The formation of the United States, as a new sovereign, did not alter these rights. The Indian tribes were still separate and distinct from the United States and dealt with the United States government through treaties. The United States Constitution, adopted in 1787, gives Congress the exclusive right to "regulate Commerce with foreign nations, and among the several states, and with the Indian Tribes." This clause acknowledged that the Indians were not a part of the United States, yet distinguished them from foreign nations.

This chapter originally appeared in *Journal of the West*, Volume 29, Number 3 (July 1990): 75–86. Copyright © 1990 by Journal of the West, Inc. Reprinted with permission of *Journal of the West*, 1531 Yuma, Manhattan, KS 66502.

In 1831, the U.S. Supreme Court determined the status of Indian tribes in their relation to the United States government. The Cherokee Nation challenged a law of the state of Georgia. The question arose whether the Supreme Court could hear the case, as its jurisdiction was limited, extending only to cases between citizens of different states, or between a state and foreign states. The Supreme Court, under Chief Justice John Marshall, found that an Indian tribe was neither a state nor a foreign nation, but rather a "domestic dependent nation. . . . Their relation to the United States resembles that of a ward to his guardian."

As the Indian tribe was not a foreign nation, the Supreme Court could not determine the rights of the parties in the case. The jurisdiction of the courts of the United States did not include matters involving Indians. The Indian tribes could not sue or be sued in the United States.

The decision in *Cherokee Nation* did not discuss Indians as individuals, only as tribes or nations. But if the tribe was not a foreign nation, nor its members foreign citizens, neither were the tribes states, nor their members citizens of states. As citizens of dependent domestic nations, there were no laws dealing with the status of individual Indians. Thus, Indians were nonentities and had no legal status.

Yet the Supreme Court in 1856, without mentioning the *Cherokee Nation* case, stated that Indian tribes had been treated as foreign governments and their citizens as foreigners. The Court was considering the question of whether Negroes, descendants of African slaves, became citizens when they were emancipated. Chief Justice Roger Taney, in *Dred Scott v. Sanford*, distinguished Negroes from Indians. Indians, "although they were uncivilized, they were yet a free and independent people, associated together in nations or tribes, and governed by their own laws." The Court continued, "These Indian Governments were regarded and treated as foreign Governments . . . and the people who compose these Indian political communities have always been treated as foreigners not living under our Government."

This language opened a way for Indians to become citizens. Foreigners could apply for and become naturalized as citizens, and if Indians were foreigners, they too could qualify for citizenship. Taney concluded:

> They may, without doubt, like the subjects of any other foreign Government, be naturalized by the authority of Congress, and become citizens of a State, and of the United States; and if an individual should leave his nation or tribe, and take up his abode among the white population, he would be entitled to all the rights and privileges which would belong to an emigrant from any other foreign people.

This part of the decision seemed to contradict the earlier *Cherokee Nation* opinion on the Indians' status as dependent domestic nations. However, because the *Dred Scott* language was in an *obiter dicta*, and therefore unnecessary to the discussion of the case, it did not overrule Justice Marshall's declaration of the tribes' status.

But if it did not overrule the tribes' status, perhaps it opened a way for individual Indians who were assimilated into the white culture to become citizens. Yet even Taney was aware of the practical application of such an idea. His decision pointed out that the current naturalization law, passed in 1790, confined the right of becoming citizens to "aliens being free white persons." Taney suggested that the 1790 Congress was not using the term "white" to exclude Indians. Congress could have authorized the naturalization of Indians, because they were foreigners. "But in their then untutored and savage state, no one would have thought of admitting them as citizens in a civilized community."

While Taney did not say so, the implication was that, even in 1856, very few Indians were civilized enough for Congress to need to change the law.

INDIANS AND THE FOURTEENTH AMENDMENT

The difference in treatment between Indians and Negroes was reversed in the years following the Civil War. While the *Dred Scott* decision gave the Indians greater rights than Negroes, Negroes gained political and legal rights through the passage of the Civil Rights Act of 1866 and the Fourteenth Amendment. The Fourteenth Amendment, ratified by the states in 1868, provides in §1: "All persons born or naturalized in the United States and subject to the jurisdiction thereof, are citizens of the United States and of the State wherein they reside." Undoubtedly, this made former slaves citizens. But the Senate was divided in its opinion as to whether Indians would also become citizens. There was no question that Indians were born in the territory of United States as this now extended to the Pacific, but were they "subject to the jurisdiction thereof"?

The majority of Senators wanted to exclude Indians. Discussion focused upon a proposed amendment to the wording of the bill (later adopted as the Fourteenth Amendment) which would add "subject to the jurisdiction thereof, excluding Indians not taxed." The Senators were uncertain whether this was necessary. Senator James R. Doolittle from Wisconsin, who proposed the amendment, did so because

> it seems to me very clear that there is a large mass of the Indian population who are clearly subject to the jurisdiction of the United States who ought not to be included as citizens of the United States. All the Indians upon reservations within the several States are most clearly subject to our jurisdiction, both civil and military. We appoint civil agents who have a control over them on behalf of the Government. We have our military commanders in the neighborhood of the reservations, who have complete control.

Senator Reverdy Johnson of Maryland also believed that Indians were "subject to the jurisdiction" of the United States.

> What I mean to say, is that over all the Indian tribes within the limits of the United States, the United States may—that is the test—exercise jurisdiction. Whether they exercise it in point of fact is another question; whether they propose to govern them under the treaty-making power is quite another question; but the question as to the authority to legislate is one, I think, about which, if we were to exercise it, the courts would have no doubt.

Illinois Senator Lyman Trumbull also wanted to exclude Indians. But his belief was that the words "excluding Indians not taxed" were unnecessary because Indians were not subject to United States jurisdiction. He stated:

> But it is very clear to me that there is nothing whatever in the suggestions of the Senator from Wisconsin. The provision is, that "all persons born in the United States, and subject to the jurisdiction thereof, are citizens." That means "subject to the complete jurisdiction thereof." Now, does the Senator from Wisconsin pretend to say that the Navajoe [*sic*] Indians are subject to the complete jurisdiction of the United States? What do we mean by "subject to the jurisdiction of the United States?" Not owing allegiance to anybody else. That is what it means. Can you sue a Navajoe [*sic*] Indian in court? Are they in any sense subject to the complete jurisdiction of the United States? By no means. We make treaties with them, and therefore they are not subject to our jurisdiction. If they were, we would not make treaties with them.

Senator Jacob Howard from Michigan expressed concern over the language "Indians are not taxed." If this language was included, any state could naturalize Indians merely by taxing them. Surely this was not wanted.

Senator Doolittle continued to argue for inclusion of "excluding Indians not taxed." If there was any doubt as to whether Indians could be included, he believed this to be the sure way to relieve that doubt. The language "excluding Indians not taxed" had been used in the Civil Rights Act of 1866, and was also used in the Constitution and the second section of the Fourteenth Amendment dealing with apportionment. Including the language in the first section of the amendment would add clarity.

The language of the proposed amendment was not adopted. Yet there was no doubt that the Senate wanted to exclude Indians. Senator Howard stated:

> I am not yet prepared to pass a sweeping act of naturalization by which all the Indian savages, wild or tame, belonging to a tribal relation, are to become my fellow citizens and go to the polls and vote with me and hold lands and deal in every other way that a citizen of the United States has a right to do.

Senator Thomas Hendricks of Indiana was even more adamant, and was against Indians and Negroes becoming citizens. He spoke of the "mad fanaticism and partisan fury of a single year" which would degrade American citizenship.

> But this is certain that the section will add many millions to the class of persons who are citizens. We have been justly proud of the rank and title of our citizenship, for we understood it to belong to the inhabitants of the United States who were descended from the great races of people who inhabit the countries of Europe, and such emigrants from those countries as have been admitted under our laws. The rank and title conferred honor at home and secured kindness, respect, and safety everywhere abroad; but if this amendment be adopted we will even carry the title and enjoy its advantages in common with the Negroes, the coolies, and the Indians.

Only one senator, Willard Saulsbury of Delaware, argued for inclusion of Indians as citizens under the Fourteenth Amendment: "If these negroes are to be made citizens of the United States, I can see no reason in justice or in right why the Indians should not be made citizens."

The Fourteenth Amendment was ratified by the states in 1868. But the question whether it included Indians was not satisfactorily settled for many senators. In April 1870, the Senate instructed the Committee on the Judiciary to determine the effect of the Fourteenth Amendment on the Indian tribes. Had Indians become citizens under the amendment? If Indians had become citizens, were the treaties between the United States and the tribes annulled? The straightforward answer from the Committee was no: "That in the opinion of your committee the fourteenth amendment to the Constitution has no effect whatever upon the status of the Indian tribes within the limits of the United States, and does not annul the treaties previously made." The Committee based this conclusion upon a close and comparative reading of the first and second clauses of the Fourteenth Amendment. The first clause states that "All persons born or naturalized in the United States and subject to the jurisdiction thereof, are citizens of the United States and of the State wherein they reside." The second clause excludes Indians not taxed from apportionment for representation. It states: "Representatives shall be apportioned among the several states according to their respective numbers, counting the whole number of persons in each state, excluding Indians not taxed." If the Indians had been made citizens by the first section, they would not be excluded in the second section from representation. The Fourteenth Amendment

> recognizes no change in the status of the Indians. They were excluded by the original constitution, and in the same terms are excluded by the amendment from the constituent body, the people. Considering the political sentiments which inspired the amendment, it cannot be supposed that it was designed to exclude a particular class of citizens from the basis of representation. *The Indians were excluded because they were citizens.*

However, the Committee pointed out that treaty relations could exist only with tribes or nations, not with individual Indians. It reiterated Justice Taney's comments from *Dred Scott*: "When the members of a tribe are scattered, they are merged in the mass of our people and become equally subject to the jurisdiction of the United States." This still left the status of individual Indians vague and uncertain, and up to the courts' interpretations.

THE COURTS' INTERPRETATION OF THE INDIANS' STATUS

The lower federal courts were not as certain in the beliefs on the citizenship status of Indians. The decade of the 1870s produced a number of disparate and conflicting court decisions.

The cases of *United States v. Elm* and *McKay v. Campbell* involve Indians seeking the right to vote. Elm was an Oneida Indian living in New York who voted in the congressional election of 1876. He was indicted and convicted of illegal voting, on the grounds that as an Indian he could not be a citizen, and only citizens could vote. The federal district court considered the question of whether Elm was, in fact, a citizen. The court recognized that "Indians who maintain their tribal relations are the subjects of independent governments, and, as such, not in the jurisdiction of the United States, within the meaning of the amendment" and therefore are not citizens. But Elm was different. "His tribe has ceased to maintain its tribal integrity, and he has abandoned his tribal relations . . . and because of these facts, and because Indians in this state are subject to taxation, he is a citizen, within the meaning of the fourteenth amendment."

The court found Elm was a citizen and overturned his conviction. The court interpreted the Civil Rights Act of 1866 as Senator Howard was afraid would happen:

> Native Indians in this state are taxed. . . . When by the civil rights bill Indians not taxed were excluded from the classes upon which citizenship was conferred, upon well-settled rules of construction those who were taxed were by implication included in the grant. In other words, those Indians who were taxed were not excepted from the class who were declared to be citizens.

The district court judge further stated that this interpretation was based not just on the Civil Rights Act, but also on the Fourteenth Amendment. "It is not necessary, however, to decide that the Indians in this state became citizens by force of the civil rights bill. I prefer to regard that act as a contemporaneous construction of the meaning of the fourteenth amendment." With the amendment, the court concluded, "The phraseology employed is sufficiently broad to include Indians who have abandoned their tribes and become so far integrated with the general body of citizens that the states in which they reside have subjected them to the duties of citizens and enforced over them the prerogatives of sovereignty."

William McKay was the son of a Chinook Indian woman and a British man. He tried to vote in Oregon, was refused, and filed a complaint with the federal district court in 1871. The court spent the majority of its decision discussing the possibility that McKay was a United States citizen through his birth (as he was born in Oregon Territory when it was subject to a treaty of joint occupation). But the court only needed a few lines to dispose of the question of whether he became a citizen through his Indian mother. The answer was no. "Being born a member of 'an independent political community'—the Chinook—he was not born subject to the jurisdiction of the United States—not born in its allegiance."

In *Ex parte Reynolds* (1879), Reynolds, a white married to a Choctaw, killed another white married to a Choctaw. Under Choctaw law, both men were Choctaws and subject to tribal law. Reynolds wanted to be tried in the Choctaw court rather than the federal court. If both were considered Indians, the federal court had no jurisdiction. The court found that Indians are not citizens. However, the victim's Indian wife had had a white paternal grandfather. As the law required that children follow the condition of their fathers, the victim's Indian wife could be considered a citizen, so the marriage did not make the victim an Indian. Reynolds was tried in the federal courts.

The 1878 case of *Ex parte Kenyon* also dealt with a white man married to an Indian woman, of the Cherokee nation. By Cherokee law, he was considered an Indian. After her death he took her property with him and their children out of Indian territory. The Cherokee nation convicted him of larceny, and Kenyon sought review by the federal courts. The federal circuit court held he was not an Indian, because he had voluntarily left the Cherokee nation and became a citizen of the state of Kansas. Citing *Dred Scott* again, the Court held:

> When members of a tribe of Indians scatter themselves among the citizens of the United States, they are merged in the mass of our people, owing complete allegiance to the government of the United States and of the State where they may reside, and, equally with the citizens of the United States and of the several states, subject to the jurisdiction of the courts thereof.

As Kenyon had abandoned the Indian nation and merged with the citizens of Kansas, the Cherokee court had no jurisdiction over him. While individual Indians could possibly become subject to the federal jurisdiction, Indians in tribes or nations, because they were not citizens of the United States, nor citizens of a foreign country, were not within the jurisdiction of the federal courts. But the Fifth Amendment, and also the Fourteenth Amendment, provides certain protections not to citizens but to "persons." The Fifth Amendment provides, in relevant part, "No person shall . . . be deprived of life, liberty, or property, without due process of law." This use of "persons" was the key to allowing Indians to seek and receive a writ of habeas corpus from a federal court.

The writ of habeas corpus allows a court to hear arguments from a prisoner that his custody is unlawful and in violation of the United States Constitution. A lower federal court found the writ of habeas corpus was available to Indians. In *United States ex rel. Standing Bear v. Crook* (1879), Ponca Indians, under the leadership of Standing Bear, left Indian Territory and tried to return to their original reservation. General George Crook arrested them on the Omaha reservation and tried to return them to Indian Territory.

Standing Bear and 25 other Indians petitioned the circuit court for a writ of habeas corpus, alleging that their arrest and custody by General Crook was unlawful. The United States challenged the authority of the court to issue a writ of habeas corpus on behalf of Indians, who were not citizens. The court disagreed:

> Now it must be borne in mind that the habeas corpus act describes applicants for the writ as "persons," or "parties," who may be entitled thereto. It nowhere describes them as "citizens," nor is citizenship in any way or place made a qualification for suing out the writ, and, in the absence of express provision or necessary implication which would require the interpretation contended for by the district attorney, I should not feel justified in giving the words "person" and "party" such a narrow construction.

The court quoted a *Webster's Dictionary* definition of person as "a living soul; a self-conscious being; a moral agent; especially a living human being; a man, woman, or child; an individual of the human race." The court stated, a bit sarcastically, "This is comprehensive enough, it would seem, to include even an Indian."

As an Indian was a person, the federal court had jurisdiction to issue a writ of habeas corpus. The government would have to prove that its custody of the Indians was proper and lawful. The government could no longer just move the Indians from one place to another; it must act lawfully in regard to the Indians. In reviewing the specific facts of the Poncas, the court found that while the government could remove them from the Omaha Reservation, it could not force them to go anyplace else.

This decision provided the Indians some protection under the Constitution. The citizenship status of tribal Indians seemed fairly certain—but that of Indians who had left their tribes was still undecided. The Supreme Court had still not addressed the issue.

THE COMMISSIONER OF INDIAN AFFAIRS AND INDIANS' STATUS

During the decade of the 1870s the Commissioner of Indian Affairs was also concerned with the status of American Indians. The Commission at this time was seeking to civilize the Indians, and the questions of civilization and citizenship often became intertwined. Citizenship was viewed as both a means to civilization and an end to the civilization process.

The 1873 Annual Report, lamenting the lack of status of the Indians, asked for citizenship as a means to civilization. "He is, so far as citizenship is concerned, a constitutional, illegal anomaly—a sort of an indefinable, hybrid citizen. If the right to all of the benefits and privileges of citizenship is placed in reach of the Indian, under proper restrictions, it will prove a powerful incentive to his progression upward in civilization." The Commissioner realized that "radical legislation will be required."

The legislation suggested was to provide a way into citizenship for those Indians who wanted it and who were able to prove themselves competent. The Commissioner, in 1874, believed that the main obstacle to civilization of the Indians was the fact of their lack of status: "I desire to reiterate my conviction of the entire feasibility of Indian civilization, and that the difficulty of its problem is not so inherent in the race, character and the disposition of the Indian—great as these obstacles are—as in his anomalous relation to the Government."

Yet a different Commissioner, in 1878, urged caution:

> Such citizenship, if conferred indiscriminately, would, in my judgment, while the Indians are in their present transition state, be of incalculable damage to them. We should move slowly in the process of making Indians citizens, until they are prepared to assume intelligently its duties and obligations. The experience of the past has shown us that to make them citizens hastily is to make them paupers.

Individual Indian agents and superintendents on reservations also called for a means of allowing Indians to be citizens. The agent would refer to Indians under his care who were striving toward civilization and making progress. Providing the lure of citizenship would encourage these Indians in efforts toward self-support and independence. There were two benefits to the Indians becoming citizens. One was encouraging the Indians toward civilization. The other was that Indian citizenship would relieve the federal government of its guardianship responsibilities.

The agents who raised the issue of citizenship seemed mainly concerned for the welfare of their Indian wards. R. M. Milroy, the agent for Washington Territory, specifically requested the enactment of an Indian citizenship law in at least four annual reports, 1873, 1877, 1879, and 1880. In 1877 he wrote:

> As there is no law by which an Indian may acquire all of the rights and privileges of a citizen of the United States, notwithstanding he may be possessed of the highest learning and Christianity. . . . I respectfully suggest the enactment of an Indian citizenship law, fixing the requirements, terms, and conditions

upon which Indians may become fully enfranchised citizens, fixing the standard high. Such a law would do much to stimulate and encourage the Indians in efforts to pass through the rough breakers that intervene between barbarism and civilization.

Francis A. Walker, a former Commissioner of Indian Affairs, took up the question of Indian citizenship in a book he published in 1874. He believed there were two options for treatment of the Indians—seclusion on reservations with the least possible contact with white men, or inclusion of the Indians as citizens. He discussed some of the reasons why people wanted the Indian as citizen—which were not for the benefit of the Indian. One reason was that it did not make a difference—if Negroes were allowed to be citizens, why not also make Indians citizens? Another reason was to get rid of the expense of providing for the Indians. The Congress spent a great deal of time and money "for a very small and not very useful portion of the population of the country," and by enfranchising the Indian, it would relieve the legislative purse.

Walker, though a cynic, was not willing to go so far as to make the Indians citizens and to withdraw all government support.

> We conclude, then, that Indian citizenship is to be regarded as an end, and not as a means; that it is the goal to which each tribe should in turn be conducted through a course of industrial instruction and constraint, maintained by the government with kindness but also with firmness, under the shield of the reservation system.

The United States Senate addressed this question in 1880, in a proposed bill to allow for allotment of land in severalty, which included making allottees citizens. The bill failed at this time, but the Senators were aware of the inequities of subjecting Indians to obligations of citizens without giving them the rights and privileges of citizenship.

The question of citizenship was also being discussed in the legal community. An 1881 *American Law Review* article reviewed the constitutional position of the Indian and the rights of Congress to deal with the tribes. This author disagreed with the lower federal court in *U.S. ex rel. Standing Bear*:

> An Indian is not a person within the meaning of the Constitution . . . but "person" has several different meanings, and a good deal of confusion results from not distinguishing between them. It may mean simply a human being, a "biped without feathers," which is the metaphysical definition; or it may mean one who is recognized at law as capable of possessing and enforcing rights, as distinguished from a slave, which is the legal definition; or lastly, it may mean one who is protected against the action of Congress by the restrictive clauses in the Constitution. Now an Indian, a member of an Indian tribe, and living with it on a reservation, is a person in the first two senses, in the metaphysical and legal sense. But he is not a person within the meaning of the Constitution. There-

fore the power of Congress over him is Supreme and absolute, like that of the sovereign Union itself.

The author of the article, George P. Canfield, did distinguish between Indians on the reservation and those who have left their tribe and live among the white population. The second group was in the same position as any foreigner, and became a person in all three senses, including the constitutional sense. The author believed that the Fourteenth Amendment did not make Indians citizens, because it was not the intent of Congress to do so. In fact, "despite all of the changes of the past fifty years . . . their legal position has remained unchanged, and is the same to-day as when Marshall, C.J., delivered his famous opinions in *The Cherokee Nation v. Georgia*." So Congress, through its treaty and commerce powers, could treat the tribal Indians any way it wished. This was the prevailing view—"the Government is only bound in its treatment of them by considerations of present policy and justice."

THE SUPREME COURT'S INTERPRETATION—
ELK v. WILKINS (1884)

The distinction between tribal Indians and those who left the tribe to live among white men had first been made by Justice Taney in the *Dred Scott* decision, but only in *dicta*. The Supreme Court finally addressed the issue squarely in the 1884 case of *Elk v. Wilkins*. John Elk, an Indian who had severed his tribal relations and had fully and completely surrendered himself to the jurisdiction of the United States, tried to register to vote in Nebraska. Wilkins, the city registrar, refused to allow him to do so on the grounds that Elk was an Indian. The Court addressed the issue of whether voluntarily leaving the tribe and living among white citizens was enough to make an Indian a citizen of the United States, as *Dred Scott* had implied. The answer was a blunt "no."

The Court rested its decision on two factors. One was that the Indians were not "subject to the jurisdiction of the United States," so could not become citizens by birth. Indians born in tribes owed allegiance to the tribes and so were not completely subject to the United States' political jurisdiction because they did not owe complete and direct allegiance to the United States. Indians were compared to children of foreign ministers and ambassadors who were born in the United States—their parents worked for and claimed allegiance to their foreign government.

The Fourteenth Amendment provided for two sources of citizenship—birth and naturalization. When the Court found that Indians were not citizens by birth, it directed its attention the second factor—naturalization. Naturalization, the Court found, required an affirmative act by Congress. Congress had to accept each individual Indian as a citizen.

Though the plaintiff alleges that he "had fully and completely surrendered himself to the jurisdiction of the United States," he does not allege that the United States accepted his surrender, or that he has ever been naturalized, or taxed, or in any way recognized or treated as a citizen by the State or by the United States. Nor is it contended by his counsel that there is a statute or treaty that makes him a citizen.

An individual Indian could not decide that he was advanced enough in civilization to become a citizen. Only Congress could make that decision. So until each Indian went through naturalization proceedings, he or she could not become a United States citizen. The mistaken belief of the past 30 years was finally laid to rest. Yet the naturalization laws still did not provide for entry by Indians. One had to be white, or (since 1870) of African descent, to be eligible for naturalization.

There was a vigorous dissent in *Elk*, by Justice John Marshall Harlan, an advocate of civil rights. Harlan argued that the Civil Rights Act of 1866, by excluding Indians not taxed, included all other Indians, who were unconnected with any tribe and who resided with the white population. He found that the Senators and President Andrew Johnson all believed the Civil Rights bill would include Indians off the reservation.

The entire debate shows, with singular clearness, indeed, with absolute certainty, that no Senator who participated in it, whether in favor of or in opposition to the measure doubted that the bill, as passed, admitted, and was intended to admit, to national citizenship Indians who abandoned their tribal relations and became residents of one of the States or Territories, within the full jurisdiction of the United States. It was so interpreted by President Johnson, who in his veto message, said: "By the first section of the bill all persons born in the United States, and not subject to any foreign power, excluding Indians not taxed, are declared to be citizens of the United States. The provision comprehends the Chinese of the Pacific States, *Indians subject to taxation*, the people called Gypsies, as well as the entire race designated as blacks, persons of color, negroes, mulattoes, and persons of African blood. Every individual of those races, born in the United States, is, by the bill, made a citizen of the United States."

The Supreme Court's denial of Elk's citizenship stirred controversy in the circles of Indian reformers. The Indian Rights Association, a humanitarian reform group based in Philadelphia, published a book in 1884 expressing its sentiments that Congress should provide a way for Indians to become citizens. It believed that giving the Indians political power would enable them to improve their condition.

Humiliating as the acknowledgment may be, much of the placid indifference on the part of public men to dishonesty and injustice toward the Indian is due to the simple fact that he is not a voter: he is of no political significance. What possible inducement can there be to do anything for men who cannot possibly affect election returns? They are nobody's constituents.

The Indian Rights Association, however, did not want immediate and total citizenship. The right of citizenship for Indians should be tied to competency, ability, or education even though this was not required for others. This would provide that Indians who did become citizens were prepared for the resulting responsibilities and duties that went with the privileges of citizenship. It would also protect those Indians who were not able to support themselves without tribal and governmental benefits. The Association feared that untutored Indians would become prey to devious whites, turning them into paupers and criminals.

Unlike others, the Indian Rights Association did seem to have the best interests of the Indian in mind. It expressed concern about the justice of requiring Indians to be bound by laws in which they had no say, and of which they were mainly ignorant. Yet other non-citizens could apply for citizenship without these requirements. The only requirements for a non-Indian who wanted to be a United States citizens were a declaration of his intent to become a citizen, a five-year residency period, 21 years of age, good moral character, and the renouncement of all allegiance to foreign leaders.

The Association advocated education, religion, and law as the means to citizenship. Every effort should be made to educate the Indian as soon as possible. Those Indians who graduated from the Indian schools at Hampton or Carlisle should be entitled to immediate citizenship, as they would be able to protect and support themselves.

The Friends of the Indians who gathered at the Lake Mohonk Conference in 1884 also considered the topic of Indian citizenship. These interested humanitarian and philanthropic individuals who gathered in upstate New York also seemed to have the best interests of the Indian in mind.

While calling for a process for citizenship for Indians, the Lake Mohonk conferees wanted adequate preparation of the Indian for the duties and responsibilities that flowed from citizenship. They too called for education of the Indians. The conferees resolved, "That all adult male Indians should be admitted to the full privileges of citizenship by a process analogous to naturalization, upon evidence presented before the proper court of record of adequate intellectual and moral qualifications."

The Commissioner of Indian Affairs agreed that some naturalization process was necessary for those "Indians who have dissolved their tribal relations and are sufficiently prudent and intelligent to manage their own affairs," but hesitated to call for complete citizenship for all Indians. He too called for education, especially in the English language, so that citizenship would be an advantage to the Indian.

Not all writers of the post-*Elk* period were so solicitous of the Indians. The *American Law Review* published an article in 1886 by G. M.

Lambertson of Lincoln, Nebraska. He began by showing all the reasons citizenship was unnecessary for the Indians and, in fact, would harm the Indians more than any benefit conferred. He noted that the laws of the country run to "persons" (as in *U.S. ex rel. Standing Bear*) and not to "citizens." The only benefit to making the Indians citizens was to give them the ballot. But,

> is it to his interest to have it, and would it prove a boon to him? Is the ballot ever a greater good than evil to the illiterate and uneducated? Is not the Indian, who craves the right to vote, in the words of Longfellow, "longing after the good he comprehends not?" (The introduction of the Indian into American politics with its evil associations, the caucus, the primary, the polls, with their attendant influences of money and rum, is to debase and degrade him.)

Lambertson also expressed concern for the Indians losing the special protection of the government, if they became citizens. "As wards of the government they are objects of special care and protection, and jealously guarded from being overmatched by the superior intelligence and cunning of the white man. As citizens, they should stand upon their own feet."

Unfortunately, Lambertson's underlying concerns also come to the forefront in the article. He commented on the absurdity of giving citizenship to those "who have made the tomahawk the arbiter of their wrongs." He then expressed, in angry racist words, his concerns about naturalization and immigrants.

> When we remember that our country is being invaded, year by year, by the undesirable classes driven out of Europe because they are a burden to the government of their birth; that as many as seventy thousand immigrants have landed on our shores in a single month, made up largely of Chinese laborers, Irish paupers, and Russian Jews; that the ranks are being swelled by adventurers of every land—the Communist of France, the Socialist of Germany, the Nihilist of Russia, and the cutthroat murderers of Ireland—that all these persons may become citizens within five years, and most of them voters under State laws as soon as they have declared their intentions to become citizens—we may well hesitate about welcoming the late "untutored savages" in to the ranks of citizenship. With 15,000,000 people of foreign descent already resident, with social habits, customs, ideas of government, widely different from the native population of America, with the vexed problem of the Chinese and negroes unsolved and possibly unsolvable, it requires great faith in our robust virtues and the saving efficacy of republican institutions to believe we can with safety absorb the Indians into our population, and make them partners in the political function of the government.

Lambertson also pointed out that the Indians were not asking for the vote—it was the reformers from the East who would inflict Indian citizens on the Western states. Lambertson recognized, however, even in his vitriolic rage, that citizenship for Indians was inevitable.

CONGRESSIONAL RESPONSE TO *ELK*

Senator Henry Dawes of Massachusetts, known as a friend of the Indians, wanted to undo the *Elk v. Wilkins* decision and allow Indians to become citizens. His belief was that giving allotments of land in severalty to the Indians would be the beginning of breaking down tribal relations and would make the individual Indian independent and self-supporting. The General Allotment Act, popularly known as the Dawes Act, was passed in 1887 and provided for the allotment of land in severalty. Section 6 of the act provided that upon receipt of the allotment the Indian would become a citizen of the United States. The section also gave citizenship to "every Indian born within the territorial limits of the United States who has voluntarily taken up, within said [territorial] limits, his residence separate and apart from any tribe of Indians therein, and has adopted the habits of civilized life." It specifically used the language that the Supreme Court had used in *Elk* and *Dred Scott*.

The citizenship provisions caused much discussion in the Senate and the House of Representatives. Not everyone wanted the Indians to be citizens.

The Senate debate was held in February 1886. Senator Samuel B. Maxey of Texas, though in favor of separate allotments, was against making Indians citizens. He argued that qualifications were needed, and compared the Indian to the Negro. The Negro had at least associated with white people, learned the English language, and was exposed to the lifestyle of civilized people. But the Indian was not aware of civilized society.

> But here are people who but a few years ago were wild tribes roaming upon the prairies, engaged in raiding upon the settlements of the white people with the tomahawk and scalping-knife; we have gathered them up into reservations; and now, because we put them on separate tracts of land, we are to say to them, "You may become citizens of the United States." It is too soon. I do not say, and I do not wish to be understood as saying, that the time may not come when I would favor the extension of citizenship to them; but I want first to educate them up to that standard.

Maxey also pointed out that the bill excluded the Five Civilized Tribes and the Seneca Nation of New York, those tribes that were the most qualified to be citizens.

Senator Dawes defended the granting of citizenship to allottees. He pointed out that such a clause was in most treaties with the different tribes since the 1817 treaty with the Cherokee, and was therefore not a new policy. He further argued for the granting of citizenship to those Indians in the position of Elk.

In the case of an Indian who has left his tribe, turned his back upon the savage life, has adopted the modes and habit of civilized life, is in all respects like one of us, why shall he not be a citizen of the United States, while the poor and degraded and ignorant African, with no better qualifications than if he was imported from the Congo coast, merely because he is born here, may be a citizen?

Rhode Island Senator Jonathan Chace went further. He appealed to the Senate's sense of right and justice. The American system is based upon the belief that all men are created equal, he pointed out, and to allow the Indians to be less than equal is an anomaly and an injustice. And if an argument to right and justice would not convince the senators, Chace also appealed to their pocketbook interests. The United States would not have to spend money fighting the Indians and educating the Indians if the Indians were given the right to vote, and sue and be sued—the rights of citizenship. This bill could settle the Indian problem.

The House debate, held in December 1886, followed similar lines. Let the Indian allottee become a citizen, Representative Thomas G. Skinner of North Carolina argued, as long as he couldn't alienate his land for a sufficient length of time to prepare him for his responsibilities. "And in the meantime, the surplus lands upon such reservations can be sold, and the money arising from such sale can be used in such manner as Congress may direct in each particular case, for the benefit of the Indians to whom the land belonged."

Indians as citizens would solve the Indian problem. The government would no longer have to provide special grants for the Indian, who would cease to be a burden. And allotting the land would allow unused land to be sold to white frontier citizens.

The General Allotment Act passed Congress and was signed into law. The Board of Indian Commissioners was pleased with the bill in its 1887 report. The bill "is a great step in advance in our Indian policy, and the day when it was approved by the President may be called the Indian emancipation day. The measure gives the Indian the possibility to become a man instead of remaining 'a ward of the Government.'" Yet the Board expected that citizenship would be a slow maturation process. "The law is only the seed, whose germination and growth will be a slow process, and we must wait patiently for its mature fruit." The Board called upon the churches and philanthropic organizations to share responsibility in educating the Indians in civilization and citizenship.

In a directive to Indian agents concerning curriculum in Indian schools, Commissioner of Indian Affairs Thomas Morgan stressed the schools' responsibility to prepare their students for citizenship.

Education is to be the medium through which the rising generation of Indians are to be brought into fraternal and harmonious relationship with their white fellow-citizens, and with them enjoy the sweets of refined homes, the delight of social intercourses, the emoluments of commerce and trade, the advantages of travel, together with the pleasures that come from literature, science, and philosophy, and the solace and stimulus afforded by a true religion.

Education was to inculcate the Indian students with patriotic fervor toward the United States. The students were to learn of the nation's great beneficence toward the Indians, its historic past and its power. Teachers were instructed to "carefully avoid any unnecessary references to the fact that they [Indian students] are Indians."

Under the General Allotment Act, citizenship for tribal Indians was tied to the granting of allotments. While the land could not be alienated for 25 years, nor a patent in fee granted until that time, citizenship devolved immediately upon the granting of the allotment. The allotment process took some time, depending upon the individual tribes and Indian agents. For most Indians, especially tribal Indians, citizenship caused no change in their lifestyle. Legally, however, they were now entitled to the privileges and immunities of citizenship, and also responsible for the duties of citizenship. And, as a citizen, the Indian was no longer entitled to special protection, but subject to the ordinary laws of society.

THE COURTS' TREATMENT OF ALLOTMENT INDIANS

The federal courts had to consider different issues that arose from the new citizenship of allotment Indians. In the 1902 case of *United States v. Rickert*, the state of South Dakota attempted to tax the lands allotted to Indians. If Indians were citizens, were their lands not subject to taxation? The Supreme Court held that the state, on its own, could not tax Indian allotments. The Court believed that this was a question for Congress, because the federal government still held the patent in fee to the land. "It is for the legislative branch of the Government to say when these Indians shall cease to be dependent and assume the responsibilities attaching to citizenship."

But in matters not dealing with the allotment land itself, the federal courts found that allotment Indians were to be treated as any other citizens. In the 1902 case of *In re Celestine*, Mrs. Celestine, a Tulalip Indian, sought a writ of habeas corpus in federal court to receive custody of her child. The federal court determined that she had to go to a state court for relief. Mrs. Celestine was a citizen by reason of allotment, and could no longer seek special protection from the federal courts. State courts normally deal with family matters, and she now had "the right to sue in the proper forum." The court continued, "Congress has relieved the government of responsibility in such cases as this by conferring the rights of citizenship upon Indians to whom allotments of land have been made."

Not only family matters, but some criminal matters were within the jurisdiction of the state. The controversial case of *Matter of Heff* (1905) illustrates this. The United States had a law prohibiting the sale of liquor to Indians. Heff was convicted of selling liquor to an Indian who had received his allotment under the Dawes Act. Heff appealed, claiming that because the Indian had received this allotment, he was a citizen and no longer a ward of the federal government, so the federal law did not apply. The Court reviewed the Dawes Act and found it gave citizenship to allottees, at the beginning of the 25-year allotment period, and not to patentees, at the end of the 25 years. The fact that the land could not be alienated for 25 years did not affect the allottee's status as a citizen. And as a citizen, he was subject to state law, so Congress could no longer regulate him. Heff's conviction was overturned, because "when the United States grants the privileges of citizenship to an Indian, gives to him the benefit of and requires him to be subject to the laws, both civil and criminal, of the State, it places him outside the reach of police regulations on the part of Congress."

The *Heff* case allowed the sale of liquor to allotment Indians. The immediate uproar from white citizens in Western states caused Congress to pass the Burke Act in 1906, amending the citizenship section of the Dawes Act. The Burke Act postponed the acquisition of citizenship until the fee patent was issued, which was 25 years after allotment was made, unless the Indian could prove earlier that he was ready for citizenship. Citizenship was tied to the patent, not to the allotment.

The Senate debate makes it clear that the *Heff* case was being legislatively overruled.

> Mr. DIXON of Montana. Mr. Speaker, I want to ask the gentleman from South Dakota [Mr. BURKE] if the purpose of the bill is not to prevent the blanket Indians by wholesale becoming citizens by allotment, and still allow the intelligent Indians on application to become citizens by allotment?
>
> Mr. BURKE of South Dakota. That is the purpose of the law, and further, to protect the Indians from the sale of liquor.
>
> Mr. CURTIS. It is a very great improvement over existing law.
>
> Mr. DIXON of Montana. I thoroughly concur.

The change in citizenship from allottee to patentee did not affect the citizenship status of those Indians who had received allotments prior to the Burke Act. The Act also allowed for the Secretary of the Interior to end the trust period by issuing patents before the end of the 25 years, to those Indians who could show they were competent to manage their own affairs.

The Commissioner of Indian Affairs in 1906 called the power to issue patents to competent Indians "a very important one, if not the most important relating to Indians that has been vested in the Department." But by 1907, the Commissioner was discussing the difficulties arising from determining the capacity of Indians. Each individual agent or superintendent had different views as to capacity, and this affected their recommendations to the

Secretary of the Interior. Some agents looked to educational requirements, others to the type of clothing or hairstyle of the Indian. The Commissioner felt there was no one standard, but suggested that

> the safest test is the industry and thrift of the applicant. If an Indian has supported himself by his own exertions, whatever calling he may have followed, it is reasonable to suppose that he has acquired enough knowledge of money, values, and opportunities to justify the Government in trusting him with his own land.

The Commissioner of Indian Affairs was also involved in approving conveyances by Indians of allotment land. In 1911, Marchie Tiger, a Creek Indian, challenged the constitutionality of requiring approval, alleging that as a citizen he should not need anyone's permission to alienate the land he inherited from an allottee.

The Supreme Court disagreed. The Court found that one could be a citizen and still be a ward of the government where land was concerned. The right to sell property is not derived from citizenship, but from the title one holds to the land. The land could not be alienated during the allotment period under the laws of Congress.

The Court also found that Congress had the right to determine when guardianship over the Indian in all aspects of his life should cease. Until that time, Congress could still regulate the Indians as guardian to ward. Citizenship was not considered incompatible with guardianship. While many cases applied this concept to the Indians, the concept was not limited to them. Minor children are citizens, but a legislature could pass laws regulating and limiting their conduct. The same was true for women, who, while citizens, could not vote, and in some states, could not own property in their own right.

The Court's concept of citizenship and guardianship was now applied to the Congressional act prohibiting the sale of liquor to Indians. While the 1905 *Heff* case had found that Congress could not regulate Indian allottees, in 1916 *United States v. Nice* affirmatively overruled *Heff*. Nice was also convicted of selling liquor to Indian allottees. The Court found that allottees remained tribal Indians and under guardianship until Congress determined they were competent to be on their own. The Court reiterated that "it rests with Congress to determine when and how this shall be done, and whether the emancipation shall at first be complete or only partial."

Congress did determine that certain Indians could be citizens, and not under the guardianship of the government. During the First World War, many Indians volunteered and fought in the United States Armed Forces. Congress honored this patriotism by granting citizenship to every Indian who served in the Armed Forces and who received an honorable discharge. The act required a discharged Indian to show his honorable discharge and proper identification before a court of competent jurisdiction.

In 1924, Congress finally determined that all Indians should be made citizens. There was little debate on the issue. The act of 2 June 1924 granted citizenship to "all non-citizen Indians born within the territorial limits of the United States." The act specifically stated that application or naturalization was not required.

The act further provided that the granting of citizenship would not affect the Indian's right to tribal property. The Commissioner of Indian Affairs in his 1924 Annual Report interpreted this to allow continued guardianship as to allotment land. This was consistent with the Supreme Court's prior decisions that guardianship and citizenship were not incompatible.

As of 1924, all native-born Indians became citizens. This gave them political and legal equality with other citizens of the United States. It allowed them to sue and be sued in federal and state courts. Male Indians could vote in federal elections but would still have to meet state election requirements before being able to vote. The federal government still retained guardianship over some Indians, but Indians could no longer legally be segregated or discriminated against purely on racial grounds.

Four years later, the government-funded Meriam Report discussed "what remains to be done to adjust the Indian to the prevailing civilization." The report found that the government had a duty to aid the Indian in adjusting to civilization. This could mean retention of regulations until the Indian was able to support himself. The report gave no indication of how long it would take to reach this state.

CONCLUSION

"The United States will be judged at the bar of history according to what they shall have done in two respects—by their disposition of Negro slavery, and by their treatment of the Indians."

Over the period of 1830–1924 the United States government treated Indians in whatever manner best served the interests of the United States. The Indian tribes were physically moved at the will of the government, requiring them to give up lands previously promised. The courts excluded them from asserting any rights. Indians were treated as children, as wards of the government. And it took almost 100 years for these children to become adults.

The policies toward the Indian can be compared to the government's treatment of Negroes. Both Negroes and Indians were considered unwanted intruders, though the Indians had occupied the land before the Europeans, and the Negroes had arrived involuntarily. As unwanted intruders, they were ignored by the government for as long as possible, and finally dealt with, as a race, because the government could no longer avoid the legal and humanitarian issues raised.

The "Negro problem" was legally resolved by the United States long before the "Indian problem" was addressed. Negroes resided mainly in the Eastern states, while the majority of Indians were in the Western territories. The Indian problem could be put off as long as there was land to move them around in and keep them separated from white communities. This could not be done with the Negro. The Western Indians could be easily forgotten, and the public was not concerned about something they would read about only in newspapers. Negroes lived in the more populated Eastern states, and their deprivation and lack of status were visible for all to see. Humanitarian groups and the population as a whole dealt with the "Negro problem" because it was their problem. The "Indian problem" was never as visible and therefore could be ignored.

Indians were denied equal protection of the laws, citizenship, and equal political and legal rights long after Negroes were legally given such rights. But the treatment of both problems was resolved along racial lines. Negroes and Indians were viewed by the government as races, and few allowances were ever made for them as individuals.

Both Negroes and Indians were segregated from the dominant white culture, by law and by fact. The case of *Plessy v. Ferguson* made segregation legal as the U.S. Supreme Court found that separate but equal accommodations for the different races were constitutional. In local communities, Negroes were separated from whites in property and home ownership by de facto segregation. Indians were segregated by reservations. While the Dawes Act had contemplated allotments of land to whites and Indians living side by side (so the Indians could learn by watching the industrious whites), this in fact never occurred. This was due partly to the fact that the land given to the Indians in allotments was land that white citizens did not want, generally because it was unsuitable for farming, raising cattle, or providing a livelihood. But it was also due to white citizens' perceptions of Indians as an inferior and uncivilized race, with whom whites did not want to associate.

The Indian and Negro "problems" both generated socially concerned humanitarian and religious reform groups who advocated on behalf of the Negro and Indian. The "Friends of the Indians" and the abolitionists used similar methods to bring the plight of the downtrodden Indian and Negro to the public's attention. These groups contacted influential citizens and government representatives, distributed tracts and pamphlets to publicize their efforts on behalf of the Indians and Negroes, and kept the Indian and Negro "problem" in the public eye. Both groups seemed motivated by their sincere beliefs in the ability to civilize and assimilate the Indian and Negro and their genuine desire to see justice done.

The problem of what to do with the Indians was also coming to the forefront during the time of massive immigration. The assimilation of the immigrants may have provided a positive example to the federal government, and allowed, over time, grudging *legal* acceptance of Indians. The Indians were able to become one more ingredient in the country's legal melting pot.

Laws passed regulating the Indians were generally done under the guise of protecting and benefitting the Indian. But the words of the people involved in making, executing, and interpreting those laws speak for themselves. Laws regulated the Indian because the Indian was a problem which had to be dealt with. In the end, giving citizenship to Indians was a way to get rid of a problem that was never fully addressed, nor ever really solved.

V

CIVIL LIBERTIES

"Congress shall make no law respecting an establishment of religion, or prohibiting the free exercise thereof." These opening words of the first amendment to the U.S. Constitution, protecting religious freedom, represent one of the most historically significant and celebrated civil liberties said to be guaranteed to all Americans. Does the Bill of Rights apply to American Indians, however? Here, as in many other areas, American Indians have a history of exclusion from these protections, as Lee Irwin's chapter makes clear. While the American Indian Religious Freedom Act, passed only in 1978, might appear to correct this particular state of affairs, Irwin argues that even this law was ineffective in protecting the free exercise of Native religions among tribal members. Thus, the civil liberties described in the Bill of Rights appear to have been limited in fundamental ways for American Indians within the United States—not just in practice but also as a matter of government policy. By this point in the volume it should be clear, however, that an argument that Indians' rights ought to be protected in the same manner as other citizens in the United States may itself be called into question. Rather than view Indians as representing a minority group whose religious rights deserve constitutional protection under the First Amendment, we might instead argue that the sovereignty retained by tribes ought to protect them from U.S. governmental intrusion into their exercise of religion.

Freedom, Law, and Prophecy: A Brief History of Native American Religious Resistance

LEE IRWIN

In August 1978, the American Indian Religious Freedom Act (AIRFA) was passed by Congress as a guarantee of constitutional protection of First Amendment rights for Native Americans. This act was passed as an attempt to redress past wrongs by the federal government or its agents. That history of legal suppression was due to "the lack of a clear, comprehensive and consistent Federal policy [which] has often resulted in the abridgement of religious freedom for traditional American Indians." The summary text of this act states:

> Henceforth it shall be the policy of the United States to protect and preserve for American Indians their inherent right of freedom to believe, express, and exercise the traditional religions of the American Indian, Eskimo, Aleut, and Native Hawaiians, including but not limited to access to sacred sites, use and possession of sacred objects and freedom to worship through ceremonials and traditional rites.

It is perhaps hard for those unfamiliar with the history of Native American religious oppression to realize that in our own lifetimes it continues to be difficult or impossible for Native Americans to freely practice their religions. The suppression of those practices has been pervasive to such a degree that AIRFA has proven to be insufficient to grant the freedom that many Native Americans feel is necessary for the complete affirmation of their respective religious identities.

What is the background that necessitated AIRFA and what directions have issues of religious affirmation taken since this act became law? Perhaps the most suppressive laws regarding religious freedom were those promulgated by the Bureau of Indian Affairs for the Indian Courts, known as the Indian Religious Crimes Code. These laws were first developed in 1883 by Secretary of the Interior Henry Teller as a means to prohibit Native American ceremonial activity under pain of imprisonment. Teller's general guidelines to all Indian agents ordered them to discontinue dances and feasts as well as instructing them to take steps with regard to all medicine men, "who are always found in the anti-progressive party . . . to compel these impostors to abandon this deception and discontinue their practices, which are not only without benefit to them but positively injurious to them."

Religious offenses on the reservations were later codified by the Commissioner of Indian Affairs, Thomas J. Morgan, in 1892 in his "Rules for Indian Courts," whereby he established a series of criminal offenses aimed at Native American religious practices. He wrote:

> Dances—Any Indian who shall engage in the sun dance, scalp dance, or war dance, or any similar feast, so called, shall be guilty of an offense, and upon conviction thereof shall be punished for the first offense by withholding of his rations for not exceeding ten days or by imprisonment for not exceeding ten days; for any subsequent offense under this clause he shall be punished by withholding his rations for not less than ten days nor more than thirty days, or by imprisonment for not less than ten days nor more than thirty days.
>
> Medicine men—Any Indian who shall engage in the practices of so-called medicine men, or who shall resort to any artifice or device to keep the Indians of the reservation from adopting and following civilized habits and pursuits, or shall use any arts of conjurer to prevent Indians from abandoning their barbarous rites and customs, shall be deemed guilty of an offense, and upon conviction thereof, for the first offense shall be imprisoned for not less than ten days and not more than thirty days: Provided that, for subsequent conviction for such offense the maximum term or imprisonment shall not exceed six months.

These laws not only abrogate First Amendment rights in a conscious and well-documented policy of religious oppression, they also reveal a systematic attempt on the part of highly placed government officials to stamp out Native American religious practices. They also represent a determined policy to reconstruct Native religions in conformity with dominant Protestant majority values in a myopic vision of what constitutes "civilized" religious behavior. Such policy is found consistently in the annual reports of many commissioners of Indian Affairs from the creation of the office in 1832 through the appointment of John Collier in 1934.

These oppressive policies can be traced through the writings of not only the Indian commissioners and other heads of state who managed Indian affairs, such as various secretaries of state (after 1849) as well as various secretaries of war (1824–1848), to an even earlier policy, that of the 1819 Indian Civilization Fund Act, the primary intent of which was to create a fund to reform and "civilize" Indian peoples in accordance with alien cultural norms imposed on them by a conquering majority. Where this proved impossible or undesirable, the Indian Civilization Act also called for the more insidious policy of Indian removal, generally to the west and thus away from encroaching Euro-American settlement. The mandate for determining Indian affairs by government officials can be further traced back to the 1783 First Continental Congress Indian Proclamation, which says, "The United States in Congress assembled have the sole and exclusive right and power of regulating trade and managing all affairs with the Indians." This set in place the legal precedent by which Indian peoples were denied religious freedom, imposing exclusively non-Native standards of legitimacy. Pushing back even further, it is significant that in the United States Constitution only five words can be found that refer to any Native peoples, these words involving only trade and taxation agreements.

What strategies have Native peoples followed in responding to this crushing onslaught against their spiritual lives, goods, and diverse religious practices? In general, there has been a range of strategies in a spectrum between two major alternatives: accommodation or resistance. As Gregory Dowd has argued, the late 1700s and early 1800s was a period of resistance by Native people against Anglo-American settlement, a time of "widespread intertribal activity" in which various Native peoples sought to solve the challenges of cultural and political encroachment while also being deeply influenced by events affecting other tribes. On the religious front, some groups, like the Cherokee and other southeastern peoples, tried to accommodate the new way of life introduced by settlement, taking up Anglo farming as well as taking a receptive interest in the teachings of Christianity. Significantly, the strategy of accommodation often was promoted by those in upper echelon leadership roles (like John Ross among the Cherokee) who often had diminishing contact with the most traditional ways of life as a result of intermarriages, exposure to Anglo-European education, or wealth accrued through non-Native economic practices.

However, this strategy of accommodation proved to be primarily a one-way accommodation; that is, while various Native groups struggled to adapt or accommodate the invading Anglo-Europeans, this accommodation was rarely if ever reciprocated. Such one-way accommodation often proved fatal, such as in the Cherokee case when, after many years of often successful adaptation and conformity to alien values and lifeways, they were forced off their lands through the greed and racist mentality of the Georgia legislature that revoked their political rights after gold was discovered on Cherokee lands. The federal government then forced Cherokees to take the Trail of Tears in the fateful winter of 1838, when so many Cherokee people died. Thus the strategy of accommodation has its own tragic history and has largely been nonreciprocal, often resulting in a subordination of Native concerns to those of the dominating political hierarchies on state and federal levels.

Over against the strategy of accommodation is the resistance or revivalist movements that increasingly emphasized the importance of traditional Native values, indigenous religious orientations, and the need to abandoned all dependency on non-Native goods or ideas. Often, the origins of this resistance came from a variety of Native religious leaders who emphatically called for an assertion of Native beliefs and practices as an affirmation of intrinsic, inherited spiritual values and as a rallying cry for the preservation of the many diverse paths found in Native religious life. At the extreme pole of this response, "nativistic" came to mean not a return to the past in an ideal or artificial, utopian sense, but a preservation of core indigenous values and beliefs as a basis for cultural survival, a survival that might include a diverse synthesis of alternative religious ideas or practices. This affirmation was strengthened by the emergence of a significant number of prophetic spiritual leaders whose visionary experiences confirmed and celebrated Native religious orientation as a primary source of empowerment for resisting colonial advancement. In many cases, this prophetic leadership was forced to advocate a militant resistance and a strategy of complex alliances, often turning hostile in the face of non-Native aggression while also rejecting any form of unilateral, submissive accommodation.

Examples of this prophetic leadership are many, extending from coast to coast in the wake of increasing patterns of political and cultural domination. The corrosive effects of trans-Appalachian conflicts through the forced migrations of east coast indigenous peoples, the uninhibited spread of the rum and whiskey trade, and various Anglo-European armed conflicts (and later American military aggression) all contributed to a necessarily defensive stance on the part of Native peoples. A responsive religious leadership began to emerge among Native peoples in the form of empowered individuals whose messages were oriented to more apocalyptic visions in which non-Native aggressors would be defeated, destroyed, or pushed back depending on the degree to which Native peoples could re-affirm traditional values corrupted by colonial advancement.

As early as 1752, Munsee religious leader Papounhan received a vision while mourning the death of his father that he should lead the Munsee people in a restoration of their Native traditions that had been nearly lost as a result of European contact. The Delaware prophet Neolin, in the 1760s, was one of four such prophetic leaders who arose to reaffirm through personal visions the importance of traditional religious values and in fact influenced Pontiac's resistance during his so-called "conspiracy" of 1763. In 1776, Wangomen, another Delaware prophet, also advocated a return to Native values and religion. He condemned a number of Euroamerican practices such as slavery and the use of alcohol and tried to lead the Delaware to a renewed affirmation of traditional Delaware values. Around 1800, Handsome Lake, a Seneca prophet, perhaps a bit more of an accommodationist, received a religious revelation that combined elements of Christianity and core Senecan religious practices. Preaching the Gaiwiio or Good Word, Handsome Lake led the Iroquois in reorganizing their economic, social, and religious lives along lines that combined traditional Iroquois religious practices and beliefs with elements from Christianity.

By the early 1800s on the Northwest Coast, many such prophetic and charismatic figures appeared in a sequence of revitalizing spiritual movements, all advocating a new rebirth of older religious patterns as a means for the affirmation and survival of indigenous tribal identities. The Spokane leaders Yurareechen (Circling Raven), the Flathead leader Shining Shirt, and the Umatilla religious leader Dlaupác all preached the importance of preserving indigenous traditions. Dlaupác predicted ominous and apocalyptic scenarios in the wake of the arrival of Euroamerican settlers, including a prediction of the complete destruction of the Indian way of life as well as the destruction of the world thorough flood or fire. In the east, prior to 1812, Tenskataaw (Open Door), the Shawnee prophet and brother of Tecumseh, sparked the first intertribal confederacy that united many thousands of diverse Native peoples around a religiously motivated resistance movement. Tenskataaw emphasized a return to indigenous values as a result of a visionary journey he had during a near death experience. He condemned intermarriage and all contact with Europeans and urged a return to traditional communal values. He traveled extensively throughout the tribes with his message of spiritual and political renewal. Around this same time Hildis Hadjo (or Josiah Francis), the Creek Prophet, also led a movement that combined resistance to Anglo-European ways with a return to Native values in the face of cultural erosion.

Throughout the nineteenth century, revitalization movements continued along the front of advancing Anglo-American settlement, as tribal displacements made life increasingly more difficult and bitter for Native peoples. In 1820, Yonaguska (Drowning-Bear), a Cherokee prophet, as a results of visionary experience at the age of 60, promulgated traditional Cherokee values, promoted anti-alcoholism, and resisted removal talk, emphasizing the need to retain ancestral ties to the Blue Ridge Mountains as intrinsic to Cherokee spiritual life. In 1832, Kenekuk, a Kickapoo spiritual leader, led the Kickapoo to Illinois when they were displaced by settlers as a result of the 1832 Indian Removal Act promulgated by Andrew Jackson. While Kenekuk assimilated some features of Christianity into his teachings, he also emphasized the maintenance of core Kickapoo religious values and practices as essential for Kickapoo survival. The Kickapoo under his leadership resisted standardized education and land division, refused to learn English, and engaged in Kickapoo dances and singing during religious ceremonies. In the mid-1850s, other Nativistic religious movements in the Northwest were underway, led by Smohalla, the Wanapam dreamer-prophet and Washani religious revitalizer. Smohalla's teachings, which emphasized a return to Native traditions and the abandonment of alien goods and ideas, acted as a catalyst for tribal confederation during the Yakima Wars of 1855–56 against Anglo-American encroachment and government plans to confine the Northwest peoples onto small and inadequate reservations. Those who kept the old Washani spiritual ways would be resurrected after death and their traditional world would be restored to them. Smohalla, like many other *yantcha*, or "spiritual leaders" of the Northwest, emphasized non-violence and peaceful co-existence with non-Natives (as did Kenekuk and Drowning-Bear) while still seeking to return to older ways and indigenous spiritual values.

From this period forward, many such prophetic movements arose, all emphasizing Native values and traditional religions, with varying degrees of accommodation with Christian beliefs—but all stressing the importance of a return to basic core values and indigenous practices. The culmination of this movement, what Leslie Spier has called the Prophet Dance tradition, was transmitted by the 1860s dreamer-prophet, Wodziwob, a Paiute of central California, to Tavibo, the father of the Nevada Paiute, Wovoca, the visionary founder of the Ghost Dance of 1889. Again, this visionary history of spirit dancing became a rallying cry for many different Native peoples throughout the Great Plains area, illustrating the intertribal effects of Native prophetic movements and their often unifying character. Many different tribes sent representatives to meet with Wovoca, who then instructed them in Ghost Dances rites. These rites were then transported back to the Plains tribes as a revelation of greatest import—the practice of the dance was to result in the return of the old way of life now rapidly diminished, a return of the buffalo, and the expulsion of Anglo-Americans from Native lands. The tragic consequence of the Lakota practice of this dance resulted in the U.S. Army's slaughter of 84 men, 44 women, and 18 children at Wounded Knee, in December 1890. The victims of this massacre are buried in a mass grave on the Pine Ridge reservation. This site, a stain on the American national conscience, continues to be a historic monument of the tragic and aggressive assault on Native religious life. Even though the Ghost Dance continued sporadically, as among the Kiowa, the unprovoked destruction of the Lakota people as they attempted to arbitrate their rights to practice Native religions had a shocking, suppressive force on all Native religious practices.

It is around the time of the events at Wounded Knee that the most suppressive measures against Native religions were promoted through the "Rules of Indian Courts" instigated by Commissioner Thomas J. Morgan, nominal head of the BIA under the Secretary of the Interior. Morgan also wrote in his 1889 Annual Report:

> The Indians must conform to "the white man's ways," peaceably if they will, forcibly if they must. . . . The tribal relations should be broken up, socialism destroyed, and the family and the autonomy of the individual substituted. The allotment of lands in severalty, the establishment of local courts and police, the development of a personal sense of independence and the universal adoption of the English language are the means to this end.

A similar Canadian law also was promoted, the 1884 Canadian Indian Act that made Native potlatch or giveaways illegal and participants subject to a misdemeanor and imprisonment from two to six months. Similarly repressive laws were introduced and approved by the Canadian legislature in 1895, 1914, and 1933.

The darkest and most difficult times for the practice of Native religions and ways of life was the post–Civil War period up to the mid-twentieth century. During this period Sun Dancing and other such rites were made illegal, suppressed by government Indian agents as "barbaric and uncivilized." In accordance with the Grant Peace Policy, the Board of Indian Commissioners was formed in 1869. Their first report noted that the duties of the board were "to educate the Indians in industry, the arts of civilization, and the principles of Christianity." This board was given joint control with the secretary of the interior over congressional funds appropriated for dealing with the Indian agencies. Christian missionaries of all denominations were given government support for the founding of missions on Indian reservation land on seventy-three agencies. In 1872, Commissioner of Indian Affairs Walker reported that agents from the mostly Protestant denominations were appointed "to assume charge of the intellectual and moral education of the Indians thus brought within the reach of their influence." During this time, Native children were forcibly shipped to Christian missionary schools where they were denied the rights to speak Native languages, to wear Native clothing, or to practice any form of Native religion. Missionary zeal specifically targeted Native religions as the bane of all civilized Christian ideology. Subsequent missionary activities caused "fractions, feuds and schisms, discredited popular leaders and imposed new ones on the Indians and in scores of ways undermined and weakened the unity of the tribes." Indian ceremonies were banned, religious practices disrupted, and sacred objects destroyed or confiscated.

Some renewal movements did continue, such as the turn of the century Four Mothers Society of the Natchez-Creek based on a return to the old Southeast ceremonial tradition. Membership in the Four Mothers Society linked traditional full-bloods from the Natchez, Creek, Cherokee, Choctaw, Chickasaw, and Seminole in Oklahoma. In 1900 there was a resistance to allotment led by the Creek spiritual leader Chitto Harjo (Crazy Snake), who formed a Chitto or Snake Society, the members of which were dedicated to preserving the old Creek spiritual way and to resisting political encroachment. In 1902 Redbird Smith, breaking away from the Four Mothers Society, led a renewal of the Oklahoma Cherokee Ketoowa or Night-Hawk Society and laid out a traditional ceremonial ground on Blackgum Mountain. This effort established a new sacred fire from which twenty-two more traditional fires were started, spreading a traditionalist spiritual movement among the older Cherokee population. In the Northwest, in 1910, the Nisqually John Slocum established the Shaker Church in Olympia, Washington. As a result of a visionary experience, Slocum and his wife promoted a religious movement that brought together Native people from many different tribes throughout the Northwest and California in a synthesis of prophetic Native indigenous beliefs and reinterpreted Christianity. In 1918 the Native American Church (NAC) was legally incorporated in Oklahoma in resistance to congressional efforts to make possession and transportation of peyote illegal, though seventeen states passed laws making the use of peyote illegal.

During the early twentieth century, however, Native religious reaffirmation movements tended to decline as indigenous peoples struggled to survive under the appalling and oppressive political circumstances. In 1906, the Act for the Preservation of American Antiquities (APAA), while making it a criminal offense to appropriate, excavate, injure, or destroy historic or prehistoric ruins or monuments or objects of antiquity located on lands owned or controlled by the U.S. government, also defined dead Indians or Indian artifacts as "archaeological resources" and converted these persons and objects into federal "property," thereby further depriving Native peoples of the right to dispose of their dead or to maintain possession of sacred objects, as reservation lands were under federal jurisdiction.

Indian religions, many still espousing a commitment to Native religious practices, went underground, into the Kivas, out of sight, into the back hills and hidden valleys of the reservations. Many religious leaders still refused to accommodate the larger cultural imperium. In 1934, John Collier was appointed as the Commissioner of Indian Affairs and the Indian Reorganization Act was passed. This act ended allotment, allowed for the appointment of Native people to the BIA without civil service requirements, and encouraged the formation of tribal governments—but only with a written constitution and accompanying by-laws approved by the Department of the Interior. Secretary of the Interior Harold Ickes approved of Collier's BIA Circular 2970 titled "Indian Religious Freedom and Indian Culture," which was sent to all agencies and stated that "no interference with Indian religious life or ceremonial expression will hereafter be tolerated." This circular represents the government's first specific policy statement made to protect Native American religious rights.

Still, the long history of religious oppression was by no means ended, as government policy and legislation continued to undermine the solidarity and cohesion of reservation life. In 1940 the Fish and Wildlife Service of the Department of the Interior "issued regulations restricting the taking, possessing and transporting of bald and golden eagles or their parts" as a result of the Bald (and later Golden Eagle) Protection Act. This made the use of eagle feathers a federal offense and individual spiritual leaders and traditional practitioners were persecuted under this act. Displacement from reservation lands in the mid-1950s to forced relocations in urban environments, as epitomized by the 1954 Mennominee Termination Act, further added to disorientation and spiritual loss as many families were paid to move into large cities, where promised job opportunities and employment failed to materialize. Thousands of indigenous people found themselves alienated from reservation life, living in "red ghettos" where crime, poverty and alcoholism escalated to extreme proportions. In 1959, a court case between the Native American Church and the Navajo Tribal Council resulted in a ruling from the Tenth Circuit Court of Appeals that "The First Amendment applies only to Congress. . . . No provision in the Constitution makes the First Amendment applicable to Indian nations nor is there any law of Congress doing so." This decision severely limited the freedom and legal rights of Native peoples to seek redress from religious oppression or discrimination. As late as 1971, Sun Dancers were being arrested on Pine Ridge by tribal police because the tribal judge issued an injunction against Sun Dancing.

The first contemporary resistance movement came with the formation of yet another Nativistic survival movement, this time led by younger Native American political radicals, in the form of the American Indian Movement (AIM). In 1968, George Mitchell and Dennis Banks (Chippewas) founded AIM in Minneapolis in an attempt to force better treatment for inner-city Native peoples harassed constantly by police and other city officials. Shortly thereafter, Clyde and Vernon Bellecourt (Chippewa) and Russell Means (Oglala) joined AIM and, in 1969, AIM members joined with other Native peoples in the occupation of Alcatraz Island as "Indian land" in the first public re-affirmation of Red Power since Wounded Knee. In August 1972, AIM members went to the Lakota Crow Dog Sun Dance at Pine Ridge, where traditional spiritual leaders gave their support to the movement. The "spiritual rebirth" of Indian rights was affirmed as a union between traditional religious and political leaders espousing a revival of Native identity and a rebirth of Native religious practices as a means for political empowerment. AIM became the spearhead in the effort to secure tribal rights, authentic religious practices, and governmental redress of past wrongs and oppression. Increasing confrontations between AIM leaders and non-Native authorities, as well as opposition from government-supported tribal leaders at Pine Ridge, resulted in numerous shoot-outs and yet another battle and standoff at

Wounded Knee (Feb.–May 1973) as AIM members confronted state and federal authorities. While no redress was given after AIM members and tribal religious leaders surrendered at Wounded Knee (562 were arrested, yet only 15 were found guilty of a crime), from this time forward visible redress of Native rights begins to surface in government policy.

In 1973, all attempts at tribal termination officially ended; in 1974 the Indian Self-Determination and Education Assistance Act (ISDEAA) authorized the Secretary of the Interior to implement "an orderly transition from federal domination of programs for and services to Indians to effective and meaningful participation by Indian people in the planning, conduct, and administration of those programs and services." This act allowed for contracts and grants to train Native people to operate programs they might want to take over in full, as well as for the disbursement of funds more directly to reservation populations and the election of Native peoples to official positions within governmental institutions and programs. In 1978, the Indian Child Welfare Act assured that there will be no more governmentally enforced education or the "forcible and systematic transferring of care of Indian children to non-Natives through compulsory boarding schools and adoption to non-Natives." And in 1978, the American Indian Religious Freedom Act (AIRFA) was passed.

In 1979, the Archaeological Resources Protection Act (ARPA) attempted to redress the 1906 Act for the Preservation of American Antiquities by ruling that permits must be obtained for excavations of sites more than 100 years old, that consent must be obtained for any work on tribal Indian lands by tribal landowners, and that work on public lands held to be sacred by any tribes requires those tribes to be notified before any permits are granted. However, human remains on federal lands are still "archaeological resources" and "property of the United States," which, if excavated under federal permit, can be "preserved by a suitable university, museum or other scientific or educational institution." This act still undercuts the rights of Native peoples to claim legitimate control over ancestral dead, territorially identified as under federal jurisdiction, and inhibits religious claims about how those ancestral dead (now or previously unearthed) should be treated.

In 1987, the National Park Service issued a policy statement in response to AIRFA, to explore means for integrating the needs of Native religious practitioners into park resource management. The statement clearly says that Native religious claims "must be within the bounds of existing legislation as well as NPS rules and policies," thereby subordinating Native religious needs and practices to pre-existing government regulations. Also in 1987, the Iroquois Recognition Bill was passed "to acknowledge the contribution of the Iroquois Confederacy of Nations in the development of the United States Constitution and to reaffirm the continuing government-to-government relationship between tribes and the United States established in the Constitution." In 1989, the National Museum of the American Indian

Act (NMAIA) provided for the repatriation of Native human remains collected by the Smithsonian Institution to American Indian tribes upon tribal request. The Smithsonian must inventory and, where possible, identify its collection of remains (18,000), notify appropriate tribal groups, and return them if the tribes request—Blackfeet reburial of 16 ancestral remains occurred in 1989; and 700 remains presently are being returned to Kodiak Island cemetery. Previous to this, in the 1980s, the Denver Art Museum returned War Gods to the Zuni; the Heard Museum in Phoenix returned Kiva masks to Hopi elders; the Wheelwright Museum returned eleven medicine bundles to Navajo; the State Museum of New York in Albany returned twelve wampum belts to the Six Nation Confederacy and a clan bundle to the Hidatsa; the Boston Peabody Museum returned the sacred pole (plus 270 other artifacts) to the Omaha; and many others have made nominal returns as well. But many museums and institutions have ignored requests. For example, the Iroquois request for return of all their sacred masks has not been met.

In 1990, the Native American Grave Protection and Repatriation Act (NAGPRA) was passed. This act protects Indian gravesites from looting and requires repatriation of all culturally identifiable tribal artifacts. According to the act, museums must inventory collections and notify tribes of their holdings. Legal procedures are established for reclaiming artifacts, though claimants must meet strict legal tests. However, NAGPRA does not apply to state land or private property. By 1991, thirty-two states had laws that dealt with reburial and repatriation of ancestral prehistoric remains; but there is little consistency among the laws passed and many do not involve goods found on private property. As Walter and Roger Echo-Hawk have written, "criminal statutes in all fifty states very strictly prohibit grave desecration, grave robbing, and mutilation of the dead—yet they are not applied to protect Indian dead. . . . [Native dead are still] 'federal property' to be used as chattels in the academic marketplace."

In 1993, the Religious Freedom Restoration Act (RFRA) was passed and signed into law, thereby compelling the government not to "substantially burden religious exercise without compelling justification" and to "provide a claim or defense to persons whose religious exercise is substantially burdened by government." While this act may help to redress future infringement of Native American religious rights, it does not mention those rights specifically. This brings us fully into the present with the 1994 Native American Free Exercise of Religion Act (NAFERA). NAFERA is a bill amending the 1978 American Indian Religious Freedom Act (AIRFA) and includes, among other things, specific protections for the use of peyote by Native American Church members as well protecting the religious rights of Native American prisoners who wish to practice traditional Native religions. The NAFERA bill was proposed as a means to put teeth into the policy statement of the 1978 act, which has been largely perceived as ineffectual in court cases involving Native American religious freedom. As of 1995, no government agency has developed actual regulations based on AIRFA; further, the U.S. Forest Service has been one of the most aggressive antagonists of AIRFA in the courts (particularly in *Lyng v. Northwest*). As Sharon O'Brien writes concerning AIRFA, "Testimony by American Indian witnesses and government officials clearly attest to the lack of federal administrative compliance with the law and congressional failure to rectify religious infringements through legislative reform."

And where is AIM today? AIM is alive and well, continuing its long struggle for political and religious rights of Native peoples. In 1993, AIM reorganized into "an alliance of fully autonomous but reciprocally supporting chapters." AIM chapters are dedicated "to advance the cause of indigenous sovereignty and self-determination within its own context and regional conditions." Decisions of local and state chapters are made independently, emphasizing their local constituencies. In April 1993, AIM held a Western Regional Conference of its many chapter organizations where AIM members were joined by John La Velle, the Santee Lakota founder of Center for the SPIRIT (Support and Protection of Indian Religions and Indigenous Traditions). San Francisco area–based SPIRIT is "a nonprofit organization of American Indian people dedicated to the preservation and revitalization of American Indian spiritual practices and religious traditions." La Velle announced a joint commitment with diverse tribal elders and the AIM chapters to continuing to work for the protection and maintenance of Native religious rights.

At the Lakota Summit V, in June 1993, an international gathering of United States and Canadian Lakota, Dakota, and Nakota nations, including 500 representatives from as many as 40 tribes, unanimously passed a "Declaration of War Against Exploiters of Lakota Spirituality." At the conference, Wilmer Mesteth, a traditional Lakota leader and instructor at Lakota Oglala College, spoke about the imitation and sale of Lakota ceremonies by non-Indian peoples. Mesteth, along with Darrell Standing Elk and Phillis Swift Hawk, drew up the declaration to warn non-Natives against the appropriation of Native spirituality. AIM also has become more visible in a walk led by Dennis Banks and Mary Jane Wilson that began February 11, 1994, from Alcatraz Island and which culminated in Washington, D.C., in July as a means to call attention to the continued imprisonment of Leonard Peltier— who many believe was falsely imprisoned and who is certainly the foremost symbol of Native American political and spiritual resistance.

The concerns of both AIM and SPIRIT are summarized in the Lakota Summit declaration of war against all "plastic Indians." This declaration expresses the frustration and anger that many Native peoples feel about the sale of Native American religious objects as well as the marketing of Native ceremonies by unqualified and (usually) non-Native people. Tourism that results in the sale of Native artifacts has been denounced as well as "New Age exhibitors [who] wrongfully [portray] themselves as Native Americans or [sell] ceremonies for profit." AIM and SPIRIT sponsor political actions against institutions of higher education and confrontations with various institutions, members of which are engaged in ceremonies that falsely claim to legitimate students as "pipe-carriers" or as representatives of Native religions. Confrontations have occurred with people claiming to lead or in other ways sponsor Native religious activities who are neither members of any tribe nor qualified by tribal standards to lead such events.

AIM and SPIRIT have adopted the terms "exploiters" and "exploitation" as part of a regional and national strategy to confront people, whether Indian or non-Indian, who profit from Native American religious traditions. Actions are presently underway by AIM to mandate tribal identification cards or tribal legal verification for anyone claiming to represent Indian people in any public forum, including powwow vendors and artisans. Anyone profiting from religious activities associated with a claimed tribal affiliation should be able to provide references from that tribe affirming the good standing of that person with tribal members. Finally, AIM delegates have resolved to work toward getting a bill to Congress making it illegal to falsely impersonate a medicine man or a medicine woman and to stop, where possible, the selling of ceremonies and sacred objects.

Other such Native groups have formed, including the League of Indigenous Sovereign Nations (LISN, May 1991, established on Piscatoway Native land in Port-Tobacco, Maryland); the Indigenous Peoples Caucus (IPC, Canada, 1993, Sulian Stone Eagle Herney, Mi'kmak); Native American Traditions, Ideals, Values Educational Society (NATIVE, 1993, founded by a Navajo mother of five, Betty Red Ant LaFontaine); and WARN (Women of All Red Nations), one of the first Native American feminist movements. This feminist element has taken a more visible form in the recent Second and Third Continental Congress of Women of the Americas (1994, Washington D.C.; 1995 in Beijing) which included women from North, Central and South America, Canada, and Russia, providing an opportunity for networking which may prove to be a formidable resource for Native political and religious actions.

In the summer of 1995, while attending a Sun Dance on Pine Ridge, I had several opportunities to discuss these issues with the full-blood traditional Lakota ceremonial leader who had invited me to that dance. In our discussions, we touched on the history and background of oppression on the Pine Ridge reservation. His comments on Black Elk were particularly salient:

> You know, Black Elk was part of a conspiracy, a cover-up here among the Lakota. What he says there about the Indian religion being dead, over, was part of a plan to stop the oppression here at Pine Ridge. It worked, too. After that book came out, things got better; we just said it was over, dead, a thing of the past. We had to still do it secretly, but things have gotten better. Now we can do it more openly and bring other people in. . . . I don't believe our religion is

something that should be hidden or kept from other people who are not Lakota or Indian. But for a long time, we had to keep everything hidden, even from other Lakota.

These comments reflect more than a personal point of view. They express in many ways both the consequences of a long oppressive history and the resistance strategies that have led to the preservation of many traditional Native religious practices in the face of religious persecution. Caution still exists—this Sun Dance was by invitation only and closed to casual outsiders. Held back in the hills, there were no signs, no indications other than a single red cloth tied on a stop sign. On entering the dance grounds, a very large sign in red paint read, "No cameras or tape recorders allowed!" The entrance was watched day and night and roped off to anyone other than those approved or known to those posted at the entrance.

Perhaps one of the most fundamental of all strategies in the struggle for spiritual survival among Native Americans has been the constant theme of maintaining traditional religious integrity and not compromising religious beliefs or practices in the face of massive oppression and coercion. Accommodation has proven, in many ways, to lead to an erosion of traditional values in the face of a long and usually uncompromising, non-reciprocal assault on Native character and identity. Yet, political resistance in the late twentieth century has been moderated by a resurgence in Native religious practices, the leaders of which have constantly promoted non-violent tactics and an ethics of preservation, mutuality, and respect for tribal differences. All too often, these leaders have been labeled as "radicals" and "troublemakers" whose actions are seen as unjustly critical of majority rule. Such a response is a symptom of cultural blindness indicating a profound lack of awareness of the real history of Native American religious oppression.

The history of prophetic leadership has been one of cultural survival with a constant reaffirmation of the rights of Native peoples to formulate, and reformulate, their religious and communal identities through a validation of their own cultural pasts. Often this has required constant, bitter negotiation with non-Native peoples whose perspective is reinforced by alien cultural values. There is nothing "radical" about such resistance—it is a natural inclination to preserve valued cultural practices that are inseparable from a way of life and identity grounded in deep, abiding spiritual principles distinct from those imposed by aggressive missionization and assimilative government policies. In many ways, Native communities are actually proponents of the conservation of culture, of maintaining continuity with the past and of preserving long-held values. The prophetic foreground of visible resistance to cultural annihilation is more appropriately seen as a bulwark protecting a long and deeply held stability than as simply a reaction to aggressive settlement.

Another theme of this chapter has been the way in which traditional spiritual movements act to facilitate intertribal cooperation without denying the diversity of religious practices or values of any particular community. This, it seems to me, is a lesson for all of us. There is a genuine need for all people involved in the study and practice of Native religious life to respect religious differences (which past generations of Euro-Americans in particular have failed to do, including academics) in order to further the cause of religious pluralism as a basis for personal empowerment and religious identity. The character of religious resistance is grounded in the confrontation between various cultural monomyths and the struggle for any people to value the uniqueness of their own spiritual practices. Only when we fully affirm those practices as living resources for our mutual betterment can we move past the need for legislation and legal protections for what is, in fact, a right of all human beings—the free exercise of their religious beliefs.

VI
GROUPS AND INTERESTS

If American Indians are discussed anywhere in your American Government textbook, it is likely to be in a section devoted to interest groups and movements. The emergence of groups such as the American Indian Movement (AIM) in the late 1960s and early 1970s may be described in tandem with the African American civil rights movement. Indeed, as Stephen Cornell makes clear, this civil rights movement did have an important influence on the rise of what he terms the "new Indian politics." Yet the context within which Indian activism emerged was quite distinct and rarely appreciated outside of Indian Country. The great strength of Cornell's chapter is that he offers insight into this context and explains both its historical and political significance. Although no longer as "new" as when Cornell wrote this essay in the late 1980s, this era of Indian political activism has had a profound effect upon more than one generation of Indians and a continuing influence upon the broader U.S. polity.

The New Indian Politics

STEPHEN CORNELL

On December 28, 1890, near the Badlands of South Dakota, a band of exhausted Sioux Indians, including perhaps 100 warriors and some 250 women and children, surrendered to the blue-clad troopers of the U.S. Seventh Cavalry and agreed to travel with them to the Indian agency at Pine Ridge. The joint party camped that night in freezing weather at Wounded Knee Creek, 20 miles from Pine Ridge. Surrounding the Indian tepees were nearly 500 soldiers and a battery of four Hotchkiss light artillery pieces.

The next morning, the Indian men were told to turn in their weapons. Few obeyed. The cavalrymen began to search the tepees. When they turned up few additional guns, the troops began to search the warriors themselves. Reports of subsequent events vary, but tension ran high.

A scuffle broke out between an Indian and some soldiers. In the struggle, the warrior, intentionally or not, fired his rifle. That did it. Instantly both Indians and soldiers began firing at each other. Within moments, the Army gunners were pouring explosive Hotchkiss shells into the Indian camp.

Most of the Sioux warriors died in the opening volleys. Others, along with a large number of women and children, were shot as they fled down adjacent ravines. By the time the firing ended, nearly 200 Indians—perhaps more, the estimates vary—had been killed.

This chapter is reprinted from *The Wilson Quarterly*, New Year's 1986, by permission of the publisher.

The survivors of this slaughter were among the last Indians to come under the direct administrative control of the U.S. government. Confined to reservations, they joined 300,000 others, from coast to coast, in a state of despondent dependency, sunk in poverty, wards of a white man's government that they had learned not to trust.

Eighty-two years later, on the wintry night of February 27, 1973, a group of armed Oglala Sioux from South Dakota's Pine Ridge Reservation joined forces with activists from the American Indian Movement (AIM) and seized the reservation village of Wounded Knee, the site of the 1890 massacre. They did so to protest corruption in the tribal government at Pine Ridge as well as U.S. violations of the 1868 Fort Laramie Treaty (which recognized Sioux sovereignty over much of what is now the Dakotas, Montana, Wyoming, and Nebraska). "We want a true Indian nation," said Carter Camp, an AIM coordinator, "not one made up of Bureau of Indian Affairs puppets."

Within 24 hours, a force of 250 Federal Bureau of Investigation agents, U.S. marshals, and Bureau of Indian Affairs (BIA) police had cordoned off the village. The much-publicized siege lasted 10 weeks, punctuated by exchanges of gunfire that left two Indians dead and several men wounded on each side. In May, after lengthy negotiations, the Indians surrendered to federal authorities. The second battle of Wounded Knee was over.

The 1890 massacre brought one era to a close. The Euro-American advance across the continent was now complete. As Black Hawk, war leader of the Sauk and Fox, had said of himself a half century earlier, "He is now a prisoner to the white men; they will do with him as they wish."

86 MILLION ACRES

The 1973 occupation also represented the culmination of an era. America's roughly 790,000 Indians still lived, for the most part, in considerable misery, afflicted by poverty, alcoholism, high unemployment, and inadequate education. But the days of dull Indian acquiescence were long gone. Beginning in the 1940s, Indians had not only been demanding a voice in federal Indian policy; increasingly, they had appropriated such a voice for themselves, forcing the surrounding society to respond. "We talk, *you* listen" was the title of a 1970 book by Sioux author Vine Deloria, Jr. And as they demonstrated at Wounded Knee, Indians did more than talk.

All in all, the path from Wounded Knee I to Wounded Knee II traced an Indian political resurgence of striking proportions. There had always been, of course, politics *about* Indians. For the most part it was non-Indian politics, carried on in Washington, among the governors of Western states and territories, and among missionaries, reformers, and bureaucrats. The situation today is dramatically different, marked by the emergence of a new and genuinely Indian politics.

In hindsight, the turning point appears to have been the Indian Reorganization Act (IRA) of 1934. Prior to its passage, two goals had guided federal Indian policy: the acquisition of Indian lands and the cultural transformation of Indians into Euro-Americans—in a word, "assimilation." Those goals were enshrined in the Dawes Act (1887), which heralded the age of "allotment." Washington broke up much of the tribal land base, withdrawing some property from Indian ownership and distributing other, often marginal, lands to individual tribal members. "Surplus" lands, more often than not the richest, were then sold off to white settlers. Between 1887, when the Dawes Act was passed, and 1934, when allotment ceased, some 86 million acres—60 percent of the remaining Indian lands—passed into the possession of non-Indians.

Allotment, which reached a peak just before World War I, was not merely a means of appropriating Indian territory. It was part of a concerted effort to break up tribal nations, of which there were—and are—several hundred, each with a distinct history, most still with a distinct culture. This effort, like everything else on the reservations, was overseen by the Bureau of Indian Affairs, established by Secretary of War John Calhoun in 1824.

"The Indians," wrote Indian Commissioner Thomas Morgan in 1889, "must conform to 'the white man's ways,' peaceably if they will, forcibly if they must." On the reservations, BIA officials put Indian children into English-language boarding schools, dispersed village settlements, moved tribal members off communal (and on to individual) tracts of land, and took control of economic resources. Indigenous religious ceremonies, such as the Sun Dance of the Plains tribes, were outlawed.

WAITING FOR FDR

By the 1920s, white America's appetite for Indian lands (the best of which had already been taken) had begun to diminish. A postwar slump in farm prices helped reduce demand. Combined with the staggering extent of poverty, disease, and other social ills now apparent on the Indian reservations, these circumstances created a climate for reform.

The reform movement can be traced in part to the ideals of Progressivism and to the growing academic interest in the notion of "cultural pluralism" as a plausible alternative to the assimilation of America's ethnic groups. In 1922, when the Harding administration backed the Bursum Bill, which threatened the land and water rights of New Mexico's Pueblo Indians, a number of liberal, non-Indian organizations—the General Federation of Women's Clubs, for example—joined the Pueblos in opposing the legislation. The thriving community of artists, writers, and intellectuals around Santa Fe and Taos supported the protest. Writing in the *New York Times*, novelist D. H. Lawrence claimed that the bill played "the Wild West scalping trick a little too brazenly." The Pueblo leaders themselves, acting in concert for the first time since the Pueblo Rebellion in 1680, declared that the bill "will rob us of everything we hold dear—our lands, our customs, our traditions." After protracted debate, the Bursum Bill was defeated in Congress.

Such protests publicized the Indians' situation. But it was not until Franklin Roosevelt's election to the presidency, and his appointment of John Collier as Indian Commissioner in 1933, that a reform package won approval in Congress.

Collier, a former social worker and educator, and champion of the Pueblo cause during the 1920s, placed great faith in the power of "community." Native American communities, he was convinced, "must be given status, responsibility, and power." Backed by FDR, Collier led a drive to reorient U.S. Indian policy. The result, in 1934, was the Indian Reorganization Act.

Indian policy did an abrupt about-face. The IRA legislation not only put an official stop to allotment; it actually allocated modest funds for *expansion* of the Indian land base. It provided money (though never enough) for economic development on Indian reservations and subsidies for Indians to set up tribal business corporations. But most important, it allowed Indians into the decision-making process by making explicit the right of any Indian tribe "to organize for its common welfare" and to adopt a constitution and bylaws for that purpose. By 1936, more than two-thirds of the tribes had endorsed the IRA in special elections (although far fewer actually organized themselves under its provisions).

The mechanisms of the IRA—representative government, for example, and the business corporation—were alien to Indian tribes. Even so, during the next few years many groups took advantage of what has been called "the Indian New Deal." The majority of today's tribal councils are one result. For some groups, such as the Papago and Apache in the Southwest or the Sioux tribes on the northern Plains, these councils represented the first comprehensive political institutions in their history. But their powers were limited. As an Apache leader from Arizona's San Carlos Reservation put it, "[BIA] Superintendent [James B.] Kitch was still the boss." Nevertheless, Indian groups enjoyed greater control over their own affairs, including a power of veto over some federal actions. For the first time in half a century, numerous Native American groups could also have federally recognized political organizations that could represent the tribal interests in Washington, state capitals, and the courts.

WORLD WAR II AS CATALYST

Another step followed. In 1944, representatives of 42 tribes founded the National Congress of American Indians (NCAI), the first major attempt to pull together Indian groups and governments in a single, supratribal organization. In the NCAI and the regional organizations that came afterwards, tribal leaders began talking to one another. The purpose of the congress, which is still active today: "to preserve Indian cultural values; to seek an equitable adjustment of tribal affairs; to secure and to preserve rights under Indian treaties with the United States; and otherwise to promote the common welfare of the American Indian." In 1948, the NCAI and other groups began a campaign designed to secure Indian voting rights—withheld at the time in both New Mexico and Arizona.

If the IRA gave Indians the legal tools with which to organize, World War II gave many of them the motivation. In what the Interior Department described at the time as "the greatest exodus of Indians from reservations that has ever taken place," some 25,000 Indians joined the armed forces and saw action in Europe and the Pacific. Some 40,000 quit the economic desert of the reservations for jobs in war industries. For many Indians, experiences in the factory or on the battlefront constituted their first real exposure to the larger American society.

The identities of Native Americans have long been rooted in tribes, bands, villages, and the like, not in one's presumed "Indianness." The reservation system helped to preserve such identities and inhibited the emergence of a more inclusive self-consciousness. As a result, Indians, unlike American blacks, have had difficulty forming a common front. World War II brought Indians from different tribes into contact with one another, and with other Americans who thought of them indiscriminately as "Indians," not as Navahos or Apaches or Sioux.

It also forcefully brought home to Indians their second-class status. One Lumbee veteran told anthropologist Karen Blue: "In 1945 or '46, I applied to UNC [University of North Carolina]. I had six battle stars. They said they didn't accept Indians from Robeson County." In the Southwest, not surprisingly, it was the Indian veterans who went to court to seek voting rights. Former G.I.s were prominent in the NCAI. In 1952, the *New York Times* reported that "a new, veteran-led sense of political power is everywhere in Indian country."

Such analyses proved premature. There had always been strong opposition to the Indian Reorganization Act, from the political Right and from politicians of all colorations in the West, partly on the grounds that it perpetuated an undesirably distinct status for Native Americans.

After the fading of the New Deal, the status of Native Americans as wards of the federal government seemed to go against the American tradition of self-reliance. Sen. George Malone (R.-Nev.) complained that Indian reservations represented "natural socialist environments"—a charge echoed by Interior Secretary James Watt three decades later. Break up the tribal domains, so the argument ran, remove the protective arm of government, and cast the Indian into the melting pot and the marketplace. Everyone would benefit.

Such, in essence, was the conclusion of the so-called Hoover Commission on governmental organization, which in 1949 proposed "integration of the Indian into the rest of the population." It recommended that Indians leave the reservations and, implicitly, the tribal framework. Assimilation, the commission urged, should once again become "the dominant goal of public policy."

ENDING SEGREGATION

By the mid-1950s it was. Under "termination," as this latest turn in Washington's policy came to be called, Congress set out to dismantle the reservation system, disband tribal nations, and distribute their assets among tribal members. What Sen. Arthur V. Wakins (R-Utah), an architect of the new policy, called "the Indian freedom program" received both liberal and conservative support. Liberal opinion during the late 1940s and '50s tended to view the problems of Indians in terms derived from the black experience and the early days of the struggle to end racial exclusion. Reservations were seen as "rural ghettoes"; termination would put an end to "segregation." As historian Clayton Koppes has noted, this view reflected the liberal emphasis on "freeing the individual from supposedly invidious group identity."

This was exactly what most Indians did not want, but Washington was not in a listening mood. Commissioner of Indian Affairs Dillon S. Myer's orders to BIA employees were explicit. "I realize that it will not be possible always to obtain Indian cooperation," he wrote in 1952. Nonetheless, "we must proceed."

During the summer of 1953, under House Concurrent Resolution 108, Congress effectively repudiated the spirit of the Indian New Deal, stipulating that Indians were to be removed from federal supervision "at the earliest possible time," with or without Indian consent. Under Public Law 280, Congress transferred to California, Minnesota, Nebraska, Oregon, and Wisconsin all civil and criminal jurisdiction over Indian reservations—previously under federal and tribal jurisdiction. Some tribal lands were broken up and sold, while many functions once performed by Washington—such as running schools and housing programs—were usually turned over to the states or other agencies.

PICKING UP THE PIECES

Meanwhile, to spur assimilation, Indians were urged to relocate to the cities. As Senator Watkins remarked: "The sooner we get the Indians into the cities, the sooner the government can get out of the Indian business."

In 1940, fewer than 30,000 Indians were city residents; almost three-quarters of a million are today. But the government is not out of the Indian business.

That is because termination did not work. Take the case of the 3,000 Menominees in Wisconsin, one of the larger groups freed from the federal embrace. When Congress passed the Menominee Termination Act in 1954, the Menominee tribe was riding high. Poverty on the more than 200,000-acre reservation was widespread, but the tribe itself had large cash reserves and a thriving forest products industry that provided jobs and income.

With termination the Menominee reservation became a county. Tribal assets came under the control of a corporation in which individual Menominees held shares, while previously untaxed lands suddenly became subject to state and local taxes. The tribal hospital once financed by Washington was shut down, and some Menominees, faced with rising taxes and unemployment, had to sell their shares in the corporation. Before long, the corporation itself was leasing lands to non-Indians in an attempt to raise money. Soon it was selling the land in order to survive. By the mid-1960s, the state and federal governments, forced to pick up the pieces, were spending more to support the Menominees than they had before termination. As more than one Menominee asked in frustration, "Why didn't they leave us alone?"

In 1969, faced with disaster, the Menominees began to fight back, organizing a major protest movement in favor of restoration of federal jurisdiction and services, preservation of the land base, and a return to tribal status. Congress acquiesced late in 1973. The Menominee Restoration Act reinstated federal services to the Menominees, and formally re-established them "as a federally recognized sovereign Indian tribe."

The assimilationist orientation of the termination policy, and Washington's complete indifference to the views of its target population, aroused Indians across the country. They saw in termination the greatest threat to *tribal* survival since the Indian wars of the 19th century.

Termination did not die officially until 1970, when President Richard Nixon repudiated it. As federal and state officials came to recognize that the policy was creating more problems than it solved, protests by Indian groups slowed. Nonetheless, some Indian groups had been irreparably harmed.

In retrospect, the chief accomplishment of termination ran directly counter to Congress's intention: It provided Indians of diverse backgrounds with a critical issue around which to mobilize. At the American Indian Chicago Conference in 1961, recalled Flathead anthropologist D'Arcy McNickle, the 500 Indians from 90 tribes gathered for the event "had in common a sense of being under attack." The termination crisis persuaded many Indians of the utility—indeed, the necessity—of united action. Strength would be found in numbers. The category "Indian," invented and named by Europeans, was rapidly becoming the basis of a new wave of minority group politics.

UNCLE TOMAHAWK

The tempest over termination coincided with a second development. Just as the late 1950s and early '60s were a time of change in the black movement for civil rights, they also saw the beginnings of change in American Indian leadership and its activity. In part, the change was one of tactics. There were glimmers of the future in actions by Wallace "Mad Bear" Anderson and other Iroquois in New York State: When the New York State Power Authority in 1958 sought to expropriate a large chunk of the Tuscarora Reservation for a new water reservoir, Anderson and 100 other Indians scuffled with state troopers and riot police, attempting to keep surveyors off the property. During that same year, several hundred armed and angry Lumbee Indians in Robeson County, North Carolina, reacted to Ku Klux Klan harassment by invading a Klan rally and driving the participants away with gunfire. The harassment stopped.

The new assertiveness reflected the emergence of a new generation of Indian leaders. During the 1950s the number of Indians enrolled in college in the United States substantially increased. According to the BIA, only 385 American Indians were attending post-secondary institutions in 1932; thanks in part to the post–World War II G.I. Bill, that number had swelled to 2,000 by 1957. On campuses, off the reservations, educated Indians from different tribes began to discover one another. That sense of discovery is apparent in Navaho activist Herbert Blatchford's description of the clubs that began to appear among Indian college students, particularly in the Southwest. "There was group thinking," he told writer Stan Steiner. "I think that surprised us the most. We had a group worldview."

In 1954, Indian students began holding a series of youth conferences in the Southwest to discuss Indian issues. The largest such conference, in 1960, drew 350 Indians from 57 tribes. Some of the participants eventually turned up at the 1961 Chicago conference—and found themselves at odds with the older, more cautious tribal leaders. In *The New Indians* (1968), Steiner quotes Mel Thom, a young Paiute from Nevada who attended the conference: "We saw the 'Uncle Tomahawks' fumbling around, passing resolutions, and putting headdresses on our people. But as for taking a strong stand, they just weren't doing it."

Two months later, at a meeting in Gallup, New Mexico, 10 Indian activists—a Paiute, a Ponca, a Mohawk, two Navahos, a Ute, a Shoshone-Bannock, a Potawatomi, a Tuscarora, and a Crow—founded the National Indian Youth Council (NIYC). "We were concerned with direct action," recalled Thom. It was time for Indians "to raise some hell."

They began raising hell in the Pacific Northwest. The trouble started during the early 1960s, when the state of Washington arrested Indians fishing in off-reservation waters. Though in violation of state regulations, "the right of taking fish at accustomed places" had been guaranteed by the Treaty of Point No Point and other agreements made during the 19th century between various Northwestern tribes and the United States. In 1964, a new regional organization—Survival of American Indians—joined the NIYC in protests supporting Indian treaty rights. They held demonstrations at the state capital in Olympia and, more provocatively, sponsored a series of "fish-ins," deliberately setting out to fish waters forbidden to them by the state.

EQUAL RIGHTS

Growing numbers of Indian tribes became involved—the Muckleshoot, Makah, Nisqually, Puyallup, Yakima, and others—and began to assert their claims in defiance of court injunctions and state actions. The protests continued into the 1970s and became more violent. In August 1970, Puyallup Indians in a fishing camp on the Puyallup River exchanged gunfire with police who had surrounded them. No one was injured, but 64 Indians were carted off to jail. A year later Hank Adams, leader of Survival of American Indians, was shot by white vigilantes as he sat in his car on the banks of the Nisqually, near Tacoma.

Adams survived, and the struggle went on. Ultimately, in 1974, a federal district court ruled in the tribes' favor on the fishing rights issue, a decision upheld by the U.S. Supreme Court five years later. But the battle is not over. In November 1984, voters in Washington approved Initiative 456, designed to undermine the Treaty of Point No Point and other similar treaties.

Jack Metcalf, a Washington state senator and author of Initiative 456, says that "the basic point is not fish—it's equal rights." But, of course, the issue *is* fish and other treaty-protected Indian resources. From the Indian point of view, it is an issue long since resolved. In the treaties they signed during the 19th century, they agreed to give to the United States most of what are now the states of Washington and Oregon as well as parts of Idaho and California. In return, the United States, among other things, recognized forever their right to fish in Northwestern waters.

Indian activism did not appear only in the countryside; it erupted in the cities as well. For many Indian migrants of the postwar period, the move from the reservation to Denver, Chicago, Seattle, and other cities merely replaced one form of poverty with another. Largely unskilled, lacking experience in the non-Indian world, victimized by discrimination in housing and jobs, Indian migrants swelled the ranks of the urban poor.

LANDING ON ALCATRAZ

They also discovered that, unlike blacks or Hispanics, they had become "invisible." In the eyes of state and local officials, urban Indians, just like reservation Indians, were the sole responsibility of the BIA. The BIA, for its part, believed that its responsibility stopped at reservation's edge. In 1963, Indians in Oakland, San Francisco, and San Jose began protesting BIA relocation policies and the failure of the Bureau to deal with urban Indian problems. They took a cue from the tactics being employed by American blacks. Observed Vine Deloria, Jr.: "The basic fact of American political life— that without money or force there is no change—impressed itself upon Indians as they watched the civil-rights movement."

The two most militant Indian political organizations took root in the cities: the American Indian Movement, founded in 1968, and Indians of All Tribes, which materialized a year later.

AIM first made its mark in Minneapolis, organizing an Indian Patrol to combat alleged police brutality in Indian neighborhoods. It soon had chapters in cities throughout the Midwest. Indians of All Tribes was founded in San Francisco in response to a specific incident. On November 1, 1969, the San Francisco Indian Center, which served the large Bay Area population, burned to the ground. There was no ready replacement for the building or the services that it provided. On November 9, a group of Indians—perhaps a dozen—landed on Alcatraz Island in San Francisco Bay, site of an abandoned federal prison, and claimed it for a new Indian center. Authorities removed them the next day. The Indians returned on November 20, now 80 strong. By the end of the month several hundred were living on the island, calling themselves Indians of All Tribes. Wary of public reaction to the use of force, federal officials pursued negotiations for 19 months. Not until June 1971, when the number of Indians on the island had dwindled and public interest had waned, did federal marshals and the Coast Guard retake "the Rock."

Alcatraz was a watershed. It drew massive publicity, providing many Indians with a dramatic symbol of self-assertion. Said occupation leader Richard Oakes, a Mohawk: "This is actually a move, not so much to liberate the island, but to liberate ourselves." During the next five years Indians occupied Mount Rushmore, Plymouth Rock, and more than 50 other sites around the country for varying lengths of time. The wave of takeovers culminated with the seizure of the BIA headquarters in Washington, D.C., in 1972, and the Wounded Knee occupation in 1973. AIM, led by Dennis Banks and Russell Means, was a major actor in both. All made for vivid television news stories.

The Indian activists, noted Yakima journalist Richard La Course, "blew the lid off the feeling of oppression in Indian country." They also provoked a concerted response from Washington. The FBI and the BIA began an effective infiltration campaign, directed in particular at the American Indian Movement. (AIM's chief of security, it would later be revealed, was an FBI informer.) More than 150 indictments came out of the Wounded Knee incident. Making headlines and the network evening news had its price. Conceded one AIM member in 1978, "We've been so busy in court fighting these indictments, we've had neither the time nor the money to do much of anything else."

GOING TO THE COURTS

Radical Indian action has abated since the mid-1970s. But the new Indian politics has involved more than land seizures and demonstrations. Beginning in the late 1960s, the Great Society programs opened up new links between Indian leaders and the federal government. By 1970, more than 60 Community Action Agencies had been established on Indian reservations. Office of Economic Opportunity (OEO) funds were being used to promote economic development, establish legal services programs, and sustain tribal and other Indian organizations. Through agencies such as OEO and the Economic Development Administration, tribes were able for the first time to bypass systematically the BIA, pursuing their own political agendas in new ways.

Indian activists have also turned to the courts. The legal weapon is especially potent in the Indian situation because the relationship of Native Americans to the United States, unlike that of any other group in American life, is spelled out in a vast body of treaties, court actions, and legislation. In 1972, for example, basing their case on a law passed by Congress in 1790 governing land transactions made with Indian tribes, the Penobscot and Passamaquoddy tribes filed suit to force the federal government to protect their claims to more than half of the state of Maine. This action led eventually to the Maine Settlement Act of 1980, which deeded 300,000 acres of timberland to the two tribes.

Behind such actions lies an assortment of Indian legal organizations that sprang up during the 1970s, staffed by a growing cadre of Indian lawyers and supported by both federal and private funds. Indeed, organizing activity of every stripe has marked the past two decades. By the late 1970s, there were more than 100 intertribal or supratribal Indian organizations, ranging from the National Indian Youth Council to the Association of American Indian Physicians to the Small Tribes of Western Washington, most with political agendas, many with lobbying offices in Washington.

Despite generally low Indian voter turnout, Indians have not ignored electoral politics. In 1964, two Navahos ran for seats in the New Mexico state legislature and won, becoming the first Indian representatives in the state's history. Two years later, 15 Indians were elected to the legislatures of six Western states. In 1984, 35 Indians held seats in state legislatures.

Of course the leverage Indians can exercise at the polls is limited. In only five states (Alaska, Arizona, New Mexico, Oklahoma, and South Dakota) do Indians make up more than five percent of the population. At the local level, on the other hand, Indians are occasionally dominant. (Apache County, Arizona, for example, is nearly 75 percent Indian.) Indians also can make a difference in particular situations. In 1963, after the South Dakota legislature had decided that the state should have civil and criminal jurisdiction over

Indian reservations, the Sioux initiated a "Vote No" referendum on the issue, hoping to overturn the legislation. They campaigned vigorously among whites and were able to turn out their own voters in record numbers. The referendum passed. A similar Indian grassroots effort and high voter turn-out in 1978 led to the defeat of Rep. Jack Cunningham (R.-Wash.), sponsor of legislation in Congress to abrogate all treaties between Indian tribes and the federal government.

THE FINEST LAWYERS

If Indians lack more than limited political clout in elections, during the 1970s they found new opportunities in the economy. The 1973–74 energy crisis and rising oil prices sent the fortunes of some tribes through the roof. Suddenly, Indian lands long thought to be worthless were discovered to be laden with valuable natural resources: one quarter or more of U.S. strippable coal, along with large amounts of uranium, oil, and gas. Exploration quickly turned up other minerals on Indian lands. For the first time since the drop in land prices during the 1920s, Indians had substantial amounts of something everybody else wanted. In an earlier time this realization would have occasioned wholesale expropriation. In the political atmosphere of the 1970s, and in the face of militant Indians, that was no longer possible. Now the tribes began demanding higher royalties for their resources and greater control over the development process. The result, for some, was a bonanza. During the 41 years between 1937 and 1978, Native Americans received $720 million in royalties and other revenues from mineral leases; during the four years from 1978 to 1982, they received $532 million.

Most of this money went to only a few tribes, much of it to meet the needs of desperately poor populations. It also had a political payoff. Michael Rogers tells the story of an Alyeska Pipeline Company representative in Alaska, who during the mid-1970s lectured pipeline workers about the importance of maintaining good relations with local Indian and Eskimo communities. "You may wonder why they are so important," the representative told his hard-hats. "They are important because they are a people, because they were here before us, and because they have a rich heritage. They are also important because they belong to regional corporations that are able to afford the finest legal counsel in the country."

WHAT DO INDIANS WANT?

This new Indian assertiveness, in its multiple manifestations, had a major impact on U.S. policy. In 1975, responding to "the strong expression" of Indians, Congress committed itself to a policy of "self-determination," to providing "maximum Indian participation in the government and education of the Indian people." From now on, the government was saying, it not only would attempt to listen to Indian views and honor Indian agendas but would grant to Indians a central role in the implementation of policy.

But self-determination raises an awkward, chronic question. What is it the Indians want?

According to Bill Pensoneau, former president of the National Indian Youth Council and now economic planner for the Ponca Tribe in Oklahoma, what the Indians want is "survival." In his view, it is not individual survival that is of primary concern. What is at stake is the survival of Indian *peoples*: the continued existence of distinct, independent, tribal communities.

Among other things, of course, that means jobs, health care, functioning economies, good schools, a federal government that keeps its promises. These have not been any easier to come by in recent years. Federal subsidies to Native Americans have been cut steadily under the Reagan administration, by about $1 billion in 1981–83. Cancellation of the Comprehensive Employment and Training Act program cost the Poncas 200 jobs. The Intertribal Alcoholism Center in Montana lost half its counselors and most of its beds. The Navaho public housing program was shut down.

Aside from those with lucrative mineral rights, few tribes have been able to make up for such losses of federal subsidies. With no economic base to draw on, most have found themselves powerless in the face of rising unemployment, deteriorating health care, and a falling standard of living.

But the survival question cuts more deeply even than this and reveals substantial divisions among Native Americans themselves. There are those who believe that survival depends on how well Indians can exploit the opportunities offered by the larger (non-Indian) society. Others reject that society and its institutions; they seek to preserve or reconstruct their own culture.

There are many points of view in between. Ideological divisions mirror economic and social ones. In the ranks of any tribe these days one is likely to find blue-collar workers, service workers, professionals, and bureaucrats, along with those pursuing more traditional occupations and designs for living. Most tribes include both reservation and city populations, with contrasting modes of life. The resultant Indian agenda is consistent in its defense of Indian peoples but often contradictory in its conception of how best they can be sustained. This proliferation of Indian factions, many of them no longer tribally defined, has made Indian politics more difficult for even the most sympathetic outsiders to understand.

The Indian politics of the 1960s and '70s, both confrontational and conventional, was too fragmented, the actors were too dispersed, the goals too divergent to constitute a coherent, organized, political crusade. What it represented instead was the movement of a whole population—a huge collection

of diverse, often isolated, but increasingly connected Indian communities—
into more active political engagement with the larger society, seeking greater
control over their lives and futures. To be sure, compared with other political and social events of the period, it was only a sideshow. It did not "solve"
fundamental difficulties. But in the world of Indian affairs, it was a remark-
able phenomenon, surpassing in scale and impact anything in Indian-white
relations since the wars of the 19th century, which finally came to an end at
Wounded Knee.

VII
CAMPAIGNS AND ELECTIONS

To many in the United States, Indian casinos—and the political controversies that surround them—are the single most visible indication of both the continued presence of Indian tribes and of the distinctive political status that these tribes maintain. California's Proposition 5 is probably the best known campaign on behalf of Indian gaming. Many of the elements that have become familiar in U.S political campaigns can be seen in the political battle over this ballot initiative. Well-financed interests, professionally managed campaign strategy, and slick television advertising were all on display. Proposition 5, however, also highlighted the voices of American Indians themselves and articulated the arguments on behalf of tribal sovereignty to many who had heard little about them before. In this chapter, Richard Maullin, a political consultant and pollster active in the campaign for Proposition 5, offers an inside look at the political strategizing that underpinned this campaign and led to its striking electoral victory in California.

Passing California's Proposition 5: The Inside Story of How the Indian Gaming Initiative Won Despite Big-Time Opposition

RICHARD MAULLIN

According to the early handicapping of California's ballot propositions, Prop 5, the Indian Gaming Initiative, was supposed to lose. The story of how this would-be loser was turned into 1998's most significant ballot winner is an intriguing case study of political strategy and campaign management.

From the start, the "Yes on 5" campaign team knew an initiative to protect Indian gaming would face highly motivated, well-funded opposition. That opposition ultimately included a broad range of unusual allies—the administration of GOP Gov. Pete Wilson, labor unions, business groups, California's horse racing industry and card clubs, Nevada gaming interests, the religious right and anti-gambling groups.

Furthermore, Proposition 5 called for a "Yes" vote on a controversial issue—an outcome that has proven historically difficult to achieve. Conventional wisdom is that a "Yes" vote requires initial public support of between 60 percent and 70 percent if a measure is to pass against a well-organized opposition campaign. Early opinion research placed the percentage of support for the measure in the low 50s.

In fact, so serious and numerous were the hurdles facing Proposition 5 that in July 1998, Harry Curtis, a senior equity analyst for the BancAmerica

Robertson Stephens Gaming Industry Report, said, "In our opinion, there is a one-in-eight chance it will pass."

But by the time Prop 5 was approved by voters on November 3, its place in history was guaranteed. Combined, proponents and opponents of the measure spent the greatest amount of money in national ballot initiative history—an unprecedented $100 million. And in spite of all predictions to the contrary, it won—and won by a substantial 63 percent to 37 percent margin.

Gaming on California Indian reservations was first regulated after Congress passed the Indian Gaming Regulatory Act in 1988. This legislation requires gaming tribes to have treaties (called compacts) with their respective state governments specifying the types of gaming permitted on reservation lands. In California, negotiation of these compacts had dragged on for several years, even as certain Indian casinos began operating with various card games, bingo and video gaming devices.

By mid-1997, the gaming tribes and Wilson were at an impasse, particularly over the tribes' desire to keep video gaming machines. The continuing impasse raised the specter that without a compact for each gaming tribe, the federal government—at the state's behest—might shut down the machines that were providing tribes with about 80 percent of their gaming revenues. Further complicating the picture were a few tribes, as yet to have gaming, who were amenable to the "Pala" compact proposed by Wilson, which restricted the number and type of gaming machines.

THE GO DECISION

With their sovereign rights and livelihood under attack, several gaming tribes began exploring the possibility of a '98 ballot initiative to resolve the stalemate with the governor. In December of '97, gaming tribes led by the Morongo Band of Mission Indians and the San Manuel Band of Mission Indians commissioned Winner/Wagner & Mandabach Campaigns to study the issue and advise them on the feasibility of a campaign.

As part of this feasibility study, our firm, Fairbank, Maslin, Maullin & Associates, conducted detailed studies of voter opinion. They revealed that while there was just marginal public support for an initiative to protect existing types of gaming on California's tribal lands, a significant majority of voters were not opposed to gambling *per se,* and supported Indian tribes having casinos on their own land. Winner/Wagner & Mandabach consulted with us regarding the research results and their implications. Then, they advised the tribes that there was a reasonable chance of success—if they could commit to putting on an intensive, highly focused campaign.

And commit they did. Thirty gaming and non-gaming tribes (a number that eventually grew to 88) joined the Prop 5 coalition, in what for many of them had literally become a battle for survival. Mary Ann Martin Andreas, chairwoman of the Morongo Band of Mission Indians, described the decision to proceed this way: "We felt we were running out of options and our backs were really against a wall. We had to go forward if we were going to secure our future."

With slightly less than a month until the petition-filing deadline, the campaign launched an all-out signature drive. Using a unique combination of direct mail, standard signature-gathering activities and supportive television advertising, the effort garnered more than a million signatures in 28 days, qualifying the measure in record time.

STRATEGIC UNDERPINNINGS

The strategic importance of unanimity among the Indian tribes—those with and without gaming—was crucial. As a result, the gaming tribes' leadership undertook an intensive effort to enlist active support for the proposition from as many California Indian tribes as possible. Ultimately, 88 tribes joined the Initiative cause, allowing the campaign to say "96 percent of all Indians living on California's reservations ask you to vote Yes on Proposition 5." Other key elements of the communications strategy included:

Inoculating the public early against opponent messages. The decision was made not to attack the federal government, the California legislature or Wilson, despite his failure to negotiate satisfactory compacts with gaming tribes. Instead, proposition supporters would focus on Nevada gambling interests as the opposition—a decision Ken Ramirez, Prop 5's campaign chairman and vice chairman of the San Manuel Band of Mission Indians, described as "smart strategy and rooted in the facts." By characterizing the opposition as "big Nevada casinos" ready to spend millions to kill off competition from Indian gaming, the campaign was able to poison the opponents' "message well" at the outset.

Positioning the gaming issue as one of "Indian self-reliance." The Prop 5 campaign characterized Indian gaming as the means tribes were using to lift themselves out of poverty and isolation and toward becoming economically independent members of society. Anchored in the bedrock of the American ethic of self-determination, pro 5 ad messages highlighted Indian efforts to achieve self-reliance, as contrasted with the Nevada casinos' desire to eliminate competition.

Using Indian spokespersons to deliver messages with emotional content. Prop 5's ads relied on simple, emotional messages delivered directly by tribal members. Mark Macarro, chairman of the Pechanga Band of Luiseno Mission Indians, was chosen as the primary campaign spokesperson. He became a recognizable symbol of the tribes' dignity and strength, voicing trust in the voters' ability to recognize the validity of the Indians' position. As Ioanna Patringenaru would remark in The *Los Angeles Times* opinion section, "The steady stream of Yes ads, starring eloquent Native Americans and beautiful western landscapes, captured the imagination of political writers up and down the state."

Implementing an "immediate response" strategy. Most ballot measure campaigns strive to stay on message, never giving the opponents' arguments a second airing through direct rebuttal. But research showed the opposition's messages were potentially very strong, so as Paul Mandabach, president of Winner/Wagner & Mandabach, put it, "We had to break with conventional wisdom, and commit to rebuttal ads. We opted for the strategy of never letting our opponents gain even a toehold of credibility." Consequently, the pro-5 campaign countered, swiftly and directly, any claim, argument or assertion the opposition made.

Its messenger, "big Nevada casinos," had been tainted by Prop 5's early framing of the issues. Now the campaign worked to show the fallacy of opposition messages while underscoring the motive behind them. The Yes on 5 campaign had rebuttal spots produced, tested and on the air within 48 hours following the initial airing of an opposition spot.

In addition to its direct counter spots, the Prop 5 campaign aired several proactive 30-second TV spots as well as a 15-minute documentary, primarily on cable. The documentary used Indian scholars and tribal spokespersons to recount the history of California Indians, and showed modern day reservation Indians telling how gaming had changed their quality of life. As Chuck Winner, partner in the Winner/Wagner & Mandabach firm, noted, "the documentary and the proactive spots were crucial in providing voters with a historical context and an understanding of why Prop 5's passage was so important to California Indians."

Finally, the gaming tribes engaged in an extensive grassroots campaign. Door hangers were hung; tribal members engaged voters in face-to-face conversations; and individual tribal members made persuasion phone calls nightly for months, thus bringing a personal Indian presence to thousands who had never met a Native American. Further, members of the tribes visited editorial boards and various organizations throughout the state to present the case for Prop 5 and obtain important third-party support.

THE END GAME

The occasional dip in Prop 5 support following some of the opponents' advertising salvos led several analysts to predict the initiative's defeat. One, Field Poll Director Mark DiCamillo, observed from their numbers, "These figures do not bode well for the measure. The trend usually continues when voters start to defect a month before election day. Undecided voters also have a tendency to vote no." Nevertheless, the campaign's voter tracking surveys continued to provide daily confirmation that the campaign's strategy was on the right track.

On the eve of the election, internal polling showed Prop 5 with majorities or strong pluralities among every major voter group except archconservatives. In fact, support actually increased about 5 percent in the last five days, causing the San Diego *Union Tribune* to comment that "Proposition 5 ran counter to historical trends, gathering momentum in the final weeks, when contested initiatives usually lose support."

In addition to our firm and Winner/Wagner & Mandabach, the pro-5 campaign team was ably supported by a team of consultants including Joe Shumate Associates, Michael Galizio, Steve Glazer, Leo Briones, Karen Waters, direct mail expert Mike Myers, opinion researchers Moore Methods and Opinion Dynamics, and tribal consultants including Rod Wilson, Waltona Manion, Nicki Symington, Cerrell & Associates and the staff of the California Nations Indian Gaming Association.

Although Robert Stern, from the Center for Governmental Studies, praised the campaign for running "one of the classic campaigns of all time," in the end, the real credit for the proposition success goes to the Indian tribes themselves. They put all they had on the line for their cause, and the public responded by providing them with an overwhelming victory.

As is the case with most significant ballot propositions in California, Prop 5's constitutionality has been challenged in the courts. Whatever the final outcome of this litigation, Prop 5's passage signals the California electorate's strong endorsement of Indian gaming.

VIII
CONGRESS

David Van Biema's chapter on the politics of American Indian concerns in Congressional committees sketches a particular budget battle that took place several years ago. No matter: the essential dynamics recur regularly. Van Biema puts a human face on a debate in which Indians themselves can be essentially marginal to Congress's calculations. Strikingly, we find conventional party positions jumbled in this debate; it's not always possible to identify consistent Republican or Democratic position among the players involved here. What this incident *does* reflect is a pattern in which the concerns of tribes—so central to the lives and livelihoods of their members—are often regarded as "minor" issues in Congress. The result that can be seen here is that these issues often become pawns in some other dispute, and the pressing needs and concerns of Indians themselves are all too rarely central to the decisions Congress makes on their "behalf."

In the end, the cuts to the Bureau of Indian Affairs' budget were not as severe as those that Van Biema describes as passing the Senate. In the interim, however, this budget was caught in the conflict between then-President Clinton and the Congress, which led to the dramatic federal government shutdowns of late 1995. Thus, once again, Indians were bit players in a wider political drama in which their voices were heard only faintly by those in power.

Bury My Heart in Committee

DAVID VAN BIEMA

As dreams go, Michael Little Boy Sr.'s is a modest one. He would like to move. Not into a mansion. But into someplace better than where he lives now. Little Boy, 41, lives in a one-room shack. Along with him live his wife, five children and two nieces: nine people jammed into a space that measures 20 ft. by 20 ft. The house, on the Pine Ridge Oglala Sioux reservation in South Dakota, has one tiny window with a plastic pane. It is made of Sheetrock and cheap wood siding. In winter the frigid South Dakota wind tears through it like a knife. When it rains, its dirt and sawdust floor becomes a swamp. Now, in a sweltering late summer, flies swarm in and out with impunity.

Little Boy does not have a job. He was a janitor once, and a tribal policeman for a while when his uncle was police commissioner. But jobs on the Sioux's Pine Ridge reservation are so scarce that only 1 out of every 3 adults has one. In fact, as in hundreds of other reservations where Third World conditions prevail, there is only one real source of income, only one source of medical services and of food. There is only one real source of hope that someday Little Boy's family will be able to move out of squalor: the federal government. But the federal government is about to pull the plug.

This chapter is reprinted from *Time* magazine, September 18, 1995, Volume 146, Number 12. ©1995 Time Inc. Reprinted by permission.

"This amounts to cultural and economic genocide," says Ada Deer, Assistant Secretary of the Interior and head of the Bureau of Indian Affairs. A ferocious appropriations bill passed last month by the Senate, outdoing an only slightly less severe offering by the House, slashes the bureau's $1.7 billion budget a third. Deer has announced that the BIA may lay off up to 4,000 of its 12,000 employees by month's end, the most drastic personnel cut currently being contemplated by any federal agency. Just as important, the Senate bill targets moneys that bulwark greater tribal autonomy. Says Kurt Russo, coordinator of the Treaty Task Force of Washington State's Lummi Nation: "What you're seeing is a smart bomb going straight to the heart of the function of tribal governments."

Language of genocide is overused in American ethnic politics, but in this case, the rhetoric of Deer and Russo was echoed by that of Senator John McCain. The Senator is a longtime supporter of Native Americans but also a card-carrying conservative Republican. Says he: "The Indians are taking it in the neck." This week representatives of more than 200 tribes will flood the nation's capital in a last-ditch attempt to influence the conference that will reconcile the House and Senate versions of the cuts. But unless they provoke a huge public outcry, most of the cuts will probably stand, and the fortunes of an already unfortunate people may take another drastic downturn.

For most of the decade, legislators have maintained the budget affecting America's 555 recognized Indian tribes at a constant level. Deploring the inefficiency of the BIA, through which most Indian-earmarked money flows, Congress has attempted to funnel more money directly through it to the tribes. This year, however, fueled partly by Republican budget-cutting fervor and partly by what some call a long-standing antipathy toward tribal rights on the part of a powerful Senator, Washington's Slade Gorton, it ripped up the playbook. "We've never seen cuts like these," says Christopher Stearns, Democratic counsel to the House Subcommittee on Native American Affairs, which allocates money to tribes.

The downsizing of the BIA's bureaucracy bothers Indian advocates far less than the cuts in money earmarked for tribal governments. Tribes' abilities to fight crime, provide sanitation, repair roads and administer dozens of other basic services would be endangered. The federal housing program that might have helped the Little Boy family would be cut 67%. The Agriculture Department's food program for Indians is scheduled to be folded into the food-stamp system, to the Indians' disadvantage. The advocates fear that the cuts will not just shatter dreams of individual Native Americans like Little Boy but also cripple Washington's efforts over the past 20 years to encourage tribal self-reliance and send Indians spinning into a void of isolation and poverty. "We are forgotten people," says Little Boy. "They are going to hurt us, but they don't care."

Defenders of the cuts argue, with some passion, that under Congress's new balanced-budget dispensation, all of government must become smaller, and Native Americans must sacrifice like other Americans. Says Senator Gorton, who as chairman of the Senate appropriations subcommittee overseeing Interior Department funding wrote some of the most drastic legislation: "To give more to the BIA would, bluntly, have required us to give less to the national parks and cultural institutions which are our national heritage for everyone." This he refuses to do.

Yet the argument for equal distribution of pain may be seriously misguided in this case, for several reasons. The first is that the BIA, which makes up 26% of the Interior Department's budget, would absorb 45% of the department's overall reductions. The second has to do with the Indians' abject destitution. Despite the arrival of gambling facilities on reservations, which has enriched a handful of tribes and made a few dozen more comfortable, a third of the country's 2 million Native Americans live below the poverty line. On the reservations, where per capita income averages $4,500, half of all children under age six live below the line; 1 out of every 5 Indian homes lacks both a telephone and an indoor toilet. Federal expenditures that reach the tribes are low enough as it is: according to Stearns, the government spends $2,600 a year for the average American's health, but the average for Indians' is only $1,300.

The cuts may also be illegal, in a profound and historic way. When Indian advocates invoke the "special relationship" between the government and members of Indian tribes, it may disturb citizens who believe all Americans to be equal under law. But few other American groups have warred as sovereign nations against the U.S. government; and none, in return for laying down its arms and accepting life on reservations, has received explicit guarantees of its well-being. The 800 or more treaties signed with various tribes, sporadically upheld by the Supreme Court under a loose philosophy of "trusteeship," obligate the government to maintain a reasonable level of education and health among tribal members and to protect their resources.

Gorton points out that health and education fall outside the ambit of his subcommittee. Yet lapses in policing, child welfare and sanitation will have an indirect impact on health. And many tribes spend the discretionary funds he is imperiling on health and schooling. "Tribes are in desperate need of resources for educating children, for protecting abused and neglected children, for combating alcoholism and drug abuse, for fighting crime, for building roads and water and sewer systems," said Senator Byron Dorgan, a North Dakota Democrat, as he argued to reinstate Indian funding earlier this month. "And we, the Federal Government, have a special trust responsibility to provide those resources to tribes." His side lost by a vote of 61 to 36.

"It's not that people don't want to work," says Joe Blue Horse, director of the Pine Ridge reservation's federal food-distribution program. "It's that

there is no work for them to do." There is no major commercial development near the reservation, which sits within South Dakota's Shannon County
in the shadow of the Badlands, and no factories or malls. Construction work
provides some labor: unemployment drops from 85% in winter to a still
miserable 65% when it is warm enough to build. Oglala who have ventured
off-reservation to find work have more often found alienation and a different kind of penury and have returned. All are almost totally dependent on
the federal government, which long ago signed treaties with the Oglalas
promising education, health and welfare.

Housing is the need that first assaults a visitor's eye. With only 1,500 units
for the reservation's 26,000 people, tribal officials estimate that an average
of 17 people are crammed into each dwelling. Many of the homes are not
in much better shape than Little Boy's; 1,800 families have been officially
designated as "in need of housing." Yet the only money in town available
for building is $285,000 derived from federal Tribal Priority Allocation ac-
counts, which probably will not even stretch to cover this year's 700 requests
for weatherproofing. If the congressional cuts go through, that money will
drop to $176,000.

Education is almost as ill-served. Leon Brave Heart, like an estimated 50%
of the tribe, had an alcohol problem; it caused him to drop out of school.
But when his father died of cirrhosis of the liver and his mother was killed
in a car crash, he dried out and returned to school. In San Francisco, he
joined the Job Corps, specializing in cooking and culinary studies. Now the
22-year-old works at a tiny convenience store on the reservation while caring for 10 extended-family members who share a shack and a trailer. Brave
Heart wants to go to college, but was told not to bother applying for a tribal
grant because the federally funded grant program had only 215 places for
524 applicants this fall. With the cuts, the number could drop to 115.

Even food is a problem, and the Agriculture Department provides cheese,
frozen ground beef, rice and other basics through its Food Distribution
Program on Indian Reservations. William Apple, a temporary $400-a-month
construction worker who must support nine relatives, says, "That's our main
staple food. It's not something we take for granted. Without a job, that's
something you depend on from month to month to supply you." The House
appropriations bill proposes reducing the program's funding, with an eye
toward eliminating it. Says Bernice White Hawk, a 63-year-old grandmother:
"We are going to starve if they cut the [food program]. But those politicians, especially the Republicans, are stingy, rich people. They don't care
about anyone except themselves."

Native Americans and their allies were hurt but not utterly shocked when
the House hacked the administration's proposed $1.91 billion for the BIA
down to $1.68 billion. Most if not all of the House cuts affected the bureau's
central and regional offices, a bureaucracy so inefficient that even friends like
McCain estimate that only 10 cents on every dollar it administers actually

reaches the tribes. Gorton's Senate subcommittee not only tacked on more than $2 million in additional cuts but, claim the injured parties, cold-bloodedly targeted the very programs crafted over two decades to sidestep the BIA's bureaucracy and nurture autonomy among the tribes by funneling money directly to them.

In defense of the Native Americans, Senators Pete Domenici and Daniel Inouye proposed amendments to the appropriations bill that would have reinstated many of those funds. But by then, Gorton had managed to frame the issue as a budget battle, with every cent restored to the Indians taken from someone else's hide. Interior Secretary Bruce Babbitt so objected to this zero-sum game that he threatened to ask Bill Clinton to veto the bill even if the Indian funds were reinstated, on the grounds that the money would disappear from other key Interior programs, putting "public health and safety in jeopardy," among other things. Similarly, several Democratic Senators apparently found that their fondness for Interior projects in their home states outweighed their party's traditional support for the Indians. Senate minority leader Thomas Daschle of South Dakota stood to lose the facility that develops photographs from the landsat satellite in his state. His defection made it easier for such key liberal colleagues as Massachusetts' Ted Kennedy and California's Barbara Boxer to do likewise.

When first asked by a reporter for Gorton's rationale for the cuts, a spokesman said the Senator had based his decision on grounds similar to Babbitt's. But given Gorton's reputation as one of environmental regulation's stauncher foes, this was a dubious rationale. In fact, the Senator's battle with autonomous—and assertive—local Indian government goes back at least to the 1970s, when as an 11-year attorney general in Washington State, he found himself embroiled in high-profile court cases against area tribes over fishing rights and criminal jurisdiction. "I do not believe there is a permanent duty, lasting not only a century and a half, but forever, to fund activities that every other American funds through local taxes and local effort," he says. "Self-determination is something the Indians desire and to which they have a right. But ultimately, self-determination carries a certain duty of self-support." The Senator insists that if health and education programs are included, Indian budget cuts will average just 8%. Gorton also maintains that Indian self-support may be well under way through activities such as "mining, fishing and gambling." Reminded that most tribes claimed to be not yet enriched through those avenues, he gives a disbelieving sniff. "Ah, they are people who have income," he says.

Standing off Highway 18 on the Pine Ridge reservation is what Slade Gorton would like to believe is a symbol of hope and self-sufficiency. It is Prairie Wind, the Oglala Sioux's venture into Indian gambling. Housed temporarily in two connected double-wide trailers, it consists of several slot machines and two tables for poker and blackjack. The casino's revenues in its 10 months of existence have run from $13,000 to $92,000 a month, of which 30% is earmarked for its investors. Thus far, after expenses, it has provided $10,000 for children's school clothes in each of the reservation's nine districts. Prairie Wind's prospects are not golden. In this sparsely peopled state, it must compete with a plethora of other gambling ventures. Says Oglala tribal council vice president Mel Lone Hill: "It is not a benefit to the tribe. It doesn't help us. If we were in an urban area, we could make millions."

An equally valid symbol of the tribe's future fortunes, at least at this particular historical juncture, can be found 19 miles away at Wounded Knee, where a band of peaceful Sioux were mowed down by the Seventh U.S. Cavalry in 1890. Here is a man in ragged, dirty jeans and a filthy red T-shirt. His face is puffy and pockmarked, and there is liquor on his breath. His hand outstretched, he claims he is the caretaker of the Oglala Sioux cemetery.

IX

PRESIDENCY

Dependent as he is upon congressional support for policy, the power of the president is often less than it appears. Presidential agendas are influenced by a host of political players, including members of his administration, members of Congress, and interested groups. Our perception of these agendas are also influenced by *time*. Samuel Cook's study of the Reagan administration's Indian policy shows us both types of influence. Regarding the first type, Cook describes both the sources of opposition encountered by Reagan when he proposed deep budget cuts in Indian programs and some presidential policy shifts that resulted from this opposition. Perhaps more surprisingly, Cook argues that policies that many then perceived as being detrimental to Indian tribes have had unexpected and ironic consequences. He sketches ways in which these policies prompted greater efforts by tribes to assert control over their destinies and ultimately influence policy more successfully. Yet, Cook suggests, only in retrospect can we see how this longer-term "success" for the tribes emerged from short-term "failure."

Ronald Reagan's Indian Policy in Retrospect: Economic Crisis and Political Irony

SAMUEL R. COOK

INTRODUCTION

Over the past 30 years, the native peoples of the United States collectively have seized a position in the national political arena that cannot be ignored. As a consequence, federal policies toward Indians have become, relatively speaking, more responsive to the will of natives than ever before. Yet this era of Indian self-determination also has been characterized by a continuing uphill battle for natives over their inherent rights as members of the first nations of this continent. When federal policymakers seemingly turn a deaf ear to indigenous voices, a crisis appears imminent, and natives become more acutely aware of how much they have lost and how little has been regained. Such was the case during Ronald Reagan's tenure as president of the United States. Reagan was infamous for slashing the federal budget in virtually all areas related to social and economic development and reform, and Indian affairs proved to be a formidable testing ground. The results were such that many tribal leaders and critics in the Indian community viewed Reagan's Indian policy initiative as tantamount to termination.

This article will examine presidential politics during the Reagan era with regard to the formulation, implementation, and aftermath of Reagan's Indian

This chapter is reprinted from *Policy Studies Journal*, Volume 24, Number 1, 1996, pp. 11–26, by permission of the publisher.

policy. In considering the aftermath, it will be necessary to examine briefly the less controversial Indian policy of the Bush administration, arguably an offshoot of the Reagan policy. With the benefit of nearly a decade of hindsight, we may consider both the negative and positive effects and implications of Reagan's Indian policy in a more conclusive light.

Before considering the Reagan era, however, it is necessary to place it within the larger historical context of the so-called "Self-Determination Era" in Indian affairs (1960–present). The term "self-determination" seems to have entered the vocabulary of Indian affairs in 1966, when the National Congress of American Indians (NCAI) convened to draft countertermination measures. Termination was the official federal policy toward Indians that emerged in the post–World War II years. Initially gaining bipartisan support on the premises of "emancipating" Indians from federal tutelage while reducing the national war debt, the termination policy purported to extinguish the federal trust relationship—that is, the political relationship of good faith—with tribes, and to discontinue all federal services to Indians. The benchmark of termination policy was Houses Concurrent Resolution (HCR) 108, which was an official congressional policy statement calling for the immediate termination of specific tribes, and eventually of all tribes. Shortly thereafter, Congress passed Public Law 280, which sanctioned the extension of state civil and criminal jurisdiction over reservations in certain states, and permitted all other states to do so, provided they passed appropriate legislation. Pursued unilaterally, the termination policy marks the most recent consolidated federal effort to assimilate natives.

The greatest irony of termination policy, however, is that it motivated natives to seize control of their destinies from the federal government. A growing awareness among natives of the workings of the larger world converged by the 1960s to cultivate a new age of indigenous political awareness and efficacy, solidarity, and action. Organizations such as the NCAI and the American Indian Movement emerged to represent natives collectively, while educated tribal leaders and specialists (economists, lawyers, etc.) emerged to represent reservation communities.

As we have seen, self-determination ideally is a tribally derived concept. Thus, it must be considered in terms of three interrelated tribal goals: (a) tribal self-rule; (b) economic self-sufficiency; and (c) cultural survival. In addition, self-determination policy initiatives hinge on the necessity of Indian participation within and without the policymaking process. Ideally, such policies are promulgated with the understanding that tribes inherently are sovereign political entities. However, the idea of tribal self-determination was endorsed easily (albeit selectively) by federal officials early on, because it was viewed as consistent with prevailing political trends. Some commentators suggest that self-determination as a policy is an offshoot of the Office of Economic Opportunity programs to bolster the "maximum feasible participation of the poor." Beginning with President Richard Nixon, the Republican party began to advocate a policy of "New Federalism," or the removal of federal barriers to the governmental autonomy of local communities, and tribal self-determination was viewed as a consistent policy initiative. Thus, as we shall see, federal policymakers have had fluctuating, and often vague or contradictory, ideas concerning the full meaning and implications of self-determination.

SELF-DETERMINATION AS A FEDERAL POLICY INITIATIVE

Although the seeds for self-determination policy were planted in the soil of the Democratic poverty programs of the 1960s, the first federal official to express an understanding of the full meanings and implications of Indian self-determination was President Richard Nixon. Nixon recognized the unique political relationship between the Indian nations and the federal government from the inception of his campaign for the presidency. In his 1970 special message to Congress on Indian affairs, he opened with a stark repudiation of termination policy, and boldly reminded Congress that the federal trust relationship with tribes was based on treaties and other binding elements of the law. Hence, Nixon became the first president in the twentieth century to emphasize the politically binding nature of treaties.

Included in Nixon's statement were a number of policy recommendations that underscored the major goals of Indian self-determination. By recommending codified procedures to allow tribes to negotiate contracts with the federal government for the tribal control of federal programs, he emphasized tribal self-rule. By advocating measures such as the Indian financing act, he emphasized economic development. In acknowledging the sacred nature of Blue Lake to Taos Pueblo and advocating the restoration of these lands to the Pueblo, he highlighted cultural integrity, while reaffirming relations of good faith between the tribes and the federal government. Moreover, Nixon opened the door for Indian participation in the federal policymaking process. It was under his administration that the preferential hiring of natives in the Bureau of Indian Affairs (BIA) and other agencies became an active practice. To support these policies, Nixon advanced an unprecedented increase in the federal Indian budget, which more than doubled during his tenure as president. Notably, Nixon realized that successful policy initiatives required the executive and Congress to cooperate in making a progressive agenda bear fruit. Thus, many of his legislative recommendations ultimately became law—most significantly, the Indian Self-Determination and Education Assistance Act of 1975.

Nixon's interest in Indian affairs was not without controversy. Indeed, his administration's dealings with Indian activists in the 1970s were questionable ethically, although there is evidence that certain of his subordinates took liberties in that arena without his consent. However, Nixon's Indian initiatives essentially formed a working blueprint for self-determination policy from a federal perspective, and his policy provides a solid example by which to gauge subsequent self-determination policy initiatives. Indeed, tribal leaders and federal policymakers continue to evoke Nixon's Indian agenda as a beacon for the intended course of Indian policy. Ronald Reagan, in fact, evoked Nixon's policy as his purported inspiration in delivering his official Indian policy statement. Yet, as we shall see, Reagan's policy contrasted sharply with that of Nixon.

THE REAGAN AND BUSH ADMINISTRATIONS

The remarks of President George Bush (Reagan's ideological and temporal successor) in June of 1991 concisely describe the premises on which both the Reagan and Bush administrations based their Indian policies. In his official Indian policy statement, Bush stated: "The government-to-government relationship [between the United States and Indian tribes] is the result of sovereign and independent tribal governments *being incorporated into the fabric of our nation*" (emphasis added). Neither Bush nor Reagan ever bothered to explain how tribes had become incorporated into the federal system without a clear constitutional delineation of their political status. Instead, both presidents treated Indian policy as merely another vein of domestic policy. Reagan perceived Indian self-determination as an exclusive matter of economic development vis-à-vis the private sector. While Bush was not as fervent as Reagan in emphasizing economic development among tribes, his administration tended to downplay the political implications of self-determination, characterizing the concept as minority self-determination.

Unlike Nixon, Ronald Reagan did not enter the presidency with a strong Indian agenda. During the campaign of 1980, Reagan made a general promise to Indian leaders to uphold the principle of "self-determination," to support treaty rights and obligations, and even to expand the scope of federal obligations. Most notably, he proposed to end tribal dependence on the federal government by helping them to develop their own natural resources. However vague, these promises were enough to win Reagan the support of many tribal leaders for his first election—particularly members of the federally funded National Tribal Chairman's Association (NTCA), and the Council of Energy Resource Tribes.

What Reagan did not address was the fact that his Indian proposals might run counter to his economic platform. The Reagan administration will be remembered for such ideological vocabulary as "private sector" and "federalism." In general, federalism denotes some degree of decentralization within a governing system. However, Reagan's version of federalism, or "New Federalism," was "to reduce the size, cost, and burden of the Federal Government and to clear the way for State and local governments to regain their autonomy in our federal system," without creating obstacles to private-sector activities. In other words, drastic budget cuts were pending with the incoming administration, and tribal leaders waited in anticipation to see if Indian affairs would be caught in the crossfire of these cuts.

One area in which Reagan was particularly gifted was in the selection of close "ideological kin" for his administration. In January 1981, he appointed James G. Watt as Secretary of the Interior. Watt had prior experience in the Interior Department under the Nixon and Ford administrations, and when he joined the Reagan administration he was president of the Denver-based Mountain States Legal Foundation. This firm, which championed the development of public lands for business enterprise, epitomized Watt's stance on conservation. He made it no secret that he opposed environmental extremists, and he took every measure within his power to appoint subordinates who would not deviate from his philosophy that "the greatest threat to the ecology of the West is environmentalism itself."

If the appointment of James Watt did not provide immediate insight into the Interior Department's position on Indian affairs, intimations soon followed, with the appointment of Kenneth L. Smith as Assistant Secretary on Indian Affairs. Smith, a Wascoe Indian, from the Warm Springs Reservation, in Oregon, had vast experience in the field of economic development. He was a successful business leader with his own tribe, and had served on the Board of Directors for the Federal Reserve Bank of San Francisco. At his confirmation hearings, Smith reiterated Reagan's preelection proposals, stating that "Indian people have the will and capacity to self-govern and exercise wisely their remaining sovereign powers," and that, while the federal trust relationship would not diminish, tribes should move away from federal dependency "in accord with the existing government-to-government relationship." Citing economic developments to follow:

> I think we have to tap the private sector. I do not think we can come back to the Government because we realize that with the economic conditions that are facing us . . . the tribes understand that there is not always going to be money from the Government. . . . I think we are going to have to tap the private sector . . . for construction and capital money.

Following Smith's appointment, Indian leaders anticipated that a statement of policy from the administration might be forthcoming. What came instead was the administration's fiscal 1982 budget proposals, which revealed that the proposed cuts indeed would apply to Indian programs. The greatest decreases were aimed at human services. Reagan's fiscal 1982 budget cut called for a $136.9 million decrease in Indian Health Service (IHS) funding, a $72.9 million cut from the BIA, and the termination of funding for the construction of reservation water and sanitary facilities. It recommended further that Housing and Urban Development funding for Indian housing be phased out entirely by 1983. At the same time, the administration proposed to cut the Bureau's Business Enterprise Development Fund from $2.4 million to $1.3 million.

Some of the most devastating cuts came in the area of employment. The 1982 Reagan budget called for an end to funding for the public-service employment portions of the Comprehensive Employment and Training Act (CETA), and for similar programs such as the Economic Development Administration. If CETA programs were discontinued, an estimated 10,000 reservation Indians automatically would be unemployed. Although these programs were not terminated automatically, CETA funding was cut drastically, and the impact was immediate. Between 1980 and 1982, overall reservation unemployment jumped from 40% to 80%. On the Navajo Reservation alone, the rate rose from 38% to 75% in less than one year. Interestingly, the administration called for more cuts in CETA funds in its 1983 budget, but requested an $8.3 million increase for BIA social services, anticipating a major increase in Indian requests for General Assistance.

One of the Reagan administration's most vicious budgeting maneuvers focused on Indian education. This assault, however, would occur gradually. Between 1982 and 1987, the proposed Reagan budget for Indian education was reduced from $285 million to $217 million. With the submission of the 1982 budget proposals, Smith announced that the BIA intended to close a number of its schools, beginning with those off reservations. In the same year, he announced that the Bureau was negotiating a contract with Alaska for the state takeover of the remaining 37 BIA schools in that state. Moreover, the administration did not bother to submit a request for Johnson-O'Malley (congressionally authorized funds for contracting with public schools for the education of Indians) funds in its fiscal 1986 proposal, holding that other federal programs (i.e., impact aid) would cover the cost of Indian education in public schools.

While the administration dismissed these measures as necessary sacrifices in the wake of trying economic times, many Indian leaders viewed them as the ultimate breach of trust. Whether for purposes of assimilation, or simply in fulfillment of treaty terms, the federal government always had highlighted education in Indian policy, but the Reagan administration made it clear that it intended to break from the norm.

Smith, as Reagan's key voice in Indian affairs, based his policy initiatives on the supposition that economic independence for tribes could occur only in the context of "traditional American free enterprise," which could flourish only in a stable tribal environment. Thus, the administration consistently requested (without proposed cuts) a $10 million appropriation for "seed money" for Indian business ventures, with the intent of tapping eventually into the private sector. During Smith's tenure, the administration also requested frequently a $5 million annual appropriation to help small tribal governments set up core management teams and to become more efficient.

Had it not been for strong opposition to Reagan's budget proposals in Congress, many Indian programs would have collapsed. Members of the Senate Select Committee on Indian Affairs, most notably John Melcher (D.-Mont.), continually rebuked BIA officials for their anemic budget requests. With regard to Indian affairs, the Reagan administration quite possibly had one of the most dysfunctional relationships with Congress of any presidency. Yet, when Congress provided obstacles to further reductions in the Indian budget, the administration turned to internal changes. The BIA began to alter its rules and regulations governing eligibility for Indian programs, setting more strenuous guidelines regarding blood quantum, tribal affiliation (federally recognized only), etc. In this manner, the administration sought to limit the number of persons eligible for Indian programs.

Interestingly, the NTCA supported Reagan until 1983, at which time James Watt launched a verbal assault on Indian Country. In a January 19 television interview, Watt commented: "If you want an example of the failure of socialism, don't go to Russia—come to America and go to the Indian reservations." Indian leaders, most notably the NTCA, immediately demanded a formal apology and/or Watt's resignation. Eventually, Watt did apologize, and in October 1983 he resigned. Watt's resignation primarily was due to his controversial environmental policies (for example, he had revised 98% of the federal strip mining regulations, adding much more leniency), and it is worth noting the effect these policies had on Indian Country. As a prime example, in 1983, Watt announced that Interior's official policy was to recognize absolute state primacy in all water resource issues. That year, tribes requested over $6.7 million in federal funds to litigate water rights cases, yet only $300,000 in such funds were provided—in spite of the administration's pledge to protect Indian natural resources.

On January 24, 1983, possibly in an attempt to buffer Watt's comments, in appeasement to Indian leaders, Reagan issued his official Indian policy statement. On the other hand, some commentators suggested that Watt made his controversial remarks to divert attention from Reagan's forthcoming statement. Whatever the case may be, Reagan claimed to reaffirm Nixon's Indian policy statement, acknowledging the endurance of the "government-to-government" relationship between tribes and the federal government, and voicing his commitment to self-determination. He also requested that Congress, once and for all, repudiate termination by repealing HCR 108. In fact HCR 108 was repealed legislatively at the end of Reagan's tenure, in 1988, though the specific provision was hidden amidst countless lines of a general education act consisting of hundreds of pages.

The heart of Reagan's message, however, laid out initiatives that were geared almost exclusively toward reservation economic development, and it was apparent that his policy was an attempt to draw tribes into the scheme of New Federalism. After expressing the key principles of New Federalism,

Reagan stated: "This philosophy applies not only to state and local govern-ments, but also to federally recognized American Indian tribes."

Reagan's policy statement can be divided into two parts. The first con-sists of measures the administration had taken to advance its policy prior to the statement. First, the President pointed out that the administration had obtained funds in 1983 to implement the BIA small tribes initiative for the development of tribal management capabilities. Interestingly, the adminis-tration never explained the specific goals of this initiative (beyond citing it as a means toward tribal self-sufficiency), though the President's Commis-sion on Reservation Economics would provide further insight in 1984. Reagan also noted that the administration obtained $10 million in "seed money" for reservation economic ventures in 1983, assured that the free market would supply the greatest amount of financing for such ventures. What Reagan failed to address was the fact that few tribes had an abundance of resources for development, and, considerably more than $10 million an-nually to prompt any noticeable amount of economic growth among all tribes.

Reagan also introduced legislation to allow tribes to enter into "creative agreements," such as joint ventures and nonlease agreements with private enterprises, in an effort to develop reservation resources. This would allow tribes a great deal of freedom in nonlease business activities, although the Secretary of the Interior remained the ultimate authority in such transactions. Finally, the president noted that he had signed into law the Tribal Govern-mental Tax Status Act of 1982, which conveyed upon tribes the same status as states for federal tax law purposes. On the one hand, this would provide an incentive for business enterprises located on reservations, as tribally im-posed taxes could be deducted for federal income tax purposes. Furthermore, tribes could generate revenue through the issuance of interest-free bonds. However, considering the economic state of most reservations, investors were not likely to take stock in tribal bonds due to a lack of security. In light of recent Supreme Court decisions that have increased state tax jurisdiction on reservations, the incentives in the Tax Status Act may become increasingly obscure.

The second category of Reagan's statement consisted of proposed and/or forthcoming initiatives. First, he requested that Congress create a posi-tion on the Advisory Commission on Intergovernmental Relations for a tribal government representative. A related measure was his proposal to move the White House liaison for federally recognized tribes from the Office of Pub-lic Liaison to the Office of Intergovernmental Affairs, which was done shortly after his message. These measures certainly would create a better line of communication among the tribal, state, local, and federal governments, and would relieve tribes of the pressure of having to compete with special inter-est groups under Public Liaison. Third, Reagan instructed the Cabinet Coun-cil on Human Resources to review and coordinate all federal programs on

Indian affairs, making certain there was no unnecessary duplication and insuring a minimum of federal interference with tribal self-governance. This measure ostensibly would alleviate unnecessary bureaucracy, though at the same time it provided a convenient excuse for budget cuts.

As a measure of compensation for budget cuts in Indian affairs, Reagan proposed legislation making Indian tribes eligible for Title XX social services block grants to states. Under such an arrangement, however, tribes would have to compete with states for dwindling federal moneys. Finally, Reagan established by executive order the Presidential Commission on Indian Reservation Economics (PCIRE), to "identify obstacles to economic growth and recommend changes at all levels, [and] recommend ways to encourage private sector involvement." on reservations.

Reagan's statement did not receive a favorable response from most Indian leaders. While the NCAI endorsed the basic framework of the policy, it also suggested major changes that ran counter to the policy Reagan set forth in his statement. Most tribal leaders interpreted Reagan's policy as a new approach to termination via the "sink or swim" philosophy of New Federalism. The rhetoric of intent behind the PCIRE particularly evoked memories of the Hoover Commission of the 1940s, an early proponent of termination, which advanced the charge to "free the Indians."

The PCIRE consisted of six Indian members and three non-Indians (two federal officials and one private-sector businessman). Ross O. Swimmer, then Principal Chief of the Cherokee Nation, cochaired the commission with Robert Robertson, former executive director of the National Council on Indian Opportunity (an advisory council of tribal leaders and federal officials under the auspices of the White House during the Johnson and Nixon administrations). The Commission operated on the assumption that "Indian reservation economies were an integral part of the national economy and not distinctly separate Third World economies." In less than eight months, the commission conducted 16 field hearings, interviewed several Indians, consulted the private sector for suggestions, and reviewed all the literature and federal programs pertaining to reservation economic development. It presented is final report in November 1984.

The Commission's report basically did little more than to elaborate on Reagan's official policy, and it offered few suggestions of merit. The report placed the greatest blame on tribal governments for the poor state of reservation economies. In support of this conclusion, the Commission listed several tribal barriers to economic development, including: the tribal emphasis on the group, rather than the individual; the rapid turnover of tribal governments, which supposedly created an unstable business climate; and weak business management by tribal governments. The Commission recommended several policy measures that would "modernize" tribal governments. This entailed, basically, the complete democratization of tribal governments, and the Commission essentially suggested that the scope of tribal governmental authority should be confined so as not to impede private-sector activities. Yet, the report was not entirely condescending. It did cite factors such as excessive BIA regulation and poor federal funding as contributing to poor reservation economies. Furthermore, it suggested that legislation be enacted to create an Indian Trust Service Administration, similar to the Trust Counsel authority that Nixon had advocated to avoid a conflict of interest when tribes employed federal legal services in grievances against federal agencies.

In the long run, what was contained in the report made little difference, for the administration did not take any substantial measures to pursue the recommendations. Robertson recalled, "[the] commission never received a formal thank you from the White House." Robertson's remarks bring into question the sincerity of Reagan's interest in Indian affairs. The recommendations of the PCIRE were compatible ideologically with Reagan's Indian policy. If Reagan intended to draw Indian tribes into the matrix of his New Federalism, it seems he was willing to make only minimal efforts to that end.

In fact, Reagan's announcement of an official Indian policy did not prompt any noticeable changes in the administration's approach to Indian policy. The BIA budget continued to diminish, dropping from $1.5 billion in 1983 to $923 million in fiscal 1987 (despite the PCIRE recommendation that it not fall below the 1986 appropriation). In 1986, the IHS budget authority was reduced by $88 million, and by another $85 million in 1987. Not surprisingly, by 1986, the NTCA was eliminated from the BIA budget. Most likely, this was the result of the NTCA's increasing criticism of the administration after Watt's "failed socialism" remarks.

To the credit of the Reagan administration, one area in which BIA appropriations increased was that of tribal contracts, through the Indian Self-Determination and Education Assistance Act of 1975 for the tribal administration of federal services. This is not surprising, for tribal contracting would place more administrative responsibility for domestic programs in the hands of the tribal governments, and might prepare tribes to assume a greater financial responsibility for such programs. In 1980, tribes were contracting $203 million in federal programs, and by 1984, that amount had risen to $315 million. In 1985, five Oklahoma tribes negotiated a contract to take over all direct services provided by the Shawnee Agency—the first time an entire agency serving more than one tribe had been contracted. It is possible, however, that many tribes sought contracts as the only sure method of obtaining federal moneys, whether they were prepared to assume such responsibilities or not.

By the time Reagan came to office, the preferential hiring of Indians in the BIA was no longer an issue or concern. A 1987 survey revealed that 82% of the Bureau's employees were Indians. Moreover, the administration did maintain an Indian desk within the White House. Yet, the negative Indian response to Reagan's Indian policy statement revealed a disturbing tendency on the administration's part, to make only minimal efforts to consult Indian leaders on policy issues. This tendency reached its climax during Reagan's second term as president.

Following Reagan's reelection, Ross O. Swimmer became Assistant Secretary for Indian Affairs. Swimmer was akin to his predecessor—Ken Smith— philosophically, but his approach to Indian policy was far more abrasive. During Swimmer's tenure, the friction between Congress and the administration over Indian affairs reached its peak, and by 1987 a majority of Indian leaders were demanding Swimmer's resignation.

Swimmer became notorious for pursuing policy initiatives without consulting Indian leaders. One of his key initiatives was to attract private-sector involvement in Indian programs, and in 1987 he attempted to pool the $1.7 billion Indian trust fund (then managed by the BIA) and, through contract, place it in the financially troubled Mellon Bank of Pittsburgh. Although Swimmer had established a board of Indian leaders to monitor such contracting, they were not consulted on this particular transaction. When several tribal leaders threatened litigation, Swimmer was forced to nullify the contract.

In fact, 1987 proved to be the most controversial of the Reagan years with regard to Indian affairs. In December 1986, Swimmer unveiled his fiscal 1988 budget proposals, which sent a shock wave through Indian Country. Without consulting tribal leaders, Swimmer announced that the Bureau planned to transfer all BIA schools to the state governments in Arizona, South Dakota, and New Mexico. Tribes would have the option to contract for these schools, but, where tribes failed to contract, states would assume authority. In addition, he proposed a tuition fee of $850 for Indian students in BIA postsecondary schools. Tribal leaders immediately protested Swimmer's plan as "a blueprint for termination."

Swimmer defended his plan, stating that public school education was far superior to anything the BIA could offer. Nonetheless, his proposals met strong opposition in the Senate, where Senator Jeff Bingaman (D.-N.M.) promptly sponsored an amendment to halt the education proposal, and required the Bureau to issue an annual education report thereafter. Despite Interior Secretary Don Hodel's (Watt's successor) protest that the bill was an "unjustified and unwise intrusion upon executive branch prerogatives," the education amendments passed, halting Swimmer's planned transfers.

In October 1987, the *Arizona Republic* published a series of articles entitled "Fraud in Indian Country," which added depth to the already dark shadow hanging over the BIA and other agencies dealing with Indian affairs. The series put forth a multitude of allegations, ranging from federal involvement in the looting of Indian resources to the Bureau's inability to account for millions of dollars in supplies. Most significantly, the *Republic* accused Swimmer of "trying to get the government out of the Indian business and to replace federal programs with those operated by private firms." Swimmer dismissed most of the allegations as "mythology," but the stark revelations of the series prompted a lengthy Senate investigation into Indian affairs.

On October 27, Swimmer was called before a special House Subcommittee on Indian Affairs to respond to the allegations in the *Republic*. His testimony defended the BIA, stating that the Bureau was overburdened and plagued by a lack of consensus between the tribes and Congress as to the priorities of his agency.

The sudden increase in congressional scrutiny apparently had a profound impact on Swimmer. Perhaps in an attempt to divert attention from the Bureau's obviously negligent conduct, he proposed that federal funds be transferred directly to tribes, rather than through the BIA. Committee chairman Sidney Yates (D.-Ill.) immediately considered this as a feasible plan. The same day, Yates met with tribal leaders on Swimmer's proposal, and, following a conference with Swimmer the next day, ten tribes volunteered to participate in such a project.

Not surprisingly, the BIA was not supportive of the Self-Governance Project, as it had the potential to dispossess the Bureau of any manipulative control over the tribes involved in the project. But the participating tribes refused to let the whims of the Bureau hinder progress, and they sought congressional direction. The Interior Department attempted to intervene by submitting legislation for the project that would waive the federal trust responsibility to participating tribes. However, with the support of congressional leaders such as Sidney Yates and Senator Daniel K. Inouye (D.-Hawaii), the legislation submitted by the tribal leaders was enacted, first as part of the 1988 Appropriations Act, and later expanded and clarified as Title III of the 1988 Self-Determination Amendments. The Tribal Self-Governance Demonstration Project (TSGDP), as codified, allowed a total of 20 tribes to receive consolidated block grants through five-year contracts for planning and implementing programs formerly administered by the federal government.

Although the BIA continued to pose obstacles to the TSGDP, under the Bush administration, the participating tribes successfully petitioned Interior Secretary Manuel Lujan to establish an Office of Self-Governance, independent of the BIA, to deal with the tribes involved in the project. This illustrates the importance of the TSGDP. The participating tribes seized the full initiative in the formulation and implementation of the project. Tribal leaders drafted the project's enabling legislation, and conducted the research and planning for the use of the federal funds they received through block grants. While it is too early to provide a definitive assessment of the project, it does represent a significant step away from federal paternalism in Indian affairs.

The Senate investigation apparently prompted the administration to be more prudent in considering Indian programs, for notable changes emerged toward the end of Reagan's term. Reagan vetoed the Indian Finance Development bill of 1988, on grounds that it would create unnecessary layers of bureaucracy and would only duplicate existing federal programs for Indian business development. However, he did agree to raise the cap on guaranteed loans for Indian businesses under the existing Indian Finance Act from $200 million to $500 million. Meanwhile, the BIA budget began to increase, reaching $1.89 billion in 1989.

Having charted the Reagan administration's approach to Indian policy, it is clear that the administration did not respect the historical implications of the sovereign political status of tribes. Reagan often spoke of tribal sovereignty, thereby distinguishing tribes from mere special interest groups, but the term "sovereign" was used in a diminished context. From the beginning, the administration spoke of "the remaining sovereign powers" of tribes, and Reagan explicitly compared tribal governments to state and local governments in his 1983 policy statement. Reagan's economic approach purported to develop tribal governments, but in a manner compatible with private-sector activities. The disturbing aspect of this approach is that it seemed to imply that tribes were inferior to state and local governments.

Reagan's position on the regulation of gambling on Indian lands provides some indication of his administration's perception of the sovereign status of tribes. Ultimately, the Indian Gaming Regulatory Act of 1988 established a federal commission to regulate such activities. However, several bills were introduced, and the Reagan administration originally had endorsed a bill that would have allowed exclusive state regulation of reservation gambling activities. Evidently, the administration viewed tribes as having a sovereign status lower than the states, but probably higher than local governments by virtue of the trust relationship.

C.P. Morris describes Reagan's Indian policy in these terms: "In words, the Reagan administration has openly called for market forces to be applied to Indian policy issues. In practice, the administration has selectively written and used federal regulations to prevent the Indian tribes from competing equally with the states and private interests." To assume that Reagan adamantly opposed the concept of Indian self-determination would be extreme, but his perception of self-determination was a matter of economic self-sufficiency and competitiveness in the private sector. If Reagan considered the enhancement of tribal self-governance or cultural integrity as goals of self-determination, he did so only marginally. Essentially, he expected private-sector activities to compensate immediately for budget cuts, without considering how tribal values might play into this scheme. It would seem, then, that Reagan embraced the classical diffusionist view that, by some process of natural law, "the Western world could civilize other less developed areas, . . . and expansion [would] combine with the spread of European values to these areas." Integrating this ideology with the assumption that tribes held a low political status within the federal system, the aftermath of Reagan's policy became manifest before he left office.

The Indian policy of the Bush administration also might be considered an aftermath of Reagan's Indian policy. On June 14, 1991, George Bush summarily reaffirmed Reagan's 1983 Indian policy statement. Bush's statement, however, placed more emphasis on tribal governmental affairs, and made no explicit reference to economic development. Unfortunately, Bush characterized tribes as "quasi-sovereign domestic dependent nations," which did little to advance tribal sovereignty, and certainly did nothing to distinguish tribes as national or subnational entities. Yet, as noted previously, it is clear that Bush believed that tribes somehow had been incorporated into the federal system. While tribal autonomy may be constrained by the primary institutions of the federal system, incorporation requires constitutional grounding. Whereas the United States Constitution clearly defines the position of states within the federal system, the status of tribes remains nebulous. Article I, section 8, states: "The Congress shall have power . . . to regulate commerce with foreign nations, and among the several states, and with the Indian tribes." Article II, section 2, grants Congress the power to negotiate treaties with tribes. While the process of making treaties with tribes was negated legislatively in 1871, these two passages remain the only constitutional benchmarks to define the parameters of tribal-federal relations. Moreover, in spite of its inconsistencies, the Supreme Court has affirmed the sovereignty inherent in tribes by virtue of their existence as political entities prior to the framing of the Constitution.

However, there were marked differences between the Bush administration's Indian policy initiatives and those of the Reagan administration. First, under the direction of Interior Secretary Manuel Lujan, and assistant Secretary on Indian Affairs Eddie F. Brown, the Bush administration acknowledged education and other human services as an integral part of the federal trust responsibility. Furthermore, the BIA budget increased steadily, reaching an all-time high of $1.9 billion in fiscal 1993. In fact, the Bush administration will not be remembered for strong Indian policy initiatives. However, it must be credited for reversing some of the pejorative trends of the Reagan administration in Indian affairs, such as the reduction of the federal Indian budget and the diminished emphasis on Indian education.

CONCLUSION: THE IRONY

In 1982, Vine Deloria, Jr., hailed the Reagan budget cuts, remarking that such reductions would allow tribes to "evaluate the strengths and weaknesses of their past activities and to plan more precisely for the future." As we have seen, Deloria's words proved prophetic. Taking advantage of a Democratic Congress that was committed to scrutinizing administrative policy initiatives, tribal leaders lobbied successfully against many of the administration's unilateral policy initiatives that could have wrought utter chaos in Indian Country. Most significantly, many tribes began not only to plan for the future, but also to assert their autonomy in controlling their destinies. The most salient example, of course, was the successful implementation of the Tribal Self-Governance Demonstration Project, which allowed the tribes involved to bypass the BIA—perhaps the greatest bastion of paternalism in the federal bureaucracy—and to take meaningful control of the programs affecting them exclusively. While the project was guided initially by temporary legislation, it was made permanent in November 1994. While it is too early to assess definitively the merits and pitfalls of the project, there now exists for the first time a means for all tribes to deal directly with Congress. Perhaps this is the first federal policy that is flexible enough to recognize that unique concerns of the numerous tribes vary widely from community to community.

With the 1994 Republican victory in both houses of Congress, the historical context and the consequences of Reagan's Indian policy provide ample fodder for speculating on the future of Indian affairs. The last time that political configuration existed in Washington, termination was the order of the day in Indian affairs—from a native perspective, a crisis that was considerably more urgent than that which accompanied the Reagan administration. The same crisis eventually prompted an unprecedented degree of Indian political activity, and ultimately led to the passage of such measures as PL 93-638. If the scale of political mobilization hypothetically is proportionate to the severity of the crisis that provokes it, then one only can speculate that the turn of the century will usher in a turbulent and revealing chapter in Indian affairs.

X

BUREAUCRACY

Political scientists have developed a number of models to describe the relationship between an administrative agency and the groups it ostensibly regulates or serves. Among the most familiar of these are the notions of an "iron triangle" and "agency capture." The general argument reflected in these terms is that the interests of the group served or regulated by a given agency can come to dominate the priorities of that agency to an unhealthy and undemocratic degree. Yet although it is likely that no group has had a more intimate relationship with an executive branch agency than American Indians have had with the Bureau of Indian Affairs (BIA), it is also clear that the history of this relationship could not be more distant from the "capture" model.

Peter Beinart's chapter illustrates one far-reaching power that this agency holds—the means to decide which tribes receive federal recognition in the first place. But the BIA's role does not end there. As then-Assistant Secretary for Indian Affairs Kevin Gover's historic and eye-opening apology in 2000 makes clear, the historical use that the agency made of its awesome power over Indians has been devastating. Although the very expression of such an apology reflects a significant change in the agency's understanding of its mission, Gover makes clear that the BIA's legacy is one that it—and the tribes—cannot easily escape.

Lost Tribes: Native Americans and Government Anthropologists Feud Over Indian Identity

PETER BEINART

Several years ago, Chief Harold Hatcher of South Carolina's Chicora-Waccamaw tribe was visited by a young man in search of an eagle's feather. The man's mother had died, and he wanted to place the feather in her grave because he believed it would guide her spirit toward heaven.

For Chief Hatcher, it was a painful encounter. He told the young man that owning an eagle's feather is illegal—illegal that is, unless you are a member of a federally recognized Indian tribe. And the Chicora-Waccamaw are not federally recognized. In fact, they are widely thought to be extinct. According to history books, most of the Waccamaw were killed by European settlers in the eighteenth century, and the few survivors disappeared into a neighboring tribe.

Hatcher, as one might imagine, thinks the history books are wrong, and he has spent five years and hundreds of thousands of dollars trying to prove it. The culmination of his efforts—a several-hundred-page petition documenting his tribe's history, genealogy, and social structure—is now almost complete. Soon, he will jump in a gray Ford van and head to Washington, D.C., to present it to the federal government.

He will take the petition to 1849 C Street, the main building of the Department of the Interior. He will be escorted past security to the third

This chapter is reprinted by permission from *Lingua Franca: The Review of Academic Life*, published in New York, May 1999. www.linguafranca.com.

floor, through a long, sparse hallway of black-beige tiles and blank white walls. From there he will hand his petition to officials of the Branch of Acknowledgement and Research, the office charged with deciding his people's fate.

Waiting for Hatcher will be Lee Fleming, the branch chief. Fleming, a cautious genealogist, seems an unlikely magnet for controversy. He would hardly appear to be a threat to American Indian identity. After all, before joining the government he spent eight years as registrar of the Cherokee nation, and he looks on his work at the branch "as service to my own people."

Yet Fleming meets his guests in a conference room because threats against him and his staff make it too dangerous to see them in his office. The branch stopped meeting visitors in its offices a few years ago, after an anonymous caller announced that unless a certain tribe was recognized, there would be ten thousand bodies in body bags. At about the same time, a canister of mace was thrown through an open window into a nearby women's bathroom. After that, the branch moved from the first floor to the third floor. Its exact location is now a secret. But the threatening calls occasionally still come.

They come because the Branch of Acknowledgement and Research sits at an obscure but volatile crossroads of social science, group identity, and state power. Three anthropologists, three historians, two genealogists, two secretaries, and one branch chief are charged with interpreting the federal government's official guidelines—its sacred standards—for what constitutes an Indian tribe. Within the Bureau of Indian Affairs, branch staffers, many of whom have Ph.D.s, are seen as an academic elite. They speak reverently about network analysis and kinship ties and public ethnohistory. They are, in a sense, inheritors of the old academic dream of bringing scientific rigor to government policy that was once arbitrary and political.

But that hasn't made them especially popular in the academy. Their work is governed by a concept—tribe—that most academics view as outdated or worse. And their passion for clear-cut, objective judgments about political and social organization is not shared by a discipline—anthropology—that has been questioning such notions for decades. Boxed in by centuries of Indian law, a clique of hostile academics, political fights over Indian gambling, and power struggles between competing tribes, the branch is understaffed, underfunded, feared, despised, and condescended to. With a mounting backlog of unresolved cases, pressure from the courts, and congressional threats to abolish the office, this band of beleaguered academics may itself soon be facing extinction. To its critics, the branch is the latest manifestation of a centuries-old government tradition of forcing Indians into categories crafted from white assumptions to serve white interests. They accuse it of "administrative genocide." But to the branch staffers, the old, unfashionable categories constitute American Indians' chief source of power, and upholding them stands within the government's best tradition of progressive guardianship over the sovereign, yet dependent, nations with whom it shares a continent.

If membership in an Indian tribe was once a hardship, today it can be a boon. Federal recognition entitles a tribe's members to a host of special services—including business loans, subsidized housing, scholarships, and health care—and it exempts them from some state and federal laws. For some tribes, recognition paves the way to the windfall profits of legalized gambling. The impact of federal recognition can be dramatic—a 1976 study showed that members of unrecognized tribes were poorer, less educated, and in worse health than other American Indians.

That was certainly true for southwestern Alabama's Poarch Creeks. Denied entrance to white schools and relegated to sharecropping for much of the twentieth century, the Poarch Creek did not even have a tribal mailing address as late as the early 1970s. But in 1984, their nine-year struggle for government recognition bore fruit. By the end of the decade, the Poarch Creek operated a fourteen-thousand-square-foot office complex, a housing project, a court system, the seventeen-hundred-seat Poarch Creek Bingo Palace, and a Best Western motel. With an annual budget of close to $8 million, the Poarch Creek had become, in five years, one of the largest employers in Escambia County.

But who should enjoy such opportunities, and why? At a time when the political appeal of identity politics coincides with ever more sophisticated academic demonstrations of the arbitrariness of group affiliation, this is no idle question. In distinguishing a real tribe from a mere social club, the branch must fashion practical solutions to multicultural paradoxes. It is not an easy task.

The branch's efforts stem from the often-betrayed principle that Indian tribes have inalienable rights that spring from their aboriginal status as sovereign nations. In theory at least, the federal government was never allowed simply to take Indian land. It had to sign treaties with tribes, as it would with any other sovereign power. In the nineteenth century, those treaties usually gave the United States the Indian land it wanted, in return for guaranteeing a tribe new land and recognizing its sovereignty. This meant, for instance, that states and individuals could not infringe on a tribe's right to self-government on its own territory. When Georgia declared Cherokee law null and void in the late 1820s, the Cherokee sued, and the Supreme Court ruled in their favor (although President Andrew Jackson refused to enforce the decision). In his opinion, Chief Justice John Marshall outlined the twin principles of tribal self-determination and federal guardianship that have guided Indian policy ever since. "A weak state," he wrote, "in order to provide for its safety, may place itself under the protection of one more powerful, without stripping itself of the right of government, and ceasing to be a state."

So the rights that American Indians today enjoy—to be governed by their own laws and to draw on special federal programs—are based not on their racial status but on their political status as members of a tribe that the U.S. government recognizes as sovereign. The problem is that, historically, the government's decisions about which tribes to recognize have been arbitrary at best.

For most of the nineteenth century, tribes were recognized through treaties in which the United States took Indian land by threatening to wage war or after successfully doing so. But tribes that didn't pose an obstacle generally weren't offered a treaty. By the time the United States came into being, for instance, the Indian frontier was at the Appalachian Ridge. Many East Coast tribes had already been in contact with Europeans for centuries, and by 1789 they no longer posed any military threat or held any territory worth taking. The federal government had no reason to recognize their sovereignty, especially since whites generally believed that eastern Indians were dying out. And even west of the Mississippi, smaller tribes were sometimes overlooked: because they were confused with another tribe; because they isolated themselves on land the settlers did not want; or because they did not make their presence known by force of arms.

Then in 1871, when the Indian wars were largely over, the United States stopped signing treaties. After that, tribes could gain recognition through an act of Congress or a presidential order. But neither the legislative nor the executive branch had much incentive to grant recognition. To the contrary, most federal Indian policy in the late nineteenth and the early twentieth centuries aimed not at extending tribal sovereignty but at undoing it through legislation like the 1887 Dawes Act, which broke up Indian reservations and tried to force Indians to assimilate with whites.

That changed briefly in 1934, when a New Deal law called the Indian Reorganization Act (IRA) provided tribes with funds for economic development and the purchase of land. In order to decide which tribes should qualify, government agents interviewed Indians and visited their communities. In the process, they discovered deserving tribes that lacked government recognition, and twenty-one were recognized under the IRA's auspices. But federal activism was short-lived. For the next several decades, Indian policy was marked by neglect. Except for the odd tribe able to interest a powerful member of Congress in its cause, unrecognized tribes remained invisible.

Then came the 1960s. Inspired, like so many historically disfranchised groups, by the civil rights movement, American Indians began to protest politically. Spectacular confrontations between Indian activists and government agents, at Alcatraz in 1968 and at Wounded Knee in 1973, captured front-page attention. But much of the real action took place in the courts. A series of lawsuits aimed at enforcing long-violated treaties made the recognition issue impossible for Washington to ignore.

In 1975, the Passamaquoddy tribe asked the United States to sue the state of Maine for land taken in violation of a 1790 federal law. The federal government refused, noting that the Passamaquoddy were not federally recognized, at which point a judge ruled that the tribe could contest its lack of recognition in court. Around the same time, several unrecognized tribes in Washington state sued to enforce an 1855 treaty promising their ancestors a share of the salmon in the Columbia River Basin, and a Seattle judge ordered the Bureau of Indian Affairs systematically to review their status.

It was increasingly clear that if the bureau did not come up with a coherent process for evaluating tribes' demands for recognition, the courts would. And to add to the pressure, in 1975 Senator James Abourezk of South Dakota, a champion of tribal rights, got Congress to fund the American Indian Policy Review Commission (AIPRC). In its report two years later, the commission identified 133 unrecognized tribes, representing more than a hundred thousand people (compared with a recognized Indian population of less than two million), and found that "the results of 'non-recognition' upon [those] Indian communities and individuals has been devastating." Abourezk then introduced legislation to the effect that any Indian group that could show it had been viewed as a tribe by the government or by other tribes, or had a functioning tribal council, deserved recognition unless the Bureau of Indian Affairs could prove otherwise.

The bureau was in a panic. Not only did it fear losing control over the recognition process; it also feared that if Congress followed the Abourezk commission (which bureau officials called A-PRIC), the doors would be thrown open to scores of dubious new tribes, each hungry for a share of the bureau's meager budget. The bureau raced to draft administrative guidelines that would quell Congress's appetite for legislation. After endless negotiations, and several revisions, it succeeded. In the fall of 1978, the bureau published its "Procedure for Establishing That an American Indian Group Exists as an Indian Tribe" and created the Branch of Acknowledgement and Research to carry it out. The bureau had worked with anthropologists before; but now a new cadre of academic experts was imported into its offices. Abourezk's bill withered, and the courts began to back off as well, instructing tribes that they would not rule on recognition unless the tribes first petitioned the branch.

The regulations, although revised in 1994, remain essentially as they were in 1978: a hybrid of legal precedent and ethnographic method. The lettered criteria require a petitioning group to show that (a) its members descend from a tribe that dates to initial sustained white contact and that (b) the tribe has remained a distinct community with (c) a structure of political authority ever since. If petitioners can meet these and additional technical criteria, they are entitled to the fruits of their tribe's aboriginal sovereignty. The men and women who wrote the regulations believed they had come up with a simple, straightforward process that could quickly dispatch a problem that the government had been bungling for generations. In 1978, an Interior Department official told a congressional hearing that the branch would eliminate its backlog in two years. It has not turned out that way.

"I've got petitions all over the damn place in binders. This has become a major cottage industry. I don't see why all this is necessary." Jack Campisi is navigating his cluttered office, which sits atop his garage in the tiny town of Red Hook, New York. On one set of shelves are boxes upon boxes bearing the names of different tribes. On a wall is a map of the United States with colored pins designating the tribes for which he has worked. He points out his eighteenth box devoted to the Lumbee tribe and sighs. "That's why the place looks the way it does."

Campisi, a genial man in his late sixties with an anthropology Ph.D. from SUNY Albany, has worked for more than two dozen unrecognized tribes since 1978. In a sense, he owes his career to the branch. But if that has engendered goodwill on his part toward the office, it is hard to find. "I think they're incompetent. I think they're arbitrary. I don't necessarily think they're racist, but I don't think they understand that they're accepting the results of racism. . . . I think they've conned Congress and conned the administration that they're somehow this superlative research center, and God, I had students at Wellesley that could write and research around them a hundred times."

Campisi is a senior member of a group of anthropologists and historians, many of whom work for petitioning tribes, who feel the branch represents a disastrous marriage of academic research and government policy. Their objections start with the concept of tribe itself, which Susan Greenbaum, an anthropologist at the University of South Florida, says "has been torn apart and pretty much discarded in anthropology." In particular, they believe that the branch's search for lost tribes relies on two particularly dubious ideas.

The first idea is that a tribe must possess a formal political structure. Criterion (c) requires that "the petitioner has maintained political influence or authority over its members as an autonomous entity from historical times until the present." Branch staffers note that their guidelines specifically state that informal leadership, exercised by people not holding an office or title, is valid. But critics claim that informal leadership is rarely documented and that the branch accords little weight to oral history not based on firsthand experience. This, they argue, leaves written documents, largely generated by government officials, as the only way to prove "political influence or authority" hundreds of years ago. Since government officials usually interpreted "political influence or authority" to mean hierarchical institutions, they often overlooked real leadership or found artificial leaders who served their interests. Raymond Fogelson, an anthropologist at the University of Chicago, puts the problem this way: "By tribe, they [the branch] have a fixed notion of a tribal government—chief, tribal council, et cetera. That's one form of social control. But in other tribes, there might be another form of social control. It might be gossip, sorcery, whatever, but the people felt themselves a community. Very often the official forms of government were formed in interaction with whites because whites needed someone to deal with."

Indeed, according to its critics, the branch fails to acknowledge that Indians from unrecognized tribes were, almost by definition, obscured from white authority's view. Writing about the nineteenth century, one American Indian historian notes that "it is difficult to locate an Indian community in the East that is not associated with a swamp, a hollow, an inaccessible ridge, or the back country of a sandy flatwoods. Secrecy meant survival during those years." It's a Catch-22: The government demands evidence of formal political authority from precisely those tribes that were not likely to exercise it.

The second attack on the branch's notion of tribe is that it envisions an unrealistic degree of cultural and even racial isolation. Even before white contact, critics note, the boundaries between tribes were often permeable and shifting; intertribal adoptions and marriages were common. Writing about the Mashpee of Massachusetts, a heavily intermarried tribe whose petition is awaiting branch review, the UC-Santa Cruz anthropologist James Clifford has argued that their "later openness to outsiders—as long as the newcomers intermarried and conformed to Indian ways—was a continuation of an aboriginal tradition, not a loss of distinct identity." Branch officials vehemently deny that the regulations demand isolation. They accept that tribal members will intermarry into other tribes and into the community-at-large. They also point to guidelines that state "as long as the group has continued to maintain tribal existence, cultural assimilation is not a problem." The Poarch Creek, for example, followed the Baptist, Episcopalian, and Holiness faiths, as did whites and blacks in south Alabama. Yet the fact that they went to their own churches provided evidence of tribal community. The Poarch Creek also included in their petition a snippet from a local newspaper of the 1930s that reported that whites and Indians both played baseball on one Fourth of July, but the Indians maintained their own diamond.

Nonetheless, critics argue that by relying so heavily on written (and, therefore, usually white) sources, the branch allows racial criteria in through the back door. The branch may insist that it is interested only in a tribe's legal status, and not with establishing the exact details of anyone's genetic makeup or skin color. But as Greenbaum has written, "This need for external validation will likely pose difficulties for several groups whose members do not 'look Indian,' especially in southern states where the smallest degree of Black ancestry is generally sufficient to overrule any other possible ethnicity." The branch, for instance, ruled that the United Houma Nation of Louisiana could not prove that its members descended from the original Houma tribe under criterion (a). But Campisi, who worked for the Houma for fifteen years, argues that since censuses in nineteenth-century Louisiana usually included categories for only "white" and "colored," such an expectation is unfair.

The branch's harshest opponents take the argument about race even further—claiming that the branch perpetuates prejudice against intermarried tribes in its evaluation of current Indian life. Russell Barsh, a law professor currently teaching at Dartmouth, represented the Samish of Washington State, the only tribe to overturn a branch decision in court. The case was less about whether the Samish constituted a community in the past than about whether they constitute one today. The branch said they do not, and Barsh believes that it overlooked strong evidence of contemporary social organization because it decided that even though the Samish "were staying in touch, going to meetings, caring about the community, they were just too white. That racially, genetically, they couldn't be an Indian tribe." He adds: "They send someone out for a few days to meet with people. You can't do anthropology in a few days. What do they find out in those few days? They find out what they look like."

Behind the specific criticisms lies a more fundamental allegation of bad faith, often tinged with personal hostility. "I really don't like these people. I'll say that up front," says Greenbaum, who was contracted by the branch to do anthropological fieldwork on the Miami of Indiana and who says its staff denied the tribe recognition over her objections. William Starna, an anthropologist at SUNY Oneonta, suspects that two papers he authored on the recognition process were rejected by journals on the advice of current or former branch officials acting as anonymous referees. He charges the branch with "a real attempt to squelch any criticism from anyone in the academic community." The branch's academic detractors mock what Starna calls its "pretensions of doing academic research" and what Campisi calls its "anthrobabble." To them, the branch's outdated notions of tribe and its credulity about government sources are simply a cover. The real issue is that the Bureau of Indian Affairs doesn't want to recognize more tribes because doing so would tax its already strained budget. The critics admit that since 1978 the branch has acknowledged as many tribes (thirteen) as it has denied. But they point to the snail's pace at which petitions are processed. Officials declared in 1978 that the branch could dispense with twenty-two cases a year, but the annual rate has been more like one and a quarter (although in the last couple of years it has been somewhat higher). The branch argues that the process moves slowly in part because tribes are allowed unlimited time to respond to various branch comments and decisions, and tribes often take a long time in doing so. But the branch's foes turn that argument on its head, claiming that the petitioners take so long gathering information because the branch's evidentiary standards are impossibly high.

In the eyes of its critics, the branch is arrogant and insular. But in person, its staff comes across as mild mannered, and a little overwhelmed. "We get hammered for this all the time and it's absolutely ludicrous," says Steven

Austin, an anthropology Ph.D., responding to allegations that the branch take government documents at face value. "We don't accept that census at face value as indicating what was definitively a person's ancestry. It's ridiculous. We can't do that. It's totally contrary to the standards of the professional disciplines that we work under." The standards of their disciplines matter a great deal to the branch officials. They give the impression of men and women guided by an uncomplicated vision of good, solid research and slightly baffled that the outside world won't let them do it in peace.

Branch staffers describe their trips to the homes of petitioning tribes as a valuable means of gathering information. The historian searches through local archives, the genealogist inspects the tribe's membership records, and the anthropologist asks about attendance at weddings, funerals, social gatherings, council meetings, and protest rallies, to gauge whether tribe members interact as a community with functioning political leaders. Michael Lawson, a former branch historian, remembers visiting one dubious petitioning tribe that claimed it was lower Creek because its members lived in lower Alabama, when in fact the lower Creek lived in upper Alabama. The tribe claimed to own a map that showed where its ancestors had lived in the early nineteenth century. But when Lawson and a branch anthropologist took the map out of the pitch-black shed in which it was kept, they found that the wrinkled piece of parchment contained no writing at all. Lawson cites the incident as an example of the way branch staffers use visits to check up on the assertions of a tribe's petition and to find new information.

Even as they hold up academic inquiry as their model, branch officials simultaneously evince annoyance with what Austin calls modern anthropology's "whims about what a tribe is supposed to be." The regulations, they note, are based less on current academic opinion than on centuries of federal law. For people like Campisi, this is exactly the problem: The branch functions within a framework built on racist assumptions. But where the critics see a legacy of oppression, the branch officials see a kind of accumulated wisdom. Rita Souther, a staff genealogist who formerly worked for the Daughters of the American Revolution, believes that "the continuity and the steadiness of following hundreds of years of Indian law and policy" allows "respectability and some credibility. If you go with a whim or a change in academic interpretation of something, ten, twenty years later that could change again and you would be in constant flux."

What the branch staff implies, some of its outside defenders say outright: While building on government precedent may have its problems, those problems are nothing compared with what would happen if recognition decisions fell into the hands of the tribal applicants and their academic advocates. If the branch's critics accuse it of bad faith, its partisans are quick to throw the charge back at people like Starna and Campisi, who they suspect would abandon any impartial standards in the name of atonement for the government's and the anthropology profession's past sins. J. Anthony

Paredes, an anthropologist affiliated with Florida State and the branch's most vociferous academic champion, took his colleagues to task in a recent article in the *St. Thomas Law Review.* "In some segments of American national culture, there appears to be a willingness to abandon any objective tests of historical, social and cultural fact," he wrote. "Instead, subjective experience is treated as the ultimate validation of social reality. This is bad news for tribal sovereignty."

For Paredes, the irony that his colleagues will not accept is that the anthropology done by the branch, with its old-fashioned belief in objective facts and its prudish insistence on firm documentation, actually serves Indians far better than the alternative. No matter how problematic the notion of tribe may be, if it is the root of what little power American Indians wield, the right thing to do is to prevent it from being watered down.

Many members of already recognized tribes agree. Several tribes have hired historians and anthropologists to rebut other tribes' petitions, and others have lobbied strenuously on Capitol Hill to keep the regulations from being weakened. In many cases, recognized tribes have a considerable interest in keeping that status to themselves. The Tulalip of Washington state, for instance, do not want to share fishing rights with unrecognized tribes living near Puget Sound. And with the legalization of Indian gambling in 1988, some tribes have an especially large incentive to deny recognition, and other privileges, to their neighbors. Secretary of the Interior Bruce Babbitt is currently under investigation by an independent counsel for possibly misleading Congress about efforts by Minnesota and Wisconsin tribes to prevent another tribe from opening a casino.

But beyond financial considerations, some tribal leaders genuinely doubt the bona fides of highly intermarried eastern tribes that speak no tribal language and possess no tribal land. For national Indian organizations, the debate over recognition cannot be removed from its larger context: a backlash against Indian sovereignty fueled by stories of tribes grown rich on gambling. Paredes hints at a nightmare scenario in which sympathetic academics, by undermining the legitimacy of the recognition process, unwittingly aid antisovereignty conservatives like Washington state senator Slade Gorton who want to rein in Indian gambling and force tribes to abide by state laws.

American Indians are split by a dilemma that faces many American ethnic groups: Will relaxing the standards for membership lead to strength in numbers, or will it weaken group identity? Yet in their case, the dilemma is even more acute. For Jews and African Americans, who can choose how to define themselves, the question is largely cultural and answered within the group. But for American Indians, who must be certified by the federal government, it is a legal and political issue over which non-Indians have most of the control.

When Chief Hatcher arrives in Washington, he will find that the compact formed in 1978—the agreement that the branch would quickly settle unrecognized tribes' claims, and Congress and the courts would defer to its decisions—seems to be breaking down. New petitions continue to stream in, with gambling interests even seeking out unrecognized tribes and sponsoring their petitions in return for the right to build a casino if they win. The backlog at the branch continues to grow. Currently, eleven unrecognized tribes are "ready, waiting for active consideration," which means their petitions are in but the branch has not even begun the several-year process of deciding on them. Six of those eleven have been waiting since 1996. Squeezed by budget constraints, the Clinton administration has cut the branch staff from fifteen to eleven, and staffers claim that they spend most of their time fulfilling administrative duties and less than half actually reviewing petitions. One of the reasons administrative work takes so much time is that tribes denied recognition now frequently sue, and the branch is required to spend enormous energy defending its decisions in court. The previous director was recently demoted, allegedly because the assistant secretary of the Bureau of Indian Affairs was upset with the pace of the branch's work.

What's more, bills to speed up the recognition process have been proposed in the last four sessions of Congress. While each has so far failed—because of administration opposition, lobbying by federally recognized tribes, and fear that reform will lead to more casinos—proponents insist they are gaining ground. Last fall, legislation proposed by Delegate Eni Faleomavaega of American Samoa garnered 190 votes in the House. William Starna predicts that as more tribes sue, the delays at the branch grow longer, and Congress becomes more restless, "the whole process is going to collapse."

Faleomavaega would create a new commission and change the regulations so that tribes need only prove continuous community and political authority since 1934, the year the Indian Reorganization Act was passed. Moving the regulations' starting date from first sustained white contact to 1934 would probably bring a welcome change. It would speed up a process that now takes so long that many of a tribe's members may die while it is pending, a particularly depressing fact considering that tribes often seek recognition so their impoverished members can receive subsidized health care. And while the new system might make it easier for a dubious petitioner to slip through, it is still very unlikely. As Arlinda Locklear, an attorney formerly with the Native American Rights Foundation, notes, a fraudulent tribe would have to have started pretending to be Indian in 1934, and "that makes no historical sense. Who wanted to be Indian in the 1930s and 1940s?"

But even if the changes go through, petitioners will probably still have to prove genealogical descent from an aboriginal tribe. In the case of the Chicora-Waccamaw, that means tracing its roots to the sixteenth century, and Harold Hatcher isn't too confident it can be done. He'll submit his petition soon, and even if reforms speed up the process, the current backlog means a final decision will probably take five to ten years. If the answer is no, he says he'll try to get the South Carolina delegation to push for a special act of Congress, which is also unlikely to happen. If that fails, he'll go to court, which often takes a decade or more.

Hatcher is nearly fifty now. It is entirely possible that the pursuit of recognition will take the rest of his life, which raises a sensitive issue. He has one eagle feather. And he thinks he'll probably have it placed in his casket. But that doesn't put his mind at rest. "For it to work, it can't be an illegal feather," he says. "If it's against the law, it's not pure."

Let the Healing Begin: Asking for the Forgiveness of the Native Americans

KEVIN GOVER

In March of 1824, President James Monroe established the Office of Indian Affairs in the Department of War. Its mission was to conduct the nation's business with regard to Indian affairs. We have come together today to mark the first 175 years of the institution now known as the Bureau of Indian Affairs.

It is appropriate that we do so in the first year of a new century and a new millennium, a time when our leaders are reflecting on what lies ahead and preparing for those challenges. Before looking ahead, though, this institution must first look back and reflect on what it has wrought and, by doing so, come to know that this is no occasion for celebration; rather it is time for reflection and contemplation, a time for sorrowful truths to be spoken, a time for contrition.

We must first reconcile ourselves to the fact that the works of this agency have at various times profoundly harmed the communities it was meant to serve. From the very beginning, the Office of Indian Affairs was an instrument by which the United States enforced its ambition against the Indian

This chapter was originally an address delivered to the Ceremony Acknowledging the 175th Anniversary of the Establishment of Indian Affairs in Washington, D.C. on September 8, 2000. At the time he delivered it, Kevin Gover was Assistant Secretary of Indian Affairs of the U.S. Department of the Interior.

nations and Indian people who stood in its path. And so, the first mission of this institution was to execute the removal of the southeastern tribal nations. By threat, deceit, and force, these great tribal nations were made to march 1,000 miles to the west, leaving thousands of their old, their young, and their infirm in hasty graves along the Trail of Tears.

As the nation looked to the West for more land, this agency participated in the ethnic cleansing that befell the western tribes. War necessarily begets tragedy; the war for the West was no exception. Yet in these more enlightened times, it must be acknowledged that the deliberate spread of disease, the decimation of the mighty bison herds, the use of the poison alcohol to destroy mind and body, and the cowardly killing of women and children made for tragedy on a scale so ghastly that it cannot be dismissed as merely the inevitable consequence of the clash of competing ways of life. This agency and the good people in it failed in the mission to prevent the devastation. And so great nations of patriot warriors fell. We will never push aside the memory of unnecessary and violent death at places such as Sand Creek, the banks of the Washita River, and Wounded Knee.

Nor did the consequences of war have to include the futile and destructive efforts to annihilate Indian cultures. After the devastation of tribal economies and the deliberate creation of tribal dependence on the services provided by this agency, this agency set out to destroy all things Indian.

This agency forbade the speaking of Indian languages, prohibited the conduct of traditional religious activities, outlawed traditional government, and made Indian people ashamed of who they were. Worst of all, the Bureau of Indian Affairs committed these acts against the children entrusted to its boarding schools, brutalizing them emotionally, psychologically, physically, and spiritually. Even in this era of self-determination, when the Bureau of Indian Affairs is at long last serving as an advocate for Indian people in an atmosphere of mutual respect, the legacy of these misdeeds haunts us. The trauma of shame, fear, and anger has passed from one generation to the next, and manifests itself in the rampant alcoholism, drug abuse, and domestic violence that plague Indian country. Many of our people live lives of unrelenting tragedy as Indian families suffer the ruin of lives by alcoholism, suicides made of shame and despair, and violent death at the hands of one another. So many of the maladies suffered today in Indian country result from the failures of this agency. Poverty, ignorance, and disease have been the product of this agency's work.

And so today I stand before you as the leader of an institution that in the past has committed acts so terrible that they infect, diminish, and destroy the lives of Indian people decades later, generations later. These things occurred despite the efforts of many good people with good hearts who sought to prevent them. These wrongs must be acknowledged if the healing is to begin.

I do not speak today for the United States. That is the province of the nation's elected leaders, and I would not presume to speak on their behalf. I am empowered, however, to speak on behalf of this agency, the Bureau of Indian Affairs, and I am quite certain that the words that follow reflect the hearts of its 10,000 employees.

Let us begin by expressing our profound sorrow for what this agency has done in the past. Just like you, when we think of these misdeeds and their tragic consequences, our hearts break and our grief is as pure and complete as yours. We desperately wish that we could change this history, but of course we cannot. On behalf of the Bureau of Indian Affairs, I extend this formal apology to Indian people for the historical conduct of this agency.

And while the BIA employees of today did not commit these wrongs, we acknowledge that the institution we serve did. We accept this inheritance, this legacy of racism and inhumanity. And by accepting this legacy, we accept also the moral responsibility of putting things right.

We therefore begin this important work anew, and make a new commitment to the people and communities that we serve, a commitment born of the dedication we share with you to the cause of renewed hope and prosperity for Indian country. Never again will this agency stand silent when hate and violence are committed against Indians. Never again will we allow policy to proceed from the assumption that Indians possess less human genius than the other races. Never again will we be complicit in the theft of Indian property. Never again will we appoint false leaders who serve purposes other than those of the tribes. Never again will we allow unflattering and stereotypical images of Indian people to deface the halls of government or lead the American people to shallow and ignorant beliefs about Indians. Never again will we attack your religions, your languages, your rituals, or any of your tribal ways. Never again will we seize your children, nor teach them to be ashamed of who they are. Never again.

We cannot yet ask your forgiveness, not while the burdens of this agency's history weigh so heavily on tribal communities. What we do ask is that, together, we allow the healing to begin: As you return to your homes, and as you talk with your people, please tell them that the time of dying is at its end. Tell your children that the time of shame and fear is over. Tell your young men and women to replace their anger with hope and love for their people. Together, we must wipe the tears of seven generations. Together, we must allow our broken hearts to mend. Together, we will face a challenging world with confidence and trust. Together, let us resolve that when our future leaders gather to discuss the history of this institution, it will be time to celebrate the rebirth of joy, freedom, and progress for the Indian Nations. The Bureau of Indian Affairs was born in 1824 in a time of war on Indian people. May it live in the year 2000 and beyond as an instrument of their prosperity.

XI

COURT SYSTEM

In this section, we have two very different chapters. The first, by Robert Yazzie, offers insight into an element of the legal system whose very existence is all-too-rarely recognized: the tribal court system. Yazzie serves as the Chief Justice of the Navajo Nation Supreme Court. His chapter not only offers an analysis of the role of the U.S. Supreme Court in shaping Indian law; Yazzie is especially interesting and provocative when he offers a firsthand glimpse of some of the unique challenges faced by a judge within the tribal courts.

David Wilkins' chapter helps us appreciate the central role played by U.S. Supreme Court decisions—and decisions by other U.S. federal courts—in defining the significance of federal "plenary power." In general, the term *plenary* is taken to mean that the U.S. Congress, as the chief lawmaking branch of the federal government, has absolute or unlimited power over the tribes. As Wilkins makes clear, however, the practical implications of this sweeping assertion of power are not self-evident. How does federal plenary power relate to the key principle of constitutional limits on governmental power? How does it relate to tribal sovereignty? Answers to these central questions have depended largely on the interpretation of the courts.

"Watch Your Six": An Indian Nation Judge's View of 25 Years of Indian Law, Where We Are, and Where We Are Going

ROBERT YAZZIE

INTRODUCTION

A friend from Rutgers University writes us and often concludes a letter with this advice: "Watch your six." That is police slang for watching out at six o'clock in military directions. In other words, "Watch your tail—cover your behind." That is the lesson for Indian nation judges for 25 years of the decline of Indian law. Now, I want to review the dangers we face, given recent defeats in the courts and legislature. I also want to identify some of the bright spots and possibilities for the future which can come from a few positive developments.

HOW WE GOT THERE: ANOTHER VIEW

Recently, there was a front-page article in *USA Today* about the power of law clerks in the U.S. Supreme Court. It mentioned a book that came out a while back—*The Brethren* by Bob Woodward and Scott Armstrong. It was an insider's view of the workings of the U.S. Supreme Court and it tells the story of the beginning of a twenty-five-year decline in Indian nation powers.

This chapter is reprinted from the *American Indian Law Review*, Volume 23, Number 2 (1998), pp. 497–503, by permission of the publisher.

The story goes that Justice Rehnquist was kind of a "dean" for the law clerks. One year, during a Christmas party, the clerks put on a skit which mocked President Ford's difficulty choosing a successor to Justice Douglas. Chief Justice Burger was not amused. He gave Justice Rehnquist an Indian case as punishment. This is what Woodward and Armstrong said about it:

> Rehnquist had nothing but contempt for Indian cases. Traditionally, Douglas had done more than his share. He had been the Court's expert. With his own Arizona background, Rehnquist was the logical replacement, but he suspected that the assignment was Burger's way of telling him what he really thought of the Christmas party. Never one to let an opportunity pass, Rehnquist turned an opinion that was in favor of Indians into an opinion that indicated that in most cases they would lose. It wiped away decades of Douglas's opinions.

That opinion was *Moe v. Confederated Salish-Kootenai*—the cigarette tax case. It has been downhill for Indian Nations ever since.

I found out something else which is quite interesting. A few years ago, when Navajo Nation Chief Justice Tom Tso went to Washington to work on Indian court enhancement legislation, he was invited to a meeting of Capitol Hill lawyers on the "Duro-fix" legislation. During the meeting, one Indian Affairs Committee staffer called down to the Justice Department to get its views on the bill. She laughed when she got off the phone, saying, "They had their usual position: all Indian legislation is unconstitutional because it is race-based." When asked whom she spoke with in the Justice Department, she replied that it was someone in the Office of the General Counsel. That is the most powerful and influential division of Justice; it is the "lawyer for the lawyers." What is even more interesting is the fact that Chief Justice Rehnquist and Associate Justice Scalia were both assistant attorneys general in charge of the Office of the General Counsel.

We know that there have been several distinct phases in Indian affairs law, from first contact, through various attempts to assimilate Indians and their nations, to today's attacks on the basic powers of Indian nations. However, to understand today's Indian law, we must look back about one hundred years. That is, up through at least 1883, Indian nations were considered to be "nations." There were few intrusions on their jurisdiction and powers. If there was a surrender of authority, it was usually done through a treaty. The "Indian Nonintercourse Acts" meant what they said: the states were to keep their hands off of Indian policy and affairs.

However, starting with the *Crow Dog* case in 1883, the U.S. Congress and Supreme Court began a process of intensive intrusion. *Crow Dog* prompted the Major Crimes Act of 1885, and the Dawes or General Allotment Act of 1887 was a major push toward assimilation. The Dawes Act checkerboarded our nations and created many of the problems we see today. Challenges to federal legislation led to the plenary power doctrine and the notion that Congress could override an Indian nation treaty whenever it felt like it.

Let's take a closer look at what was really going on. Shortly before Congress decided to intentionally intrude into Indian nation affairs and the Supreme Court upheld it, a man by the name of Herbert Spencer came to the United States. Spencer was a British railroad engineer who looked at Charles Darwin's theory of evolution and did something with it. Spencer is the person who coined the term "survival of the fittest." Spencer said that some humans are superior to others; that some folks are just naturally better than others. Who were the "superiors" who were said to be better than the others? Primarily white, Protestant males were superior. "Irish need not apply." Indians, of course, were "savages." (You actually see that kind of language in the court opinions of the day; read *Crow Dog* as one example.)

The name for Spencer's theories is "Social Darwinism," and it is a thoroughly racist doctrine. It led to Nazi atrocities. Unfortunately, Spencer's books were best-sellers in the United States and had a great deal of influence on law and policy, including Indian law.

There was another follower of Herbert Spencer from around the same period. His name was John Austin. Austin was a failed lawyer who was a friend of an English philosopher. This philosopher got Austin the first chair in legal philosophy at a university. After studying legal theory in *Germany* for several years, he returned to England to teach *English* legal philosophy. His lectures were a flop. The reason we know Austin today is that his wife published his works after his death.

Austin developed what we know as "legal positivism." It is the legal version of Social Darwinism and "survival of the fittest." That is, Austin said something is not "law" unless it is made by one in authority. Who is that? According to Austin, it was the British Parliament. Again, you have the racist notion that a small and privileged class has the sole power to make law. If you look closely at the philosophy of the right wing U.S. Supreme Court, where Justice O'Connor is the "moderate," you will see Social Darwinism, legal positivism, and parliamentary supremacy at play.

We know that Indian affairs law began as a struggle between the states and the central government. Following a failed experiment under the Articles of Confederation, of shared Continental Congress and colonial authority to make Indian policy, the U.S. Constitution has the sole authority. The idea was that the Indian nations would be protected from the states. That is not how things worked out.

Until the appointment of Justice Rehnquist to the U.S. Supreme Court, there was a general principle that the states had no authority in Indian Country. However, the Rehnquist Court pulled a rabbit out of the hat. This rabbit was the new trick that somehow the Supreme Court can "imply" that Indian nations have lost certain powers. That is, Indian nations have no "inherent" jurisdiction over non-Indians or nonmember Indians because somehow that is "implied." Isn't it strange that if Congress is the primary source of Indian affairs policy (and we know that these days, Congress can do no wrong), then the courts, and not Congress, get to "imply" that Indian nations lost their power?

Sovereignty is only a "backdrop" these days—whatever that means. Isn't it strange that the Supreme Court is striking down Indian nation powers under a vague doctrine that can be abused, yet talking about congressional plenary power and the separation of powers at the same time? What we are actually seeing is a states' rights agenda and the federal players are M.I.A. (missing in action).

There is something else which is quite interesting: While there is a general movement away from civil rights enforcement in the United States, there is a movement toward it in the corporate world. Today, it is the corporate lawyers who raise the banner of civil rights to attach Indian nation authority. For example, in the recent Ninth Circuit Court of Appeals decision, *Wilson v. Marchington*, the court says that comity is the rule of recognition in the Ninth Circuit. Thus, a federal court there need not recognize an Indian nation court decision if its judges are politically controlled by a council. That gives mere ammunition to use against Indian nation courts and judges.

So here we are: Every time I sit on a jurisdiction case, I've got to watch my six.

LOOKING OVER YOUR SHOULDER

These days, an Indian nation judge has to indeed cover his or her six. If you look over one shoulder, there is the anti-Indian mob. Who are its members? First, there are the state attorneys general. We are horrified by Senator Slade Gorton and his anti-Indian legislation. But remember that he is a former state attorney general and there are a lot of others who think like him. Then there are the corporation lawyers, who represent interests that want to exploit Indians and Indian Country without regulation and control. Finally, there are the actual members of anti-Indian hate groups—an interesting association of the hate groups, the corporate giants, and politicians. Most of the hate group members are people who own fee land in Indian Country, and their fears of Indian government are fueled by absentee Indian Country landlords. Their battle cry is "No taxation without representation," and they cry a lot of tears about "corrupt" Indian councils and courts. They have a lot of money for litigation and, of course, that is why Senator Gorton wants to waive Indian nation sovereign immunity and send cases against Indian nations into state courts.

Who is over the other shoulder? We have to be very careful. Every time an Indian nation council interferes in the operations of Indian courts, it is used by non-Indians as a tool for attack. For example, several years ago, Chief Justice Tso terminated one of our probationary judges for insubordination. In November 1991, that terminated judge was called as a star witness to attack the Navajo Nation during Indian court enhancement hearings.

Similarly, last year, when Senator Gorton had a hearing on his move to abolish sovereign immunity, he asked the lawyer for an anti-Indian hate group to get anti–Navajo Nation testimony from a corporation that was in litigation with the Navajo Nation. Fortunately, the corporation saw that it was not in its best interest to cooperate. Every time a council does something to its own court or its own judges, that may be used in litigation or in testimony for legislation which is hurtful.

It is difficult being a judge when you have to watch your rear to make certain that those folks do not push you into something that can be the basis for review of one of your decisions by a federal court, or meat for testimony in Congress about how bad your court may be.

SOME BRIGHT SPOTS

It is not all gloom and doom. On March 12 and 13 [1998], something very nice happened. Chief Justice Zlacket of the Arizona Supreme Court invited me, Chief Justice Francini of the New Mexico Supreme Court, and Chief Justice Zimmerman of the Utah Supreme Court to sit down and talk informally about mutual concerns and interests. I was delighted to find that the justices were interested in the Navajo Nation courts, traditional Navajo law, peacemaking, who we are and what we do. I told the justices a story which applies to this discussion.

In 1994, the Navajo Nation Supreme Court sat at the Stanford University Law School in California. After the oral argument, there was a reception. One of the members of the law school faculty talked about how complex Indian jurisdiction law is and asked how we dealt with such problems. A member of our group said, "Simple—we make friends!" The professor did not quite know how to take that, but it is true. At one point, a litigant before the Arizona Supreme Court was bashing me and my decisions, and a justice told him to stop it, saying, "I know Judge Yazzie personally."

The lesson for me is that if I am to do a good job watching my six, I need friends. I find that most state judges do not know what an Indian court looks like. They do not know how we operate. They do not know us. Recently, we have been meeting with the state judges in northern Arizona and we find that as we make friends with them, we are getting things done. We find that state judges share our desire to solve problems, to stop family violence, to collect child support, to teach each other, and to share resources.

Another lesson is that Indian nations should return to their traditional law. The Navajo Nation Supreme Court has ruled that Navajo common law is the law of preference in the Navajo Nation and it is often used in our decisions. Our Navajo peacemaking program is successful and people visit us from around the world to learn about it. After all, if we apply state law in our courts, someone is always going to come back and say, "They got it wrong." I remember one decision written by our Associate Justice Raymond D.

Austin. A law professor wrote about the case and said its decision was wrong under principles of contract law, although the result was correct. Of course, Justice Austin was not pleased with the article. When you make a ruling using traditional Indian law or have a traditional process which is based on consensus, then the outside cannot criticize it.

There are a lot of agonizing law review articles coming out these days about what a mess Indian law happens to be. Do the state and federal judges read them? Probably not. If they do, they ignore them. Charles Wilkinson once wrote that while Indian nations were losing in the courts, they were winning in Congress. Is that true today?

Recently, when the Senate Indian Affairs Committee held the first hearing on the Gorton Bill to abolish Indian nation sovereign immunity, there was a lot of talk about Indian nations refusing to collect cigarette tax and other taxes. Nobody questioned the stupidity of a store owner in Indian Country having to collect a tax on the basis of someone's identity as an Indian or not. It is a bad policy. It is an unworkable policy. Despite that, we see no moves in Congress to push state taxation out of Indian Country. Instead, Indian nations get the blame for not collecting taxes for the states. On top of that, many Indian leaders will tell you that while the state counts Indian noses to get block grants, they do not share those funds with Indian nations, for the most part. Few people know that Indians actually do pay state taxes, usually sales and excise taxes, and a lot of money goes to the states, with little return for the Indians who pay the taxes.

The law journal articles are read by few and Congress is unresponsive. What do we do about that? There is one major area where we are falling down. We are not getting the word out. We are not putting our case before the American people. A few years ago, they said that since *Dances with Wolves* was so popular, Indians could get anything they wanted. That was not true because we did not know how to use the opportunity. When I get attacked or my court gets attacked, I cannot say anything because of judicial ethics. Courts do not do business by press release. Who is going to speak for us? Who will advocate our position? We know that the *Minneapolis Tribune* and the *Arizona Republic* ran a series of negative articles on Indian courts and social problems in Indian Country. When are we going to get some positive press? I think that we need to think about how to educate the American public on the legitimacy of Indian nation courts and the fact that we do have outstanding judges.

CONCLUSION

There are frightening times. As an Indian judge, I need to be creative and work with my fellow judges. You will remember that in the 1978 *Oliphant* decision, the Supreme Court said that Indian nations have no inherent jurisdiction over non-Indians in criminal cases. They said the same thing about nonmember Indians in the 1990 *Duro* decision. How closely do we read the law? In *Oliphant* and *Duro* the Supreme Court did not say that we have "no" jurisdiction over those people. They have an "adoption" exception. In 1996, the Navajo Nation Supreme Court looked closely at *Oliphant* and *Duro* and ruled that in some instances, such as when a non-Indian marries into the Navajo Nation, we will exercise criminal jurisdiction. We used Navajo common law to meet the "adoption" exception. More recently, we are getting several challenges to our personal injury jurisdiction under the *Strate v. A-1 Contractors* and the Ninth Circuit *Wilson v. Marchington* decisions. What are we doing about that? We are dusting off the Navajo Nation Treaty of 1868 with the United States and reading it closely.

It may be a losing battle. I may end up hearing traffic ticket appeals, or presiding over an enrollment case or two. It may get so bad that if I am to participate in making decisions about my people and activities on my Nation's lands, I will have to run for Justice of the Peace in Arizona or New Mexico. At least I will get paid more than I get now.

However, I am not ready to give up. I am going to try to play the cards as they are dealt to me. I am also going to try to make friends, use my Nation's original law, and get the word out that the justices, judges, and courts of the Navajo Nation are competent and legitimate organs of government. I am going to thumb my nose at the anti-Indian hate mob and try to point out that Indian governments and courts do serve legitimate interests that should be honored. While doing that, I am going to watch my six.

The U.S. Supreme Court's Explication of "Federal Plenary Power": An Analysis of Case Law Affecting Tribal Sovereignty, 1886–1914

DAVID E. WILKINS

The 200-year-old political relationship between American Indian tribes and the United States remains both problematic and paradoxical because of the conjuncture of geographical, historical, political, and constitutional issues and circumstances that influence tribal-federal affairs. A central feature of this dynamic dialogue is the incongruous relationship between the United States Congress's exercise of plenary power and the tribes' efforts to exercise their sovereign political rights. This chapter traces the historical, legal, and political origins and transformation of this pivotal concept from 1886 to 1914, an important period in its development. Analysis of 107 federal court cases and of the plenary power concept reveals that congressional plenary power has several distinctive definitions. Depending on which definition is used by the court, and whether the term is based on constitutional or extra-constitutional doctrine, determines whether the court's decision will adversely or positively affect tribal sovereignty, political rights, and resources.

One of the perennial puzzles in intergovernmental relations and constitutional law is the following question: What is the relationship between American Indian tribal governments, which exercise certain sovereign rights, and the United States government, which presumes a plenary power with

This chapter is reprinted from the *American Indian Quarterly*, summer 1994, by permission of the University of Nebraska Press. Copyright © 1994 by the University of Nebraska Press.

regard to tribes? Despite the federal government's presumption of vast authority over tribes, plenary power remains a problematic concept, particularly when paired with the doctrine of tribal sovereignty.

There is also considerable disagreement among scholars on whether plenary power is a necessary congressional power which protects tribes, or whether it is an abhorrent and undemocratic concept because it entails the congressional exercise of wide political authority over tribes. While the principal focus of this chapter is to detail the history and evolution of plenary power as defined by the Supreme Court during a critical historical era, it is important first to provide some discussion of an equally pivotal concept: tribal sovereignty.

There is a startling array of interpretations of tribal sovereignty. For years the classic reference has been that of Felix Cohen, who asserted that "from the earliest years of the Republic the Indian tribes have been recognized as 'distinct, independent, political communities,' and as such, qualified to exercise powers of self-government, not by virtue of any delegation of powers from the Federal government but rather by reason of their original tribal sovereignty." John Marshall, in the pivotal case *Worcester v. Georgia*, 21 U.S. (6 Pet.) 515, defined tribal sovereignty as a function of collective political rights. He described tribes as "distinct peoples, divided into separate nations, independent of each other and of the rest of the world, having institutions of their own, and governing themselves by their own laws."

For Vine Deloria, Jr., on the other hand, sovereignty has less to do with self-government and political rights and more to do with "continuing cultural and communal integrity." "Sovereignty," Deloria said, "in the final instance, can be said to consist more of continued cultural integrity than of political powers and to the degree that a nation loses its sense of cultural identity, to that degree it suffers a loss of sovereignty."

For the purpose of this chapter, we define tribal sovereignty as an understanding that every tribal person has the right and the responsibility to be an actor, not merely an object, in decisions affecting his or her community. It is the political will of the people that ensures the vitality of sovereignty.

The usage of plenary power to describe the Congress's political relations with North American tribes distinguishes America's indigenous groups as the nation's original peoples. On the other hand, the fact of its persistence entails an exceptional political status for tribal nations that find their preconstitutional sovereign political and legal status can be radically reaffirmed or unilaterally altered, even quashed, at any time by congressional laws, judicial opinions, or administrative actions of the Bureau of Indian Affairs.

The vacillations in the way the term plenary has been defined and the manner in which it has been institutionalized indicates a critical difference between the political status of American states and tribes with respect to their relationship to the federal government. The Supreme Court has held that while "the sovereignty of the States is limited by the Constitution itself,"

Garcia v. San Antonio Metro Transit Authority, 469 U.S. 528, 548 (1984), states do enjoy legal and constitutional protections against arbitrary federal action because of the doctrine of enumerated powers. In other words, while Congress can exercise significant power over the states, it is doubtful that it could legislate a state out of existence. Regarding tribes, however, the Congress has acted to "legislate tribes [and bands and rancherias] out of existence," through the termination policy initiated in 1953 and continuing into the 1960s.

However, a little-known dimension which further complicates tribal-federal intergovernmental relations involves the fact that both before and even during the period 1886 to 1914, when congressional plenary power (defined as unlimited-absolute) was exercised in its most virulent and unabashed form, there were numerous occasions where Congress and the executive branch could not or would not employ the plenary power doctrine to force tribes to comply with a particular treaty, agreement, or federal statute. Frequently, tribal leaders and their constituencies simply voted down pending bilateral agreements or laws perceived as potentially injurious or unfair. These laws, treaties, or agreements would then be returned to Washington for revision or tabled indefinitely if Washington could not secure tribal consent.

This prompts an important question. If the Congress did indeed have unfettered plenary power over the tribes—and the Supreme Court in a 1903 decision, *Lone Wolf v. Hitchcock*, 185 U.S. 553, went so far as to say that Congress had always had this power—why did it not simply use it all the time? "Why," as Deloria asked, "all the hoopla over treaties and agreements? Why, at that very moment, were a number of treaty and agreement commissions in the field on several reservations asking the tribes to make treaties and agreements with the United States?"

In this chapter we explore the following questions: What does "plenary power" mean? What conjuncture of events accounts for its eruption in the area of Indian law and policy in the 1880s? What factors led the Supreme Court to suggest a modicum of moral constraint on the Congress's exercise of power in 1914, without foreclosing the possibility that Congress could still wield unfettered political authority over tribes so long as the action is not "arbitrary" and is founded on some "reasonable basis"? Finally, how and why does the concept of plenary power continue to be a viable political doctrine in a democratic country founded on the principles of limited government?

SCHOLARLY VIEWS AND EXPECTATIONS

Research on plenary power has increased considerably since the 1970s. These were the halcyon days of tribal self-determination and Indian political activism, when Vine Deloria, Jr., in a number of publications, urged tribal people and the scholarly community to systematically investigate the linchpin legal and political doctrines that undergirded the tribal-federal relationship.

One of the first scholars to focus some attention on the relationship between federal plenary power and tribal sovereignty was Robert Coulter. He wrote two articles in the late 1970s that briefly examined how plenary power had worked to seriously disadvantage tribes in fundamental legal ways. Coulter admitted, however, that "the origins of the plenary power doctrine and the legal foundations were unclear."

In the 1980s two important legal studies sought to bring clarity to the subject. They focused on the origins and the factors involved in the perpetuation of the plenary power concept. These articles, the first a note titled "Federal Plenary Power in Indian Affairs After *Weeks and Sioux Nation*" and the second, an excellent piece by Nell Jessup Newton called "Federal Power over Indians: Its Sources, Scope, and Limitations," went far toward explaining the legal history of the concept.

Other researchers also employed the term. Most of these commentators, excepting Shattuck and Norgren (political scientists) and Hauptman (historian), and those previously cited, are legal scholars. While law is certainly a fundamental discipline, political scientists—who should be concerned about a subject that encompasses institutional autonomy and interaction, constitutional allocations of authority, legitimate use of power, and federalism—have paid negligible attention to this concept and its relation to tribal sovereignty.

Moreover, there has been no systematic or long-term examination of empirical data on the Supreme Court's activities during the critical era in which the plenary power doctrine as applied to tribes by the Supreme Court first appeared, was then expanded to unparalleled proportions, and was finally dampened in the 1914 Perrin case.

This three-decade period comprised the federal government's most intensive effort to assimilate American Indians. The General Allotment policy, inaugurated in 1887, whereby the Congress sought to turn American Indians into Christianized private property landowners, was the central weapon in the federal government's assimilative arsenal. There was a multi-pronged effort to detribalize indigenous peoples. The principal components in the federal government's assimilation policy were:

> Land loss via surplus land sales, specific allotment acts, amendments to the allotment policy, and fraudulent activities by land speculators and some state officials; Sponsorship of efforts to Christianize tribal members; Imposition of federal criminal jurisdiction over certain crimes in Indian Country; Eradication of Indian culture as a federal goal. This was facilitated by the establishment of Courts of Indian Offense.

Most commentators agree that the plenary power era for Indian tribes and their relations to the federal government was inaugurated with the Supreme Court's decision in *U.S. v. Kagama*, 118 U.S. 375 (1886), though the term was used in previous cases outside Indian law.

Although the term "plenary" is absent from *Kagama*, other language evidences the court's support of Congress's efforts to diminish tribal sovereignty by affirming the constitutionality of the Major Crimes Act. The court exercised what Deloria has termed plenary interpretive power to rationalize Congress's "exercise of plenary legislative power." Unable to locate a constitutional basis for its decision, the court crafted an ingenious and bizarre two-pronged explanation: Indian helplessness and land ownership. First, Justice Miller transmuted John Marshall's analogy of Indians as "wards" to their federal "guardians" (see *Cherokee Nation v. Georgia*, 30 U.S. [5 Pet.] 1, 1831), to a principle of law. Miller said: "These Indian tribes are wards of the nation. They are communities dependent on the United States."

The court said that federal power over these "weak" peoples was "necessary to their protection, as well as to the safety of those among whom they dwell." This power, the court held, "must exist in that [United States] government, because it never has existed anywhere else." However, scholars have pointed out several untenable errors in the court's analysis.

First, how could Congress apply its laws to tribes that until that time had not been subject under the Constitution to congressional jurisdiction?

Second, if the Constitution limits the authority of the various branches to enumerated powers, why did the court cite extra-constitutional or extra-legal reasons for holding a congressional statute to be constitutional?

Finally, "consent of the governed" is a treasured democratic principle. The fact that most Indians were excluded from the American political arena because they had an extra-constitutional status and treaty-defined rights and were not U.S. citizens seemed irrelevant to the court.

Coincidentally or not, the same day as *Kagama*, the court unanimously held in *Santa Clara v. Southern Pacific Railroad*, 118 U.S. 394 (1886), that the Fourteenth Amendment's due process clause protected corporations as "legal persons." In effect, one could argue that corporate property rights were extended constitutional protection, while tribal political and property rights could be quashed.

In 1914 the Supreme Court in *Perrin v. United States*, 232 U.S. 478, suggested that congressional authority was limited: "As the power is incident only to the presence of the Indians and their status as wards of the Government, it must be conceded that it does not go beyond what is reasonably essential for their protection, and that, to be effective, its exercise must not be purely arbitrary but founded upon some reasonable basis."

The Perrin court, however, remained extremely deferential to Congress. In fact, Justice Van DeVanter conceded that Congress, because of its exclusive status as the branch denominated to deal with tribes, be "invested with a wide discretion, and its action, unless purely arbitrary, must be accepted and given full effect by the Court."

Without stating it, the Perrin court had invoked a different definition of "plenary power" than the one developed in *Kagama* and *Lone Wolf*. Here the court was referencing Congress's "exclusive" power to "preempt" state law and authority.

Perrin arose during a time of flux in federal Indian policy, some of which was beginning to favor a degree of tribal self-governance. It was an era of federal administrative incompetence and Bureau of Indian Affairs corruption; an era in which a growing number of federal policymakers accepted that tribal cultures could not be physically or intellectually eradicated and that the country would be better off if it preserved some aspects of indigenous cultures.

It was also an era in which some efforts were made at political reform. In fact, several bills were introduced between 1912 and 1916 that were designed to allow reservation Indians the right to nominate and even to recall the Indian agents. Most important, the first two decades of the twentieth century represented a period in which federal Indian legislation focused less on protecting Indians from whites and more on "providing a form of trust for Indian property. Indians became an attachment to their lands rather than owners, and although the avowed policy was that of assimilation, the change in emphasis within the executive branch of the federal government meant that the vested interest of the Interior Department would always work to thwart whatever initiatives Congress might take in resolving the Indian problem."

Hence, while Perrin represented a victory of sorts for tribes in that the court urged the Congress not to act "arbitrarily" when dealing with Indians, administrative agencies like the Bureau of Indian Affairs remained largely unaccountable to Congress and especially to tribes. More important, Congress's power was not constrained in any fundamental way.

PLENARY POWER DEFINED

First cited by the Supreme Court in the seminal case *Gibbons v. Ogden*, 22 U.S. (9 Wheat.) 1, 197 (1824), plenary power often has been used in cases dealing with the extent of federal powers. It is a confusing concept "because it conceals several issues which, for purposes of constitutional analysis, must be kept clear and distinct." Engdahl incorrectly posits, however, that "no federal power is plenary in the full sense of the term, because as to all of them at least the prohibition of the Bill of Rights apply." The Bill of Rights, however, is somewhat problematic as applied to tribes because tribal governments were not created pursuant to the Constitution. While the Indian Civil Rights Act of 1968 applied portions of the Bill of Rights to tribal governments in regard to their activities over reservation residents, the Bill of Rights still does not protect tribes or their members from congressional actions aimed at reducing tribal sovereignty, political rights, or aboriginal Indian lands.

In addition, the concept of plenary "merge[s] several analytically distinct questions." This is the crux of the scholarly and public confusion about the term. First, and most important for our purposes, there is plenary meaning "exclusive." This is the definition Congress uses most frequently in enacting Indian-specific legislation, such as the Indian Reorganization Act, or when it enacts Indian preference laws that withstand reverse discrimination suits (*Morton v. Mancari*, 417 U.S. 535 [1974]). This is an exclusively legislative power Congress may exercise in keeping with its policy of treating with tribes in a distinctively political manner or to provide a recognition of rights (i.e., American Indian Religious Freedom Resolution, which Indians have been deprived of because of their extra-constitutional standing). As Deloria astutely observes:

> There may indeed be some kind of establishment of religious freedom for American Indians. If so, it is because Congress has dealt with the question of the practice of Indian religions and felt it to be necessary to extend the protection of federal laws further in the case of Indians than the Constitution allows it to extend to ordinary citizens. In this instance Indians are not to be regarded as "supercitizens"; rather, the practice of Indian religion is to be regarded as under the special protection of the federal government in the same way that Indian water rights, land titles, and self-government are protected. Congress has always dealt with Indians in a special manner; that is why Congress and the federal courts cherish and nourish the doctrine of plenary powers in the field of Indian affairs.

Plenary also is an exercise of federal power which may preempt state law. Again, Congress's commerce power is an example, as is the treaty-making process, which precludes state involvement. Constitutional disclaimers, which a majority of western states had to include in their organic documents before they were admitted into statehood, are also evidence of federal preemption. Typically, these disclaimers consisted of provisions in which the state declared that it would never attempt to tax Indian lands or property without both tribal and federal consent.

Finally, there is plenary meaning "unlimited" or "absolute." This third definition includes two subcategories: a) power which is not limited by other textual constitutional provisions; and b) power which is unlimited regarding congressional objectives. There is ample evidence in Indian law and policy of plenary power being applied by the legislative branches and the federal courts to tribes and individual Indians in all three ways.

When Congress is exercising plenary power as the voice of the federal government in its relations with tribes, and is acting with the consent of the tribal people involved, it is exercising legitimate authority. When Congress is acting in a plenary way to preempt state intrusion into Indian Country, absent tribal consent, it is properly exercising an enumerated constitutional power.

However, when Congress is informed by the federal courts that it has "full, entire, complete, absolute, perfect, and unqualified" (*Mashunkashey v.*

Mashunkashey, 134 P.2d 976 [1943]) authority over tribes and individual Indians, something is fundamentally wrong. Canfield, writing in 1881, long before individual Indians were enfranchised, observed that congressional power over tribes was absolute because tribes were distinct and independent, if "inferior" peoples, "strangers to our law, our customs, and our privileges." He went on to say that "[t]o suppose that the framers of the Constitution intended to secure to the Indians the rights and privileges which they valued as Englishmen is to misconceive the spirit of their age." But by the time *Mashunkashey* was decided, in 1942, all Indians had been enfranchised and yet they were informed by the court that absolute power was a reality confronting them. . . .

DATA AND FINDINGS

This chapter separates the concept of plenary power into three categories. First, we inquired whether the concept was contained in the court case, a yes or no question. In some cases where the concept plenary was not mentioned, it was evident, by the court's use of words such as "unlimited," "absolute," or "no restrictions," that plenary power was still being exercised (i.e., *Kagama* and *Lone Wolf*). This required the addition of a third component, "implicit."

Most Indian law scholars and historians assert that *United States v. Kagama*, 118 U.S. 375 (1886) is the seminal case presenting the advent of the plenary power era. However, as noted earlier, the term "plenary" does not appear in the decision, though it is clear by the court's unambiguous language that it was intent on establishing the political superiority of the federal government, no matter the constitutional cost. The first appearance of the term *plenary* regarding tribal sovereignty was in *Stephens v. Cherokee Nation*, 174 U.S. 445, 478 (1899), in which a split court held that Congress had "plenary power of legislation." In this case the Supreme Court was using two of the three analytically distinct definitions: unlimited and exclusive.

Second, if plenary power was cited we asked two further questions: 1) How is it defined—exclusive, preemptive power precluding state law, or unlimited, absolute? and 2) What is the basis of plenary power—constitutional provision(s) (commerce or treaty clauses), or extra-constitutional doctrine(s) (federal property ownership, Indian wardship, the theory of Indian "dependency"), or was it unclear what basis was used?

Scholars have often combined the analytically distinctive categories of plenary power into one monolithic term. This is both confusing and inaccurate. By breaking down the concept into its three components a more dynamic and slightly less complicated pattern emerges. . . . A plenary power citation alone does not ensure a legal defeat for American Indians in the court although there is certainly a greater likelihood of a loss (12-3-1 in the cases in which it was found). In the three Indian legal "victories," the court used the exclusive definition of plenary power.

When plenary power was defined as unlimited and absolute and when it was based on an extra-constitutional doctrine, tribal sovereignty and individual Indian rights were negatively affected (10-1).

DISCUSSION

An important concept in the field of Indian law and policy introduced by Ball is that of "irreconcilability."

Ball posits, "we [Americans] claim that the 'Constitution, and the laws of the United States which shall be made in pursuance thereof . . . shall be the supreme law of the land.' But we also claim to recognize the sovereignty of Native American Nations, the original occupants of the land. These claims—one to jurisdictional monopoly, the other to jurisdictional multiplicity—are irreconcilable."

A primary irreconcilable difference centers on the dissonance of the following concepts: 1) congressional plenary power (as absolute and unlimited), and 2) tribal sovereignty (a culturally distinct people within territorial limits with a leadership capable of making governmental arrangements).

Tribal sovereignty, like the sovereignty of nation-states, is a dynamic, not an absolutist concept. Plenary power, on the other hand, is considered static and absolutist whether it is wielded by proponents of federal supremacy over tribes or by advocates of tribal sovereignty. Nevertheless, as described earlier, plenary power has three meanings. Congress and the courts are the entities which unilaterally transmuted the bilateral relationship between tribes and the United States and they, not the tribes, are in the position of choosing which definition of plenary power to apply. Tribes lack such a definitional luxury.

To improve intergovernmental relations, a way should be found to reconcile these two terms. The United States could settle on one of the two following definitions of plenary power: a) exclusive or b) an exercise of federal power preemptive of state law. The United States would then disavow use of the unlimited/absolute definition as being violative of enumerated powers, limited government, consent of the governed, and the rule of law.

This action would pay immediate dividends in improved tribal-federal relations, especially from the tribal perspective, because it would send a strong message to tribal groups and individual Indians that the federal government was prepared to return to a genuinely bilateral political stance regarding those tribes.

Furthermore, tribes would welcome steps by the United States to reduce its use of non-constitutionally enumerated powers over their territories and sovereign rights. More important, tribes have a clear understanding of the doctrine of consent, and they realize that in the past 130 years or so this treasured democratic principle has sometimes been ignored (e.g., the BIA's administrative power over tribal resources; the acquisition and alienation of tribal lands and resources; the tribes' inability to punish non-Indians and non-member Indians; and tribes being denied the right to enter into foreign agreements).

The legislative branches of the federal government have begun to seriously consider the need to reestablish bilateral relations with tribes. Congress has established the experimental Tribal Self-Governance Demonstration Project, which is a major step toward restoring the tribal right of self-determination. Congress also is discussing re-establishing a more constitutionally grounded policy with tribes—"New Federalism." This policy would resemble the bilateral agreement period (which followed in the wake of the treaty period that ran from 1775 to 1868) between tribes and the United States, which lasted from 1875 to 1914.

On the executive side, the Clinton Administration is on record being supportive of tribal sovereignty. In his plan Clinton noted that while "Republican administrations have given nothing but lip service over the past twelve years to an affirmation of the government-to-government relationship," his administration would "give tribal governments more say in the distribution of federal funds geared toward economic growth, universal access to quality, affordable health care, and improved education." The Clinton Plan consists of three parts:

Guaranteeing Rights
- support tribal sovereignty and self-determination
- reaffirm the government-to-government relationship
- protect Indian religious sites and freedoms
- reform the Bureau of Indian Affairs
- support tribal efforts to resolve local disputes with states in accordance with federal law
- reaffirm U.S. citizenship of Indians and improve their voting access

Economic Development
- generate innovative strategies to develop self-sufficient economies
- create public-private partnerships to give low-income tribal etrepreneurs assistance
- implement a New Enterprise Tax Cut and create community development banks
- expand Earned Income Tax Credit
- repair infrastructure of reservations

Health Care

- incorporate goals of the Indian Health Care Improvement Act
- provide a core benefits package to ambulatory physician care and mental health services
- develop more effective measures to combat Fetal Alcohol Syndrome and AIDS
- keep hospital clinics open longer . . .

Returning to our historical discussion, why did the Supreme Court sporadically apply the "unlimited-absolute" definition of plenary power to tribes, their members, and their resources in the 1880s? The judicial, political, and historical evidence supports what many other scholars have maintained: Broadly put, it was to legitimate the unabashed and forced congressional policy of assimilation and acculturation of tribal members into the American mainstream. As John Oberly, Commissioner of Indian Affairs, noted in his 1888 Annual Report, the Indian "must be imbued with the exalting egotism of American civilization, so that he will say 'I' instead of 'We,' and 'This is mine' instead of 'this is ours.'"

It needs to be reiterated, however, that even the doctrine of plenary power, when defined as unlimited/absolute, was enforced only sporadically. As the case law attests, in several important decisions the Supreme Court—using the exclusive and preemptive definitions of plenary power—acknowledged the government's lack of jurisdiction in Indian Country, although it never denied that the United States could exert its jurisdiction if it chose. In fact, when the courts relied upon Congress's enumerated exclusive authority to deal commercially with tribes, it employed plenary power in a more viable sense.

The idea of enumeration embodies the soul of the constitutional conflict between tribes and the federal government. In constitutional law matters not involving tribes, the court has maintained, as it did in *Kansas v. Colorado*, 206 U.S. 46 (1907), that the United States "is a government of enumerated [explicitly identified] powers." The court acknowledged that the Constitution "is not to be construed technically and narrowly," and went on to say that "it is still true that no independent and unmentioned power passes to the National Government or can rightfully be exercised by the Congress."

However, when Congress deals with tribes, additional variables must be factored in: the treaty-defined, not constitutionally-defined, political relationship, and the pre- and extra-constitutional status of tribes. The combined effect of these factors is illustrated by the statement that "general acts of Congress do not apply to Indians, if their application would affect the Indians adversely, unless congressional intent to include them is clear." Moreover, there is also ample historical, political, and legal precedent for the principle that "Congress has no constitutional power over Indians except what is conferred by the Commerce Clause and other clauses of the Constitution."

As Deloria noted: "Indians receive the protection of the federal government precisely because they are outside the protections of the Constitution; they need and receive special consideration when the federal government interacts with them and handles their affairs. We have often called the government's power to accomplish this task 'plenary' because we supposed that it needed to be immune from arbitrary challenges which might otherwise hamper the wise administration of the affairs of Indians."

CONCLUSION

This chapter has attempted to explain the origins and clarify the confusion surrounding a pivotal concept undergirding the tribal-federal relationship: plenary power. The evidence shows that two of the analytical definitions of plenary power—preemption and exclusivity—sometimes are used in a constitutionally permissible way that recognizes and protects tribal autonomy. This needed protection is most evident when states and private interests have sought to make jurisdictional inroads into tribal territory or over tribal rights.

However, there remains the reality that although many tribes remain extra-constitutional political bodies, their political status has sometimes been characterized by the courts as "inferior" to the "superior position" Congress is said to occupy in relation to tribes. Tribes, despite a preponderance of evidence of their "foreign" political relationship to the states and the federal government, were informed beginning in the 1880s that they were to be treated as "wards of the nation," and that they were in a "condition of pupilage or dependency" (*Cherokee Nation v. Southern Kansas Railway Co.*, 135 U.S. 654 [1890]). Although the Perrin decision appeared to place some moral constraints on congressional power over tribes, the last eighty years bear out a stark reality: there are no constitutional restrictions on what the federal government may do to tribes or the remaining vestiges of tribal sovereign rights or aboriginal lands.

This is evident in the Indian reorganization era of the 1930s, which resulted in the forced abandonment and delegitimation of some traditional tribal governments. It is evident in the federal government's termination and relocation policy of the 1940s–1960s. It is most recently evidenced by a host of Supreme Court decisions effectively disregarding the rights of tribes and their citizens in several areas of law: non-member Indian criminal jurisdiction (*Duro v. Reina*, 110 S.Ct. 2053 [1990]); double taxation (*Cotton Petroleum Corporation v. New Mexico*, 57 USLW 4445 [1989]); zoning regulations of Indian land (*Brendale v. Confederated Tribes and Bands of Yakima*, 109 S. Ct. 2994 [1989]); and most significantly the free exercise of religion (*Lyng v. Northwest Indian Cemetery Protective Association*, 484 U.S. 439 [1988] and *Employment Division v. Smith*, 108 L. Ed 2d 876 [1990]).

Tribal nations, as pre- and extra-constitutional political-cultural-economic entities, will continue to occupy a distinctive position in the United States.

Tribes have a political status that is both dynamic and extremely tenuous. Tribes face the structural disadvantage of having rights which the federal government is not constitutionally mandated to protect. Notwithstanding the Commerce Clause and the treaty relationship, tribes remain "beyond the pale of the constitutional framework . . . [a]nd unless and until there is some positive move by the federal government to accept limitations on its exercise of naked political power over the tribes, Indians will remain people without a status and, more importantly, without the ability to protect themselves from the continuing exploitation visited upon them by the U.S." Until this disparity in tribal-federal political power is rectified, it is doubtful whether a viable domestic solution is possible to tribal-federal relations.

XII

POLICY ISSUES

Toward the end of many introductory courses in American Government and Politics, a week or two might be reserved for consideration of "public policy." This, of course, is a somewhat artificial distinction, since it might be plausibly argued that the central mission of government and politics is to address issues of public policy and it would be impossible to complete other aspects of this course without considering this. Nonetheless, at its best, a focus on particular policy concerns—economic policy, social welfare policy, foreign policy, and so forth—can teach us something about those particular concerns while also drawing together our understanding of the various aspects of the political system within which these policies are identified, adopted, and implemented.

Jace Weaver's chapter allows us to do just that. On the one hand, Weaver informs us about issues of natural resource use and environmental policy in Indian Country. On the other hand, he also highlights the ways in which Supreme Court interpretation of the Constitution, congressional plenary power, executive branch agency decisions, and especially the "triangulated" relationship between the three sorts of sovereignties in our federal system in the United States (federal, state, and tribal) all play out in the context of environmental policy.

Triangulated Power and the Environment: Tribes, the Federal Government, and the States

JACE WEAVER

In 1631 John Winthrop, the recently arrived governor of Massachusetts, wrote concerning the indigenous inhabitants of the "new England": "This savage people ruleth over many lands without title or property; for they inclose no ground, neither have they cattel to maintayne it, but remove their dwellings as they have occasion, or as they can prevail against their neighbors. And why may not Christians have liberty to go and dwell amongst them in their waste lands and woods (leaving such places as they have manured for their corne) as lawfully as Abraham did among the Sodomites?" He went on to justify the conquest with a detailed exegesis of the Hebrew scriptures, envisioning the Europeans as the ancient Israelites and the Natives as the Canaanites driven from the Promised Land. What makes this bit of articulated conquering ideology noteworthy is that Winthrop preached it almost verbatim in 1629 in England, before he ever set eyes upon the North American continent, and later repeated it aboard the *Arbella*, the ship bringing him to his new appointment.

In 1823 Chief Justice John Marshall incorporated the doctrines of discovery and conquest into the law of the youthful United States. In *Johnson v.*

This chapter is reprinted from *Defending Mother Earth: Native American Perspectives on Environmental Justice*, Jace Weaver, ed. Copyright © Orbis Books 1996. Reprinted by permission.

McIntosh he wrote: "We will not enter into the controversy, whether agriculturists, merchants, and manufacturers, have a right, on abstract principles, to expel hunters from territory they possess, or to contract their limits. Conquest gives a title which the Courts of the conqueror cannot deny, whatever the private and speculative opinions of individuals may be, respecting the original justice of the claim which has been successfully asserted." Five years later, however, Chancellor James Kent, often called the father of American jurisprudence, codified the principle that Marshall refused to entertain. Citing the work of Swiss jurist Emerich Vattel, he pronounced that "cultivators of the soil" had priority over hunters in terms of rights to property. He adopted fully Winthrop's vision of the continent as "a wilderness, sparsely inhabited" by Indians who merely roamed over the land with "no fixed abode."

Kent's view, and not that of Marshall, ultimately was to prevail. In 1985, in one of the leading cases in environmental law, the Ninth Circuit Court of Appeals observed, "Indian reservations may be considered as potential locations for hazardous waste disposal sites ... because they are often remote from heavily populated areas." To those in the dominant culture, Indian Country is still sparsely inhabited by rude hunters. The environment of Native lands can be sacrificed to the greater good of society because both they and those who inhabit them are of lesser value than more densely "settled" areas.

Indian lands have suffered from the polluting effects of heavy industry, toxic dumping, contamination of air and drinking water from off-reservation sources, and from fallout from nuclear testing and arms production. Most particularly, they have been damaged by the impact of mining operations on reservations or adjacent to them. To some extent, all mining degrades the environment. *In situ* mining (traditional deep mining) is the least harmful in this respect, but traditionally it has the potential for considerable damage due to mine waste and geological subsidence. New techniques of exploitation, however, can reduce this risk.

By contrast, surface mining, a common technique of coal exploitation on western reservations, has a severe environmental impact because a great deal of earth must be moved in order to extract resources. Surface mining takes one of three basic forms: strip mining, open-pit mining, or terrace mining. Although these techniques are safer and easier than *in situ* mining, "gas, dust and noxious odors can be expected near the mines. Both the overburden and the tailings from the processing plant . . . present substantial disposal problems." Strip mining is capable of extracting minerals to a depth of approximately 180 feet in relatively flat terrain. Reclamation normally consists of flattening the piles of overburden, replacing topsoil, and replanting. Open-pit mining is feasible for deeper deposits and irregular terrain. Overburden and minerals are removed together and carted out of the pit by means of a series of haulage roads or conveyor belts. The minerals are taken to processing plants, while the overburden normally is dumped distant from the pit. It is generally considered impractical to backfill the pit with overburden. Terrace mining is a variant of open-pit mining employed when deposits cover an extended area but are relatively shallow. Overburden is trucked away and stored, at least temporarily, rather than being dumped directly back into the pit. The process results in a very large worked-out area, which must be reclaimed.

The impact of mining in western states has placed a severe burden on the environment. The associated problems, perceived need for development and resources, and a myriad of other environmental issues have created tensions among Native nations and the federal and state governments. Historically, western states have pressured the federal government and the tribes to permit a sharing of responsibility with regard to Indian lands. They have done so under the banner of proper balance between environmental protection and development. With the onset of the energy crisis in the 1970s, states became determined "to acquire additional control over developmental activities within their borders regardless of whether such development occurs on private, state [tribal], or federal lands." In the absence of federal or tribal authorization to regulate Indian lands within their borders, states unilaterally sought jurisdiction over such lands.

Dialogue among the three levels of government (tribal, federal, state) has revolved principally around three interrelated issues. The first is the question of federal plenary power over, and trust responsibility to, Indians. The second is the question of federal preemption and the right of states to pass reasonable regulations relating to lands within their borders pursuant to their police power when such regulations do not conflict with federal legislation. Third is the inherent sovereign power of tribes recognized by treaty and the United States Constitution. Each of these strands must be kept in mind when discussing environmental regulation on Indian lands.

The Articles of Confederation gave Congress "sole and exclusive power of . . . managing all affairs with the Indians, not in any of the states, provided that the legislative right of any state within its own limits be not infringed or violated." Article I, section 8 of the Constitution dropped the states' rights proviso, granting to the Congress exclusive authority "to regulate commerce . . . with the Indian tribes." With this power came a concomitant responsibility. In *Cherokee Nation v. Georgia*, Chief Justice Marshall determined that Indian tribes were "domestic dependent nations." The federal government stood in a protective relationship toward the tribes, similar to a "guardian" over a "ward." From this grew the trust relationship between the federal government and Natives. "Later courts stretched the notion of a protective duty to tribal governments into almost unbridled power over them." The doctrine of Congress's "plenary" power over Indians evolved.

Such plenary power has been interpreted as giving the federal government authority concerning Indian lands equal to that exercised by it over federally owned lands in the public domain pursuant to the Property Clause. The United States Court of Appeals for the Eighth Circuit declared in *Griffin v. United States*: "The power of Congress over the lands of the United States wherever situated is exclusive. When that power has been exercised with reference to land within the borders of a state neither the state nor any of its agencies has the power to interfere." While the power of the federal government may not be restricted by state regulation, the states may prescribe reasonable police regulations insofar as those regulations do not conflict with congressional action and are thus preempted. Once Congress has acted, however, such action overrides conflicting state laws. As the Supreme Court noted, "A different rule would place the public domain of the United States completely at the mercy of state regulation."

The third leg in this triangle of relationships is that of the sovereignty of the tribes themselves. According to Felix Cohen, "Perhaps the most basic principle of all Indian law, supported by a host of decisions . . . , is the principle that *those powers which are lawfully vested in an Indian tribe are not, in general, delegated powers granted by express acts of Congress, but rather inherent powers of a limited sovereignty which has never been extinguished.*" For Cohen, treaties and legislation were not grants of power to tribes but to the federal government. "What is not expressly limited remains within the domain of tribal sovereignty." Tribal governments thus exercise over Indian lands what is commonly referred to in the law as a "clipped sovereignty." The precise extent of such inherent sovereignty is a much debated point. According to Getches, Wilkinson, and Williams, "In challenges to state assertions of authority over Indians, however, the existence of congressional plenary power has proved to be a formidable shield guarding the reservations as enclaves for the exercise of tribal governing authority. A tension persists between the federal trusteeship obligation, with its preemptive exclusions of state intrusions that impede tribal sovereignty, and exercises of congressional powers that often remove or denigrate Indian rights and tribal sovereignty."

For many years states largely acquiesced in the exercise of federal and tribal power over Indian lands within their borders; when conflicts did arise, they were resolved by cooperation rather than conflict. Beginning in the 1920s, however, energy-producing states enacted measures for the conservation and orderly production of petroleum and natural gas. These enactments provided for prorationing, spacing of wells, and the pooling and unitization of land overlaying a single reservoir. Conflict arose when a common source of supply underlay both private or state land and federal or Indian lands. States felt that the conservation laws of the state in which the wells lay should govern, particularly in cases where state lands lay over the same pool. Otherwise state attempts at regulation largely would be rendered ineffective. The situation was resolved by federal and tribal deference to the states.

During the early days of drastic prorationing in Oklahoma, the Osage, the richest energy-producing tribe in the state, frequently appeared before hearings of the Oklahoma Corporation Commission concerning allowable production on controlled lands. Although they steadfastly maintained their jurisdictional immunity, the Osage always abided by the orders of the commission in the interest of conservation. Similarly, the federal government acquiesced in the conduct of lengthy spacing hearings, under the laws of Utah, concerning the Aneth Field, which underlay controlled lands in that state.

In the early 1970s, with a growing awareness of degradation of the environment and the end to inexpensive, seemingly limitless resources, good will and cooperation among the three levels of government disintegrated. In response to increasing pressure for both land and natural resource development, western states began to enact comprehensive land-use legislation. Contending that any effective land-use system must include federal and Indian lands within their borders, the states undertook to legislate controls for such lands, drawing little or no distinction between them and private or state-held property. The question quickly became whether state governments would be permitted to effectuate their plans and impose environmental requirements on controlled lands.

The answer was a series of court challenges in Idaho, Oregon, and California. In *Andrus v. Click*, involving state regulation in a national forest, the Idaho Supreme Court ruled that standards more stringent than those set by the federal government were not preempted. It stated that "the mere fact that federal legislation sets low standards of compliance does not imply that the federal legislation grants a right to an absence of further regulation." Facing a nearly identical issue, the Oregon Court of Appeals, following the logic of *Click*, found "the preservation of the environmental quality of its lands is a subject particularly suited to administration by the states." When a federal court finally addressed the issue, however, it found the broader view of federal power over controlled lands to be dispositive. Since that time, western states have continued to assert aggressively the right of states to regulate the environment on Indian lands. The result has been ever-increasing conflict between the states, on one hand, and the federal government and tribes, on the other.

There is little dispute that tribes have the authority to regulate conduct affecting the environment when it occurs on trust lands within the boundary of a reservation, subject to the plenary power of the federal government. Such conduct can be regulated even when it involves nonmembers of the tribe in question. States sometimes have attempted, however, to assert jurisdiction over conduct of both Indians and non-Indians on trust lands. When such an assertion takes place, courts are called upon to undertake a careful balancing of tribal, state, and federal interests in order to determine the appropriate regulatory power.

Because of the General Allotment Act of 1887 and similar laws, which allocated reservations into individual parcels and opened "surplus" lands for settlement, significant portions of land within the exterior boundaries of many reservations are held by non-Indians. The result is a "checkerboard," in which adjacent parcels may be owned by Indians and non-Indians. Controversies arise as to which level of government has the power to impose environmental regulation upon these fee lands in non-Native hands. The issue is especially critical because of the migratory nature of resources such as air, water, and wildlife. Activities on non-Native property can have substantial effects on Indian lands.

Recognizing the potential for environmental damage to tribal trust lands from activities on adjacent lands held by non-Indians on reservations, the United States Supreme Court found that tribes had the right to regulate such conduct under certain circumstances. While the high Court overturned a ruling by the Ninth Circuit Court of Appeals that took a broad, traditional view of tribal sovereignty, it nonetheless recognized the inherent sovereign power retained by tribes. In delivering the opinion of the Court, Justice Potter Stewart stated that a "tribe may . . . retain inherent power to exercise civil authority over the conduct of non-Indians on fee lands within its reservation when that conduct threatens or has some direct effect on political integrity, the economic security, or the health and welfare of the tribe." In the ensuing years, lower courts have utilized this "*Montana* exception" to recognize tribal regulatory authority over non-Indian conduct affecting natural resources within reservations because of potential effects on "the health and welfare of the tribe."

In 1989, however, the Supreme Court's decision in *Brendale v. Confederated Tribes & Bands of Yakima* created a controversy concerning the continued vitality of the exception. *Brendale* involved the attempt of the Yakima Nation to impose zoning restrictions on two parcels of land owned by nonmembers on its reservation. The first property was located in a part of the reservation that was 97 percent tribal land. The other was in a heavily checkerboarded area. While the Court ultimately decided that the tribe could regulate the first lot but not the second, it was badly divided, with none of three separate opinions speaking for a majority. In his opinion, speaking for four Justices, Byron White raised questions about the *Montana* exception permitting tribal exercise of authority over non-Indians.

Most commentators agree that "considerable care is necessary to divine rules" from *Brendale*. Lower courts have struggled as to its meaning. The Environmental Protection Agency (EPA) does not recognize it as a controlling authority, instead continuing to rely on the clearer *Montana* decision, with which it finds the *Brendale* "fully consistent." Western states, however, have been quick to seize upon the latter case as a means to attempt to gain control over reservation lands. The Conference of Western Attorneys General points to Justice White's opinion and repeatedly overstates the scope and reach of the case, writing "*Brendale* effectively replaced the *Montana* criteria and limited tribal jurisdiction over nonmember fee lands to circumstances where such lands constitute a small percentage of distinct reservation units maintained in a natural state." The attorneys general contend that the EPA's stance with regard to the decision "diverges from Supreme Court requirements and raises questions whether determinations controlled by [its] regulations will accurately reflect the relative limits of state and tribal authority within Indian reservations." Such a disingenuous reading of *Brendale* only serves to confirm Joseph Singer's statements concerning the assumptions underlying power and property in America. In analyzing *Brendale* and other recent cases, Singer writes:

> The Supreme Court has assumed in recent years that although non-Indians have the right to be free from political control by Indian nations, American Indians can and should be subject to the political sovereignty of non-Indians. This disparate treatment of both property and political rights is not the result of neutral rules being applied in a manner that has a disparate impact. Rather, it is the result of *formally unequal* rules. Moreover, it can be explained only by reference to perhaps unconscious assumptions about the nature and distribution of both property and power. This fact implies an uncomfortable truth: both property rights and political power in the United States are associated with a system of racial caste.

The EPA refusal to recognize *Brendale* is, in fact, totally consistent with its longstanding policy of encouraging tribes to assume regulatory and management responsibilities for environmental programs. In the absence of such assumption, EPA will tend to assume direct implementation and enforcement within reservation boundaries. State regulation is strongly disfavored. Though the EPA gained considerable support for its position in the mid-1980s, when amendments to various federal environmental protection laws were enacted, its position took shape as early as 1982 when the EPA Administrator commissioned a study of environmental programs on reservations that would take into consideration "the unique political status of Indian tribes." Six months later President Reagan issued an "American Indian Policy Statement," which reaffirmed that "tribal governments had the primary responsibility for meeting the needs of tribal members," and the agency responded with its own policy, declaring that tribes were "the primary parties for setting standards, making environmental policy decisions and managing programs for reservations." With its policy in place, the EPA began to limit state authority over reservations and act on the opinion that "tribal governments retain civil-regulatory authority over all reservation lands, regardless of ownership." Pursuant to standards of federal regulatory law, courts have been willing to give extreme deference to EPA determinations denying state jurisdiction within reservations.

The federal leg of the triangle of power is clearly implicated in decisions involving Indian lands. They have responsibility for controlled lands. Beyond this, however, the U.S. Supreme Court in *New Mexico v. Mescalero Apache Tribe* stated that the federal policy of promoting tribal sovereignty includes fostering economic development. According to the Conference of Western Attorneys General, "Thus, federal interests are implicated where a tribe attracts an industry onto its reservation to broaden the tribe's economic base, and may be recognized as a factor against allowing states to impose strict regulations that would restrict or prohibit the industry's operations."

Since 1963 with the passage of the Clean Air Act, Congress has enacted a series of laws that evidence a broad public commitment "favoring preservation of resources and protection of fragile and life-supporting ecosystems." In general, these laws permit the EPA or, in the case of the Surface Mining Control and Reclamation Act, the Office of Surface Mining to delegate to states the authority to enforce minimum federal standards or, in some cases, stricter state requirements.. As these enactments came up for renewal in the 1980s and early 1990s, they were usually amended to permit tribes to assume jurisdiction as "states" in lieu of direct federal administration.

Such a delegation, however, is probably unnecessary. Inherent tribal sovereignty should be sufficient to support tribal authority over both trust and fee lands within the confines of a reservation. For instance, in *Nance v. EPA*, the Supreme Court let stand a determination by the Ninth Circuit Court of Appeals that the Northern Cheyenne had sufficient independent authority to regulate its reservation in order to prevent significant deterioration of its air quality. Likewise the Resources Conservation and Recovery Act (RCRA) contains no provisions permitting tribal assumption in lieu of the federal government. Yet the Ninth Circuit affirmed the EPA's decision allowing tribes in Washington State to administer hazardous-waste programs despite the absence of specific legislative grants. Further, the EPA itself does not view environmental legislation as delegating federal power to the tribes. As recently as July 1991 it affirmed its position that tribal governments are "the appropriate non-federal parties for making decisions and carrying out environmental program responsibilities" on reservations.

The Clean Water Act (CWA) has been a particular point of contention in the struggles among federal, state, and tribal governments. Section 518 of the CWA provides for tribal assumption of responsibility for protection of water resources held by the tribe, held by the United States in trust for them, held by a tribal member if it would be subject to trust restrictions upon a change in ownership, "or otherwise within the borders of an Indian reservation." Tribes and the EPA have interpreted the section as permitting tribal exercise of power within the entirety of the exterior bounds of reservations. States, however, argue that the statute cannot be read in such a manner. To do so, they contend, renders the first three clauses of the sentence, which apparently set limits on tribal authority, meaningless.

In the debate, the EPA and the tribes clearly have the better case. Other federal environmental statutes have similar language and have been interpreted in like fashion. The agency maintains that Congress made a legislative determination that conduct affecting water quality would have a serious and detrimental impact on tribes with the meaning of the *Montana* exception. Therefore, it concludes that "any impairment [of water quality] that occurs on, or as a result of, activities on non-Indian fee lands are [*sic*] very likely to impair the water and actual habitat quality of the tribal lands."

The migratory nature of water makes it imperative that tribes be permitted to regulate its quality throughout the borders of reservations. Any other rule would have the potential to frustrate their regulatory schemes entirely. Checkerboarded authority over migratory resources (air, water, wildlife), mirroring the checkerboard ownership patterns, is a recipe for disaster. In making such an argument, one must be aware that it is a double-edged sword. It could easily be used to justify state regulation over reservations within their borders. Such a rule, however, would be contrary to the inherent sovereignty of the Native nations and must therefore be dismissed. "Spillover" effects from activities on reservation have been used by states to argue for on-reservation regulation by them. Those who advance this argument must be equally aware that "spillovers spill both ways." Thus off-reservation pollution affecting the health and welfare on reservations should provide a basis for assertion of tribal jurisdiction beyond the boundaries of their territory. The Conference of Western Attorneys General contends, however, "Tribal sovereignty . . . is more limited [than that of states], and the mere allegation of on-reservation effects would not be sufficient to restore authority divested from the tribe as a matter of federal law." In early 1993 Isleta Pueblo in New Mexico set water quality standards for the Rio Grande, requiring that the water be clean enough for ceremonial and recreational purposes, and the EPA approved such standards. The city of Albuquerque, located five miles upstream of Isleta, routinely discharges sewage into the river and in order to meet the tribally determined standards will have to spend an estimated $250 million over the next decade. Consequently, the city has sued to overturn the EPA action.

Other aspects of EPA policy have been equally contentious. The western attorneys general argue that the administrative agency errs when it labels all property within reservations as "Indian lands," thus permitting tribal jurisdiction. The EPA definition is, they aver, in actuality that used for "Indian country," a term which includes fee lands. Federal courts have tended to define "Indian lands" as those in which Indians have a property interest. In the *Washington* case, however, the Ninth Circuit accepted the EPA's synonymous definitions as "a reasonable marker of the geographic boundary between state authority and federal authority." Similarly, the attorneys general question whether the EPA can act as a neutral mediator in disputes over the proper reach of tribal jurisdiction because of federal trust responsibilities to tribes. They fear that the agency "may be pressured to err in favor of tribes." Judicial review, however, should provide an adequate check upon erroneous or capricious exercises of administrative power as a result of such "pressure."

The triangulation of powers over Indian lands is virtually certain to become increasingly conflictual. No federal or state program is likely to take adequate account of Native cultural and spiritual considerations. Meanwhile, states will continue to grasp for regulatory control over Indian lands contrary to inherent tribal sovereignty. According to a study commissioned in 1986 as part of amendments to Superfund legislation, there were twelve hundred hazardous waste sites located on or near twenty-five reservations studied. Natives continue to fear that reservations will become "dumping grounds" for off-reservation wastes if states are permitted to control land use and environmental regulation on reservations—thus evoking the specter of disparate treatment spoken of by Singer and perpetuated by the attitude, evinced by Winthrop and Kent, that Indians sparsely inhabit the land and have no real sense of modern concepts of land use or tenure.

Currently [1995], the entire system of environmental protection in the United States is under assault at both the federal and state levels. Despite the fact that polls show that Americans want more—not less—environmental legislation if it will lead to a cleaner environment, the newly empowered Congress stands poised to roll back protections provided by a number of laws, including the Endangered Species Act, the Clean Air Act, the CWA, the Safe Drinking Water Act, and Superfund. Also in the works is a "takings bill," which would require compensation to landholders for any loss in value as a result of environmental controls. Known as the Private Property Protection Act, the bill would have a chilling effect on any future regulations as the "cost" required to be paid by the federal government becomes prohibitive. A similar provision has already passed the Washington state legislature. Montana and Idaho have enacted legislation that will permit higher levels of pollution in the watersheds of streams and lakes. Wyoming recently placed a bounty on wolves reintroduced into Yellowstone National Park.

Both federal and state governments appear intent on abandoning any pretense of national stewardship over natural resources. It seems that the only ones who will speak out for the earth in Indian Country are the Indians themselves.

For Further Reading

There are many excellent books on the American Indian experience. The following is a small selection of recent books that focus on the political and governmental themes central to this volume. They provide a starting point for interested students.

Alfred, Taiaiake. *Peace, Power, Righteousness: An Indigenous Manifesto*. Oxford University Press, 1999.

American Indian Lawyer Training Program. *Indian Tribes as Sovereign Governments: A Sourcebook on Federal-Tribal History, Law, and Policy*. AIRI Press, 1988.

Cornell, Stephen. *The Return of the Native: American Indian Political Resurgence*. Oxford University Press, 1988.

Deloria, Vine, Jr. and David E. Wilkins. *Tribes, Treaties, and Constitutional Tribulations*. University of Texas Press, 1999.

Johnson, Troy R., ed. *Contemporary Native American Political Issues*. AltaMira Press, 1999.

Josephy, Alvin M., Jr., Joane Nagel, and Troy Johnson, eds. *Red Power: The American Indian's Fight for Freedom*. Second edition. University of Nebraska Press, 1999.

Mason, W. Dale. *Indian Gaming: Tribal Sovereignty and American Politics*. University of Oklahoma Press, 2000.

O'Brien, Sharon. *American Indian Tribal Governments.* University of Oklahoma
     Press, 1989.
Wilkins, David E. *American Indian Politics and the American Political System.*
     Rowman and Littlefield, 2001.
Williams, Robert A., Jr. *The American Indian in Western Legal Thought: The Dis-
     courses of Conquest.* Oxford University Press, 1990.

Index

About the Editor and Contributors

JOHN M. MEYER is assistant professor of Government and Politics at Humboldt State University, where he has been a participant in the American Indian Civics Project. He is author of *Political Nature: Environmentalism and the Interpretation of Western Thought* (2001).

TAIAIAKE ALFRED (Kahnawake Mohawk) is director of the Indigenous Governance Program at the University of Victoria. He is the author of *Heeding the Voices of Our Ancestors: Kahnawake Mohawk Politics and the Rise of Native Nationalism* (1995) and *Peace, Power, Righteousness: An Indigenous Manifesto* (1999).

PETER BEINART is editor of *The New Republic*.

SAMUEL R. COOK is assistant professor in the Center for Interdisciplinary Studies at Virginia Tech. He is Coordinator for American Indian Studies and teaches both American Indian Studies and Appalachian Studies.

STEPHEN CORNELL is director of the Udall Center for Studies in Public Policy and professor of Sociology and of Public Administration and Policy at The University of Arizona. He also is codirector of the Harvard Project on American Indian Economic Development and has written widely on

Indian affairs, economic development, collective identity, and ethnic and race relations.

JEDON A. EMENHISER is professor of Government and Politics at Humboldt State University, where he has been a participant in the American Indian Civics Project. He works in the area where democratic theory, public opinion, elections, legislative behavior, constitutional law, and quantitative analysis converge.

KEVIN GOVER (Pawnee) is the former Assistant Secretary for Indian Affairs in the U.S. Department of the Interior (1997–2000). He is a partner in the Washington, D.C., law firm of Steptoe and Johnson, LLP.

LEE IRWIN is associate professor of Religious Studies at the College of Charleston. He is the author of several books, including *The Dream Seekers: Native American Visionary Traditions of the Great Plains* (1994).

JILL E. MARTIN is professor and chairperson of the Legal Studies Department at Quinnipiac University in Hamden, Connecticut.

RICHARD MAULLIN is president of Fairbank, Maslin, Maullin and Associates, a California-based polling and Democratic consulting firm.

SHARON O'BRIEN is associate professor of Political Science and Indigenous Nations Studies at the University of Kansas. She is author of *American Indian Tribal Governments* (1989).

DAVID VAN BIEMA is a religion writer and associate editor at *Time* magazine.

JACE WEAVER (Cherokee) is associate professor in the American Studies Program and Religious Studies Department at Yale University. His publications include *That the People Might Live: Native American Literatures and Native American Community* (1997) and *Defending Mother Earth: Native American Perspectives on Environmental Justice* (1996).

DAVID E. WILKINS (Lumbee) is associate professor of American Indian Studies, Political Science, and Law at the University of Minnesota. His two most recent books are *American Indian Politics and the American Political System* (2001) and *Uneven Ground: American Indian Sovereignty and Federal Law* (2001), coauthored with Tsianina Lomawaima.

ROBERT YAZZIE (Navajo) is Chief Justice of the Navajo Nation Supreme Court, a position he has held since 1992.